Consultancy, Organizational Development and Change

Consultancy, Organizational Development and Change

A practical guide to delivering value

Julie Hodges

KoganPage

First published in Great Britain and the United States in 2017 by Kogan Page Limited

Apart from any fair dealing for the purposes of research or private study, or criticism or review, as permitted under the Copyright, Designs and Patents Act 1988, this publication may only be reproduced, stored or transmitted, in any form or by any means, with the prior permission in writing of the publishers, or in the case of reprographic reproduction in accordance with the terms and licences issued by the CLA. Enquiries concerning reproduction outside these terms should be sent to the publishers at the undermentioned addresses:

2nd Floor, 45 Gee Street	c/o Martin P Hill Consulting	4737/23 Ansari Road
London EC1V 3RS	122 W 27th Street	Daryaganj
United Kingdom	New York, NY 10001	New Delhi 110002
	USA	India

www.koganpage.com

© Julie Hodges 2017

The right of Julie Hodges to be identified as the author of this work has been asserted by him in accordance with the Copyright, Designs and Patents Act 1988.

ISBN   978 0 7494 7863 6
E-ISBN 978 0 7494 7864 3

British Library Cataloguing-in-Publication Data

A CIP record for this book is available from the British Library.

Library of Congress Control Number

2016961116

Typeset by Integra Software Services, Pondicherry
Print production managed by Jellyfish
Printed and bound in Great Britain by Ashford Colour Press Ltd

To Michael for his patience and unerring support

CONTENTS

LIST OF FIGURES

LIST OF TABLES

ACKNOWLEDGEMENTS

I am very grateful to everyone who has supported me in writing this book and provided their thoughts and advice, from which a great number of people will benefit, including consultants, students, academics and other managers.

My special thanks go to Luca, Bruce, Claire, Dinah, Fiona, Greg, Kamales, Lindsey, Olga, Perry, Peter, Ronald, Simon and Steven who sacrificed their own time to write their personal stories to share in this book; to Michael for his advice and sense-checking my writing (and for his unwavering support); to Amy for her feedback and gently pushing me to keep to the timelines; and to all at Kogan Page for giving me the opportunity, yet again, to work with them.

Introduction

Change is part of everyday life in organizations. We are, as David Boje and Tonya Henderson so eloquently describe it, neck deep in the deluge, whether we like it or not. The choice, Boje and Henderson say, is 'not whether to embark on a journey of change, but whether we swim with the current, take action to affect the river's course, or desperately cling to the rocks' (2016: 35). For the journey to be successful it needs navigation through the rapids. Organizations need help to cope with the turbulence they are facing. For change in organizations is rarely black and white but a fusion of different colours.

Although we live in an era where transformation is seen as the norm, successful change is still viewed as elusive, for despite the many approaches to organizational transformation and the plethora of advice and advisers, it is commonly agreed that the vast majority of transformation initiatives fail (Burnes and Randall, 2016). A wide range of reasons are given for the failure of change, ranging from impractical theories to ill-informed practice (Burnes and Jackson, 2011), yet despite this recognition it appears that being able to sustain change is still a challenge (Hodges and Gill, 2015).

This book proposes that a consultancy approach to change has a role to play in helping organizations to navigate change more effectively. This approach emphasizes that consultancy is about people and therefore about the interactions between people. At the heart of this is an organizational development (OD) orientation, where there has traditionally been a focus on the client–consultant relationship, which distinguishes consultancy from other forms of helping. This is especially relevant for consultancy for change, as working with and through people, by forming relationships, is an important aspect of sustaining change in organizations (Hodges, 2016).

If implemented effectively, such an approach can contribute, catalyse and influence organizational change, and help to create, realize and sustain the benefits of transformations.

Consultancy for change is therefore about working with and through people by building and maintaining relationships in order to sustain change in organizations. The value of this approach to change is explored in this book from a theoretical and practical perspective.

Aims

A multitude of books have been written on consultancy, many of which make excellent reference guides and provide valuable suggestions for managers and consultants. The general approach offered tends to focus on the broader aspects of 'management' consultancy and on either theoretical or practical approaches, with relatively few books managing to bridge the gap between theory and practice. There is also a wealth of material offering helpful prescriptive guidelines and checklists for consultants to follow, although few that adapt such advice to the change and uncertainty that businesses across the globe face.

To address this gap, this book aims to explore the theoretical and practical aspects of an OD consultancy approach to change and to provide practical guidance for postgraduate students and professionals. The book achieves this aim in a number of ways. First, it focuses on the theoretical and practical aspects of consultancy for change. Most books and articles are written on either organizational change or consultancy, and few of them manage to bridge the gap between theory and practice or attempt to combine change and consultancy. By focusing on consulting for change this book provides a theoretical and practical basis for effectively sustaining change in organizations, Second, it includes contributions from consultants and managers who write about their experience of consulting for change. By giving a voice to consultants and managers, this book helps to focus on what consultants actually do during organizational transformations, how they do it and the outcomes.

Although the book will focus primarily on internal consultancy, many of the points made will be applicable to both internal and external consultants. Similarly, since very few consulting situations involve only people working on their own, anything referred to in this book is relevant not only to individual consultants but also the teams in which they work.

Learning outcomes

This book will aim to help you to:

- enhance your knowledge about what consulting is and how it can be translated into practice;
- increase your understanding of the theoretical concepts of consultancy;

- apply models and frameworks in practical situations;
- apply culturally transferrable tools and techniques;
- develop your skills and employability so that you will be more effective in consultancy for change in different organizational settings;
- identify good practice from practitioners and leading edge thinkers;
- apply an ethical approach during consultancy activities;
- build your consultancy capability.

Audience

This book is deliberately constructed to be helpful to readers from a wide range of professions and not just a narrow band of consultants. This is because the book is about consultancy for change, where the aim is to achieve sustainable change and realize benefits. In this way the book will be of benefit to postgraduate-level students, practising and aspiring managers and leaders, and those interested in becoming a consultant. The book will also provide practising consultants (external and internal), managers in specialist functions such as human resources and individuals who want to enhance their consulting skills with the tools to effectively consult on organizational change and transformation.

Structure

The book is divided into three parts comprising relevant chapters. Each part focuses on a theme that is central to the overall aim of the book.

Part One (The context of consultancy) contextualizes consulting and provides an overview of the nature of consultancy. Chapter 1 (The nature and value of consultancy) begins by focusing on the global context in which consultancy operates. This is followed by a discussion of the theoretical perspectives of consultancy, change and OD. An overview of the key concepts used in the book, such as 'consultancy', is then provided. This pays attention to what consultancy is, what it is not and why it is important. The second part of the chapter explores the value of consultancy and what constitutes value for clients. The chapter considers key questions such as: What are the structure and dynamics of the global consulting world today?

What are the benefits of consulting? And in what ways can consulting add value? Chapter 2 (Roles and responsibilities of consulting) commences by examining the different types of consultancy, such as reactive, proactive, expert and process consulting. The various roles and responsibilities that consultants can play during change are considered, as are the differences between internal and external consultants. The benefits of using consultancy and OD for change are then discussed. The chapter concludes by exploring how managers can decide whether internal and/or external consultants are the most appropriate for their organization.

In Part Two (The consultancy for change cycle) a proposed approach for consultancy for change is introduced. Chapter 3 (Preparation and contracting) explains the first stages of the approach. In the first part of the chapter consideration is given to what needs to be done when preparing to consult, followed by how to clarify what the issue is that needs to be addressed and the expectations of the client. The second part of the chapter discusses the contracting phase, including what it is, who needs to be involved and what the outputs should be. Key questions are considered, such as: How can the client and their problem be understood? How can a consultant contract effectively with a client? Throughout the chapter particular attention is given to building and maintaining relationships from the start of the consulting for change cycle.

In Chapter 4 (Diagnosing the need for change) the focus is on how to gather and analyse data about the root causes of key issues in order to identify the cause and effect of the client's problem. The chapter examines the different ways of analysing the data from the diagnosis, and presenting it to key stakeholders. Key questions are addressed, such as: What tools can be used to diagnose and analyse the need for change in an organization? How can these tools be adapted to different organizational contexts? What types of methods should be considered for analysing the data and presenting findings to the client and other key stakeholders?

The design and implementation of interventions are the focus of Chapter 5 (Designing and delivering interventions). The first part of the chapter explores identifying and designing appropriate OD interventions to address the issues raised in the diagnosis (as outlined in Chapter 4). Consideration is also given to how to identify the readiness for change. The chapter goes on to discuss approaches for identifying interventions. The second part of the chapter looks at different types of interventions at an individual, team and organizational level.

The aim of Chapter 6 (Transition) is to identify how consultants can transfer full ownership of a change intervention to managers so that it becomes business as usual. This includes examining how interventions can be embedded and sustained, particularly through monitoring, measuring and evaluation. Consideration is also given to how consultants can maintain their visibility with clients during and after a change has been implemented. The chapter concludes by exploring how change can be sustained and benefits realized.

In Part Three (Consultancy capabilities), Chapter 7 (Building capabilities for consulting) examines how individuals and organizations can build the capabilities (skills, knowledge and attitudes) needed for consultancy for change. This chapter emphasizes that consultancy is about people and therefore about the interactions between people. The following key capabilities are discussed: building and maintaining relationships; managing emotions; gaining commitment and engagement; facilitating creative dialogue; being self-aware; being resilient; having a tolerance for ambiguity and uncertainty; political astuteness; and managing political dynamics. The importance of the key skills of listening, questioning and summarizing are also emphasized. The chapter concludes by considering how consultants can develop and enhance their capabilities.

The ethical side of consultancy is examined in Chapter 8. The chapter begins by critically evaluating the individualization and professionalism of ethics. This is followed by a discussion of the key ethical issues in consultancy and how they should be addressed. Key questions addressed in this chapter include: What ethical considerations need to be considered when consulting? How can an ethical approach to consulting for change be applied?

Finally, Chapter 9 (Conclusions and reflections) provides a synthesis of the main points made in the book and summarizes the practical perspectives on how consultancy and OD add value during organizational change.

Each chapter includes: key points; learning outcomes; practical examples; a summary, references, discussion questions, as well as practical considerations and recommendations that point the way ahead for those practising consultancy now and in the future.

In sum, this book is intended to provide a platform for the theory and practice of consultancy for change; coalescing what is already known, identifying the priorities for what more needs to be known, and proposing how consultancy can be of value to ensure change is sustained in organizations and benefits accrued from it. It attempts to address some of the key issues related to consultancy for change from a practical and realistic perspective as well as a theoretical one. The experiences of individuals and organizations have been included to provide insights into what makes consulting for change successful and what makes it fail, as well as lessons learned.

References

Boje, DM and Henderson, TL (eds) (2014) *Being Quantum: Ontological storytelling in the age of antenarrative*, Cambridge Scholars Publishing, Cambridge

Burnes, B and Randall, J (eds) (2016) *Perspectives on Change: What academics, consultants and managers really think about change*, Routledge, London

Burnes, B and Jackson, P (2011) Success and failure in organizational change: An exploration of the role of values, *Journal of Change Management*, **11** (2), pp 133–62

Hodges, J (2016) *Managing and Leading People Through Organizational Change: The theory and practice of sustaining change through people,* Kogan Page, London

Hodges, J and Gill, R (2015) *Sustaining Change in Organizations.* London: Sage

PART ONE
The context of consultancy

The nature and value of consultancy

KEY POINTS

- Consultancy contributes to, catalyses and influences organizational change and can help to create, support and embed change.

- Consultancy for change is about working with, and through, people by building and maintaining relationships in order to sustain change in organizations.

- At the heart of consultancy for change is organizational development (OD), which is a process for initiating, implementing and sustaining change.

- Defining the value of consultancy and determining whether or not it has been achieved are highly subjective, as what constitutes value for one client may be different for another, and vary in different situations.

Introduction

The aim of this chapter is to contextualize consultancy, OD and organizational change. The chapter begins by focusing on the global context in which consultancy is operating. Kamales Lardi, a Managing Partner at consultants Lardi & Partner Consulting, describes her personal experience of how the digital revolution is impacting on consulting. This is followed by a discussion of the theoretical perspectives of consultancy, which concludes by proposing a shift from the traditional process-driven approach to a people-driven approach. Perry Timms describes how he has used the latter approach, which he terms 'people-powered' change. The chapter then goes on to provide overviews for each of the key concepts used throughout the book. Attention is paid to what consulting is and is not, and why it is important. The chapter concludes by considering the value of consultancy and what constitutes value in the eyes of a client.

Learning outcomes

By the end of this chapter you will be able to:

- differentiate between the functionalist and critical view of consultancy;
- define key concepts such as 'consultancy' 'change' and 'organizational development';
- appreciate the importance of consultancy for change;
- identify how consultancy can add value; and
- recognize the different types of clients who require consultancy.

The structure and dynamics of the global consulting world

The growth of consultancy

The consulting industry is a multifaceted, global business sector that has evolved quickly. The era of strategy consultancy began in the 1960s, when the demand for engineering-based advice on the shop floor declined and there was an increase in international trade and corporate expansion, which began to shift the demand for consultancy to the senior executive level. With the growth of global consultancy firms in the 1980s and 1990s the consultancy market exploded. This was marked by the emergence of an elite group of strategy consulting firms, including McKinsey, Boston Consulting Group (BCG) and Bain & Co. These firms applied a fact-based, integrative and analytical approach to solving clients' issues, which has been mirrored by other global firms, including the Big Four professional services firms – Deloitte, PwC, EY, KPMG – and Accenture, which also provide implementation and operational improvement services, as part of their consultancy offerings.

Commercially, consulting firms are successful; the research company Gartner has calculated that the Big Four professional services have a combined 40 per cent of the global consulting market and have significantly increased their share over the past decade through organic growth and acquisitions, with an increase in their consulting income by 11.5 per cent to £2.55 billion in 2015 (Sourceforconsulting.com, 2016). The growth of such consultancy firms is, according to the Management Consultancy Association (MCA, 2016), because of the industry's ability to deliver high-quality services that create sustainable value to organizations.

Critics are more sceptical and instead portray the consulting industry as one in which consultants benefit from crisis or underperformance on the part of clients. Their view is that consultants are healers of corporations in need of salvation, and that they are ready to provide all sorts of solutions to clients who would otherwise not know what to do (Sorge and van Witteloostuijn, 2004). This would suggest that the consultancy sector benefits from economic decline and moves counter-cyclically to the economy. Thomas Armbruster says that this is, however, an erroneous assumption. Instead he points out that consultancy not only 'breathes with economic cycles, but it does so in a strongly reinforced, procyclical way: the highs of consulting growth are much higher than general economic highs and the lows are even lower than general economic lows' (2006: 92). So a weak economy or recession pulls consulting revenues down while a growing economy boosts consulting revenues. Armbruster concludes that consultancy 'depends on and responds to blossoming or recovering client firms, rather than feeding on corporations in crisis' (2006: 93). This is supported by Andrew Hill (2015), who points out that demand for consultancy comes from improving economic conditions and a sense of being in a position to act on new visions of the future. Hill concludes that investment in consultancy is based on discretionary spend and that the consultancy market represents a buyer's, rather than a seller's, market.

The drive to succeed and to increase buyer demand shapes the structure and organization of consultancy firms and influences recruitment (Matthias, 2013) with many firms operating an 'up or out' culture (O'Mahoney and Markham, 2013) which underpins the sink or swim aspect of having a successful career. Consultants at global firms may each earn significant salaries in return for long working hours, high sales targets and utilization rates, high levels of stress and weeks spent away from home. Despite these pressures, because of the high pay and the prestige, students at business schools frequently aspire to jobs in consulting. In an article in the *Financial Times* entitled 'MBA graduates' love affair with consultancy endures', Ian Wylie

(2016) writes that 'Google, Facebook and Amazon might grab more of the headlines, but consulting firms are still snapping up the most students at top business schools as they remain the largest recruiters'.

Despite this continuing increase in popularity amongst potential recruits, the consultancy industry is facing disruption. In an article published in the *Harvard Business Review* entitled 'Consulting is on the cusp of disruption', Clayton Christensen and colleagues (2013) describe major change in the consulting industry with firms moving away from judgement-based and bespoke diagnoses towards knowledge asset solutions. Although in general the size and influence of big-name consultancies such as McKinsey and BCG are still strong, early signs of a pattern of disruption by increasingly sophisticated competitors with non-traditional business models are evident. In the article, Christensen and colleagues point out that the share of work that is classic strategy has been steadily decreasing and is now about 20 per cent, down from 60–70 per cent some 30 years ago (Christensen *et al*, 2013).

The industry is facing significant changes. A report by Sourceforconsulting.com (2011) identifies six trends impacting on the sector which are causing disruption:

1 Context. The globalization of clients is a crucial source of growth, but at the same time it is reshaping the consultancy industry.

2 Purchase. The increasing use of multinational purchasing models is impacting on the historic influence of relationships.

3 Resources. Clients are choosing to staff more projects internally.

4 Delivery. Competition is now between firms and freelancers rather than between firms.

5 Outcome. The majority of consultancy firms now sit in the middle between advice and implementation.

6 Margin. Clients are expecting lower fee rates and higher value for their return on investment.

A factor to add to this list is the digital transformation, which is driving change in organizations and consequently impacting on the consultancy industry.

The impact of the digital transformation on the consultancy profession

The digital revolution is characterized by a fusion of technologies that is blurring the lines between the physical, digital, and biological spheres and resulting in transformational change in the behaviour of people across the world. There is unlimited potential from billions of people connected by mobile devices, with unprecedented processing power, storage capacity, and access to knowledge (Schwab, 2016). Digital consumers are now expecting the same level of responsiveness and intuitive user experience from their interactions with companies. The demand for digitization of products and services has impacted traditional business models, with the emergence of digital businesses across various industries. These purely digital companies have developed their business models to accommodate the growing population of digital consumers, and are proving disastrous for traditional business models. A survey conducted by the Global Center for Digital Business Transformation of 941 business leaders in 12 industries across the globe found that an average of four of the top 10 industries (in terms of market share) will be displaced by digital disruption in five years (Bradley *et al*, 2015). As organizations seek help to cope with new technology and demand expertise in areas such as data analytics, social media and artificial intelligence, the consultancy industry is diversifying rapidly. As a result, Alan Leaman, Chief Executive of the Management Consultancies Association (MCA), says that 'beneath the surface the industry is facing seismic change' (Plimmer, 2016). What is emerging is hybrid consultancy that offers the benefits of strategic consulting along with digital knowledge or big data expertise. Nearly a third of all consultancy work now involves strategic advice on digital technologies (MCA, 2016). The shift is also evident in the types of consultants being recruited to consultancy firms. The number of recruits to the £5.5 billion a year management consultancy industry in the UK, which has traditionally specialized in project management and financial services, grew by 9.5 per cent in 2015, taking the total employed to 45,000. Twelve thousand of these were digital technology specialists (MCA, 2016).

As organizations look for integrated solutions to their management and information technology (IT) requirements, many consultancy firms are entering into alliances with software suppliers, telecoms or communications firms in order to provide a broader range of services and extend their global reach and expertise. For instance, Deloitte has aligned with data mining company Kaggle; KPMG has an alliance with the McLaren Group to use predictive analytics; and PwC has linked with Google. Consultancy firms that historically have competed are now working together on client projects and there is continuing convergence within and outside the industry as firms cooperate and merge in order to better serve their clients (MCA, 2016).

Organizations have relied on the external expertise of consultancies in order to go beyond the knowledge that exists within the company. As the digital revolution impacts the global business landscape, the type of services needed from consulting firms is evolving. Traditionally, companies have relied on consulting firms to provide innovative solutions, as well as insights into best practices, based on broad implementation experiences across multiple clients. Existing in a high-opacity industry, consulting firms act as gatekeepers to a vast knowledge base – a black box of experiences, methodologies, best practices and experts, all accessible to companies at a premium fee. However, in the digital economy, knowledge is now democratized. Today, information is freely shared and quickly accessible, creating a more sophisticated and knowledgeable client base. The needs of these informed clients have evolved to include more in-depth transformative improvements and solution implementation support. Consultancy therefore has to adapt and innovate to address global trends and provide value within the turbulent global environment in which it operates.

The growth of internal consultancy

Organizations are building their own internal consulting teams in an effort to address business issues themselves and control costs; some of these teams even offer consultancy services to outside clients. This is increasingly found in industries such as hospitality and training; for example, at the Walt Disney Company a consulting unit called The Disney Institute provides consultancy to other firms in how to improve their engagement with their customers. Similarly, the Ritz-Carlton Leadership Center, part of Ritz-Carlton Hotels, offers consultancy to other companies on how to provide high levels of customer service. Large, multifaceted consulting firms are facing growing competition from these internal consultant teams as well as from smaller niche companies.

'Gig' consultants

One of the significant trends in consultancy is the increase in consultants who are setting up their own business and becoming part of the so-called 'gig' economy, in which organizations contract with freelance workers. This is already evident in companies such as Airbnb, Uber, Deliveroo and TaskRabbit. Online platforms are enabling individuals with specific experience to offer their services directly to companies. Platforms such as UpWork (a merger of Elance and oDesk), Amazon Mechanical Turks, TopTal and

Guru offer easy access to freelancers. These sites offer the credibility and quality assurances through user ratings and recommendations, while avoiding the long process and heavy overhead costs of large companies. 'Gig consultants,' writes Andrew Hill (2016), are, 'these freelancing corporate advisers, often alumni of big professional services firms or management consultancies.' Consider, for example, Hourlynerd. Such companies tend to compete for projects in teams coordinated by intermediaries, sometimes pitching against their former employers for contracts. This shift supports the prediction made by Christensen and his colleagues (2013) of the disruption of established consultancy as clients start using alternatives to the big brands for all but a core of critical work.

A survey by McCallum (2016) of 251 independent consultants suggests that there are various types of 'gig' consultants, including 'young stars', 'family-balance seekers', 'experienced classics', such as ex-partners who trade on their expertise, 'soft landers' who are gliding to retirement on the back of occasional projects, and 'specialists'. Like other gig workers, these groups are attracted to independent consultancy because of the flexibility it offers. However, this is offset by the volatility in the demand for consultancy which means gig consultants need to be resilient and tap into a network of other freelance consultants for work (Hill, 2016).

The nature of consultancy is, therefore, beginning to transform as forces for change impact on organizations and the type of consultancy they require.

Questions for discussion

- Why has the use of consultants increased over the years?
- What has been the impact of the digital revolution in the organization in which you work, or one you are familiar with? In what ways has it affected how the organization employs consultants?
- What might be the impact of 'gig' consultants on the future of the consultancy industry?

In the following case study Kamales Lardi, a Managing Partner at consultants Lardi & Partner Consulting, GmbH describes how the digital revolution is impacting consultancy.

CASE STUDY

The impact of digital disruption on consulting

As the digital revolution impacts the global business landscape, the types of services needed from consulting firms is evolving. Traditionally, companies have relied on consulting firms to gain innovative solutions, as well as insights into best practices, based on broad implementation experiences across multiple clients. Existing in a high-opacity industry, consulting firms act as gatekeepers to a vast knowledge base – a black box of experiences, methodologies, best practices and experts, all accessible to companies at a premium fee. However, in the digital economy, knowledge is now democratized. Today, information is freely shared and quickly accessible, creating a more sophisticated and knowledgeable client base. The needs of these visionary clients have evolved to include more in-depth transformative improvements and solution implementation support. However, consulting firms have only recently started to explore new business models.

Although in general the size and influence of big-name consultancies such as McKinsey and BCG are still strong, early signs of a pattern of disruption by increasingly sophisticated competitors with non-traditional business models are evident.

Triggers for change

Digital disruption has triggered several critical changes in the consulting industry, including the following.

Unbundling of consulting services
The traditional consulting model offering integrated solutions, designed to conduct all aspects of the client engagement, is coming undone. With increasingly easy access to specialized content online, companies are looking to work with modular providers specializing in supplying in-depth expertise and knowledge of a specific part of the value chain. Additionally, there is a preference for smaller players, who are perceived to be more agile and innovative.

Disruption in consulting customer journey
Digital technologies have disrupted almost every aspect of the consulting customer journey. For example, in the past, current or potential client contact lists were managed internally. These lists were a carefully guarded competitive advantage for senior consulting people, and were used to source potential

acquisitions. Today, however, with online platforms such as LinkedIn and Twitter, there is an abundance of information available to all. Executives from all the Fortune 500 companies are on LinkedIn, and accessing them is as simple as a click of a button. Every stage of the buyer model has been similarly disrupted by digital technologies.

I founded Lardi & Partner Consulting (LPC) in 2012, after leaving Deloitte Consulting Switzerland where I led social media and enterprise collaboration. Several weeks into starting the new business, I quickly found that the traditional consulting approach to customer acquisition was less effective in the digital age. By adopting digital channels to identify and engage with key client contacts, I was able to quickly create new relationships. I also actively used social media channels to build the LPC brand, position myself as a topic expert, as well as share knowledge and insights relating to LPC services offerings. The approach has proven effective, since today more than 80 per cent of LPC business leads are generated through online platforms.

New niche companies

The digital economy has paved the way for small, niche companies to access the global market. With e-commerce platforms and social media, it has become easier for smaller firms to promote their brand and position their expertise. These companies are also able to operate in a flexible manner, for example assembling leaner project teams of freelance consultants for clients at a small fraction of the cost of traditional consulting firms. Many of these companies are digital businesses and do not carry the expensive overheads of traditional consultancies, such as fixed costs of unstaffed time, expensive downtown real estate, recruiting and training. Niche companies may not be able to deliver the entire value proposition of traditional firms, but are typically staffed with topic experts who can bring a greater degree of practical implementation knowledge.

Overall cost pressures in companies have forced clients to abandon the easy assumption that price equals quality. Where possible, they are reducing their reliance on solution-shop providers. They are savvy about assessing the jobs they need done and funnel work to the firms most appropriate for those jobs.

Access to technologies and platforms

As companies scramble to keep up in the digital economy, new technologies and platforms are adopted, even in industries that are traditionally not tech-related. For example, the use of social media, big data analytics and apps have provided companies with new access points to their consumer base and insights about their needs. Additionally, big data analytics offering speed and quantifiable insight is creating a level playing field for new players in the market by reducing opacity in the industry (Christensen, 2013). Consulting firms have been forced to become tech-savvy in a bid to stay relevant and competitive in the eyes of companies looking for advice and support on how to adopts and apply these new technologies for business.

In addition, platforms such as LinkedIn are becoming a critical part of recruiting and talent sourcing. Consultancies have started using these platforms to position their brand as an attractive employer in the highly competitive market.

Consulting in the digital age

The consulting industry has demonstrated the ability to move smoothly from big idea to big idea, as trends in the global business landscape evolve. Consulting firms will now have to tap into this agility and initiate several fundamental changes in order to respond flexibly to the threats of disruption.

Modularize business model

Consulting firms have typically been structured as 'solution shops' that bundle a range of services into a single, high-priced package. But as companies face increasing cost pressures and have more access to knowledge, they are less inclined to engage end-to-end consulting services. By unbundling the services into modular links in the value chain and using technology platforms to roll out the services, consultancies will be able to stay relevant and cost effective. The modular business model will enable firms to refocus human capital towards highly complex, transformational projects. McKinsey and Deloitte have already demonstrated the potential for modular business models through McKinsey Solutions and Deloitte Digital.

Keeping up with new technology trends

New technologies are emerging on an almost daily basis. The success of consulting firms will depend on the ability to stay at the cutting edge of business. In the digital economy this means staying on top of the latest technology trends and having a good understanding of the potential impact on companies. Apart from the impact within an industry, consultancies will need to be able to foresee, as much as possible, the impact technology may have across industry. This is where consulting can really add value for companies. For example, in Phoenix, Arizona, Google is seeking drivers to test their autonomous cars on real streets. The cars will have an obvious impact on the transportation industry. However, they could also completely disrupt the insurance industry, raising critical questions on liability and responsibility.

Update consulting skillsets

The impact of digital technologies in the business environment goes beyond functional boundaries, forcing companies to assess and initiate organization-wide changes through digital business transformation. Traditional business approaches of trying to adopt new technologies will not be sufficient to compete in the digital economy. Creating an app or using social media and online platforms to communicate or interact with customers is only scratching the surface; real digital transformation goes deep into the company's operations, transforming traditional business models to meet the needs of both traditional customers and new digital customers.

In relation to this, the role of consultants today requires a general understanding of digital technologies and their impact on business, despite the functional focus. Consulting firms will now need to ensure their workforce is sufficiently knowledgeable about digital technologies, where in the past only technology consultants were required to understand technology. Clients in every functional business area are questioning the impact of technology trends, and looking to consultants for answers.

Open to collaboration and partnerships with specialized players

In the digital economy, open collaboration is the key to success. Incumbents across industries are exploring strategic collaborations and partnerships with specialized companies and platform providers to gain access to talented people and innovative solutions. Additionally, by partnering with smaller players, such as app developers, data analytics companies or topic experts, consultancies may gain access to new and varied clients and engagements. For example, when a company engages with a platform provider across many functional areas of the business this may offer a greater breadth of new consultancy engagement across the various functional areas. Additionally, development of new consulting services may arise from this strategic partnership. For example, over the last few years, PwC has been boosting its digital expertise through a series of acquisitions, including Ant's Eye View, Intunity and Optimal Experience (Tadena, 2016). This year, PwC unveiled its Experience Center initiative that aims to widen the breadth of the company's digital services business. The centre will be an exploratory environment that includes 'sandboxes', physical labs for PwC's growing team of designers to experiment with, and prototype, digital products and services for clients. PwC has plans to set up several centres in the US, Europe, the Middle East and China.

Summary

As digital technologies disrupt the global business landscape, the consulting industry will have to update its traditional business models to meet the needs of the digital economy. Consumers are more sophisticated and knowledgeable, and they demand the same level of responsiveness that they receive from digital technologies. Digital technologies have disrupted almost every aspect of the consulting customer journey. In order to remain relevant in the digital age, the consulting industry will need to consider adopting new operating models, skillsets and technology platforms in order to accommodate the evolving business landscape.

Theories of consultancy

Many business writers and academics have strong views about consultancy, which are reflected in book titles ranging from *The Trusted Adviser* (Maister *et al*, 2002) and *Value-based Consulting* (Czerniawska, 2002) to *Consulting Demons* (Pinault, 2000) and *Flawed Advice* (Argyris, 2000). From the academic literature we can distinguish two broad schools of thought: the *functionalist* and the *critical*. The functionalist perspective sees consultancy as the carrier and transmitter of management knowledge (Armbruster, 2006). From this perspective, the methods to generate data and information outside and inside an organization constitute the primary driver of consultancy. Systematic knowledge management enables consulting firms to stay up to date with industry practices and market information, and allows them to distribute knowledge in a way that is unequalled by conventional organizations (Hansen, 2002). Consultancy is, therefore, seen to add value by providing knowledge that clients do not have.

In contrast, the critical school of thought assumes that consultants have ample opportunity for opportunistic behaviour and exert it. This critical perspective does not necessarily doubt the usefulness of consultancy, but argues that the view that consultants are experts and provide knowledge to clients is too narrow a definition to fully appreciate what is going on in consultancy (Clark and Fincham, 2002). Instead, consultants are portrayed as persuasive opinion formers who impose solutions and methods on clients who do not really need them but who may be powerless to resist. Such an opinion highlights the ways in which consultancy and client–consultant relationships are open to distortion, such as through the promotion of management fads and fashions that fuel the demand for consultancy. This perspective also criticizes the use of impression management and rhetoric by consultants to stimulate such demand. As such, consultants are seen as 'systems of persuasion creating compelling images which persuade clients of their quality and work' (Clark and Salaman, 1998: 18).

The functionalist and critical schools of thought characterize much of the literature on consultancy. However, both views have limitations. The functionalist perspective lacks analytical grounding in why clients hire external consultancies rather than carrying out the work themselves or developing internal consultancy capabilities, while the critical view lacks an acknowledgement of the economic processes and rational deliberations of clients. Instead it is preoccupied with consultants' truth claims, with consultants' supposedly unscientific approaches, and with an ostensibly dark side to consultancy, as well as appearing to focus on an anti-consultancy attitude portraying consultants as opportunists (Salaman, 2002). The critical perspective also fails to appreciate the wisdom and economic deliberations of clients in knowing what they are doing in selecting consultants, and the conditions in which social ties and reputation preclude opportunistic action by consultants (Armbruster, 2006). So both perspectives have limitations, but despite its critics the consultancy industry continues to flourish.

Consultancy

What consultancy is and isn't

Consultancy has an impact on every one of us, from the structures of government and the provision of education and transport, to the very language that we use and the way that we think about the world (O'Mahoney and Markham, 2013). When James McKinsey founded his consultancy company in 1926, he described it as a group of accountants and management engineers, even though no engineers were employed. Since then the term 'consultancy' has been widely used – even for work that is not really 'consultancy'. It is one of these words like communication or motivation that mean different things to different people and is, therefore, not an easy concept to define.

In an attempt to provide some clarity, the MCA describe consultancy as 'the creation of value for organizations, through the application of knowledge, techniques and assets, to improve business performance. This is achieved through the rendering of objective advice and/or the implementation of business solutions' (MCA, 2016). In other words, consultancy adds value by taking organizations further than they would go on their own. It does this by providing advice, solving problems and providing different perspectives. Consultancy can, therefore, be said to generally be about providing help.

This view of consultancy as 'helping' is, however, broad and is open to being exploited, with the result that the term 'consultancy' has become overused. Indeed not everything that is called consultancy is really consultancy – as some of what the term is used for is often really 'a need for an extra pair of hands', 'buying expertise', or simply 'getting a job done'.

Although there is a long history of calling many forms of help in organizations 'consultancy', it is possible to differentiate 'true consultancy' from other forms of help (Buono and Jamieson, 2010). True consultancy is based on the interaction between people. Edgar Schein (2002) points out that a consultant must create a relationship that will re-establish the client's sense of self-esteem, that will equilibrate the status between the client and the helper, and that will reduce the sense of dependency or counter-dependency that the client may feel initially. This definition of consultancy can be extended to include the guiding and influencing of the client's decisions and helping them to diagnose and identify the most appropriate intervention to address an issue. This can involve transferring knowledge and expertise, and helping clients to learn and build capability. Such a definition derives primarily from an OD orientation, where there has traditionally been a focus on the client–consultant relationship, which distinguishes consultancy from other forms of helping. This is especially relevant for consultancy for change since working with and through people, by forming relationships, is an important aspect of sustaining change in organizations (Hodges, 2016). As Buono and Jamieson say, to be truly effective, change-related consultancy requires 'a unique client–consultant relationship, a special set of consulting skills, and expertise in human and organizational systems and significant personal qualities' (2010: vii). Consultancy is, therefore, about building and maintaining relationships to achieve sustainable change.

Change

Organizations face incredible pressure to change within the complex and increasingly global environment in which they operate. It is not just that the amount of change has increased in recent decades but also that the speed of change has intensified and is, for some companies, overwhelming. This idea that organizations are constantly engaged in change to a greater or lesser degree is a common but not a new view. In 1947 the psychologist Kurt Lewin postulated that life is never without change, rather there are merely differences in the amount and type of change that exist. The same can still be said today.

In terms of defining what change is, the simplest approach is to describe it as altering something with the introduction or experience of something new or different, and can range from relatively short-term alternatives to highly complex transformations. Change can, therefore, be defined as an opportunity to make improvements and realize benefits through new ways of working or behaving (Hodges and Gill, 2015).

The nature of change is not always the same, as change comes in a variety of shapes and sizes. It can be proactive or reactive. Proactive change is initiated in response to a perceived opportunity or a threat as a result of the assessment or recognition of external or internal factors. In contrast, reactive change is a response to factors in the external environment or within the organization that have already occurred rather than being anticipated in the future. Organizational change can also be planned or emergent; slow or fast; continual or sporadic; incremental or transformational; and can also differ in a number of dimensions according to how it happens, its magnitude, focus and level.

Planned change

Sometimes change is deliberate, a product of conscious reasoning and action. This type of change is called *planned change*. Planned change is an intentional intervention for bringing about change to an organization and is best characterized as deliberate, purposeful and systematic (Tenkasi and Chesmore, 2003). The process of planned change is rational and linear.

The fundamental assumptions underlying planned change are derived originally from Kurt Lewin (1947). Lewin's model proposes three phases: unfreezing (identifying the need for change); moving (changing); and refreezing (embedding the change). Although widely adopted and adapted, the idea that organizations, and especially the people in them, are frozen, much less refrozen, has been heavily criticized (Dawson, 2003). To address such criticism, it is important to appreciate that this approach is not meant to be used in isolation. For, as Bernard Burnes (2013) points out, it needs to be recognized that Lewin intended his model to be used with the three other elements that comprise planned change – Field Theory, Group Dynamics and Action Research. Lewin saw these elements as forming an integrated approach to analysing, understanding and bringing about change, thus providing a sequential prescription for the processes of change.

Planned change models map out the processes to follow from the first recognition of the need or desirability for change through to the practicalities of implementation (Price, 2009). These models may vary in the number of steps they propose and the order in which they should be taken (see, for example, Kotter, 1996; Kanter *et al*, 1992). However, what unites them is the proposition that change can be achieved as long as the correct steps are taken.

Planned linear conceptions of change are increasingly being challenged. Critics argue that those who advocate planned change are attempting to impose an 'order and linear sequence on processes that are in reality messy and untidy, and which unfold in an iterative fashion' (Buchanan and Storey, 1997: 127). The difficulty with linear models, according to Paton and McCalman (2008), is that they create the view that change is a highly programmed process that takes as its starting point the problem that needs to be rectified, then breaks it down into constituent parts, analyses possible alternatives, selects the preferred solution and applies this relentlessly. In reality we know that change is not as easy as an x-step approach may suggest – if it was then the failure rate is likely to be lower.

Rather than seeing the process of planned change as linear, it is more appropriate to consider it as curvilinear or cyclic. This reframing has led even the most traditional of advocates of the planned staged approach to reconsider how change is managed. For example, John Kotter (2012) has redesigned his step model into a circle – which is a better reflection of how planned change can progress and be sustained.

Emergent change

In contrast to being planned, change can unfold in an unpredictable, spontaneous and often unintentional way. This type of change is known as *emergent change* – which is change as it happens. Karl Weick defines emergent change as consisting of 'accommodations, adaptations, and alterations that produce fundamental change without a priori intentions to do so' (2000: 237). In this way change can emerge without being planned. Weick's view that this type of change is small and often goes unnoticed is, however, flawed. There are many instances of emergent change that has had a massive impact, for instance the eruption of the volcano in Iceland in 2010 that caused chaos in the airline industry. Such disruption was neither planned nor small-scale but was of a significant magnitude, with losses for the airline industry running into billions of pounds. The essential unforeseeable character of this type of change means that it cannot be predicted and that the outcomes are often only understood in retrospect.

Advocates of emergent change, such as Patrick Dawson (2003), say that the applicability and validity of the approach is suitable for all organizations that operate in dynamic, complex and unpredictable environments. Despite such advantages, the emergent change theory does have a number of limitations. Research has found that a more emergent approach to change takes longer to deliver results and can be messy (Shaw, 2002). It has been criticized for its lack of coherence and its potential to create confusion and uncertainty in an organization due to a lack of clear objectives (Bamford and Forrester, 2003). This uncertainty can be unnerving to people in an organization. People need to be able to tolerate the unknown and to cope with the paradoxes that emergent change brings about. Not everyone will have the skills or the inclination to participate in such an unplanned, open-ended approach to change. So as with the planned approach to change the emergent approach has pros and cons, which need to be considered.

Magnitude of change

The magnitude or scale of change can range along a continuum from small-scale discrete change (incremental) to more radical transformations. Nearly 95 per cent of organizational changes are considered to be incremental, which means they are constant, evolving and cumulative (Burke, 2002). A key feature of this type of change is that it builds on what has already been accomplished and has the flavour of continuous improvement.

Incremental changes are the outcome of the everyday process of management and tend to be when individual parts of an organization deal increasingly and separately with one problem and one objective at a time (Burnes, 2009), such as the updating of processes, methods or regulations. Examples of incremental change include changing a product formula in such a way that customers notice no difference; for example, Cadbury's, the multinational confectionery organization, adding more or less sugar to its chocolate bars. Or a human resources (HR) department changing the format, but not the content, of its policies, procedures or job descriptions. Such changes can be incremental and gradual in nature, the risk of failure tends to be low but so are the returns in terms of benefits, which means that they often go unnoticed.

The turbulent environment of the twenty-first century means that the slow, plodding process of incremental change is not sufficient for all organizations, instead they rely on *transformational change*, which aims to redefine their strategic direction, structure, cultural assumptions and identity. This kind of change is also referred to as 'strategic', 'radical' or 'revolutionary' (Kanter *et al*, 1992). It can be described as a 'metamorpho-sis' – a transformation from one state to another, like a caterpillar evolving into a butterfly (Hodges and Gill, 2015). This is evident, for example, in how cloud technology has transformed how we store, access and share information. MasterCard, for example, has been on a journey, transforming itself from a traditional payments processing company into a technology company that provides the infrastructure that connects consumers, banks and businesses, with its underlying business model evolving to address new opportunities and competitive threats. Transformational change impacts on the deep structure of an organization. The key areas that represent an organization's deep structure are culture, strategy, structure, power distribution and control systems. This can involve a paradigm shift and completely new behaviours not only in one company but also across an entire sector or even country – it means doing things differently rather than necessarily doing things better. It might even mean doing different things, such as Amazon moving from being an e-commerce bookseller, to a producer of films and TV series. So compared to incremental changes, transformations are much more disruptive to what people do in organizations since their ways of working and behaving are radically altered.

Rather than change being either incremental or transformational, an alternative position that has gained widespread currency is that more attention needs to be paid to the interplay between incremental and transformational change – known as *punctuated equilibrium* (Gersick, 1991). This occurs when change oscillates between long periods of incremental change and short bursts of transformational change. For example, after centuries of incremental changes to printing books the publishing industry has had to reinvent itself with the advent of e-readers, such as Kindles and iPads. This pattern of change repeats itself with some degree of regularity and variation across sectors, for example periods of transformational change may follow a 10-year cycle of incremental change in the public sector, whereas in the technology sector the cycle of change may be much shorter. As the rate of change increases across industries, the time between periods of incremental and transformational change will start to decrease, thus perpetuating the need for organizations to be able to lead and manage people through different types of change (Hodges, 2016).

Levels of change

The focus of transformational change is often *strategic*, whereas incremental change tends to be more *operational*. De Wit and Meyer emphasize the difference between operational and strategic change in the following terms: 'while operational changes are necessary to maintain the business and organisational systems, strategic changes are directed at renewing it' (2004: 163).

Strategic change can include restructures, mergers, acquisitions or outsourcing, while operational change involves anything affecting day-to-day operations, such as changes to manufacturing processes.

Change can also vary depending on the level of its focus – which can be *individual, team* or *organizational*. These three levels tend to be related since change at one level will often result in change at another level and so act like a 'waterfall'. This means that if the target of change is the organization as a whole, the intervention will frequently cascade down to the teams that make up the organization and ultimately down to the individuals who make up the team. So change can vary in how it emerges, its size, scope, magnitude and level depending on the context in which it is occurring.

Pace and sequence of change

Change is enabled through its pace and sequence. The speed at which change occurs can vary and subsequently have different impacts. Fast-paced changes, for instance, can create energy and momentum, while slow-paced change can help to facilitate learning and allow all organizational members time to understand what needs to be changed and in what way. Alternatively, a slow pace can allow time for opposition to grow to the proposed change, while fast-paced change can lead to change fatigue – where people are worn out by too much change too quickly. So there needs to be caution against moving too quickly and too slowly, as organizations are littered with the debris of getting the pace of change wrong. Michael Schrage (2012) quotes examples such as Ron Johnson, CEO of JC Penney, as moving too fast and Meg Whitman of Hewlett-Packard, Jack Welch of GE, Bob McDonald of Procter and Gamble, as moving too slowly. This, Schrage says, is in contrast to IBM's Lou Gerstner who, through a practised, cultivated deliberateness, ensured that the right pace was employed. So how quickly or slowly the change is implemented needs to be considered.

Related to the pace of change is how it is sequenced. Sequencing of change refers to the order in which different elements of the change are introduced. The available time for each stage or phase of change is important because changes that are transformational often require people to learn new behaviours and ways of working. Such major adjustments take time and can be hindered when changes are implemented too quickly (Bennebroek Gravenhorst *et al*, 2003). To address this Brown and Eisenhardt (1997) suggest 'time pacing'. Time pacing creates a regular, rhythmic and proactive approach to change that can increase the capacity for change and gives people a sense of control as it makes change more predictable, focused and efficient. This does, of course, need to be adapted to the organizational context and the type of change that is being implemented.

Questions for discussion

Consider a change you are facing either in your organization or home life:

- What should the pace of change be – will it be easier if it is introduced quickly or over a longer period of time?
- How should the change be introduced – what should be the phases or sequencing of it?

Process-driven or people-driven change

Change is changing as the process approach to change is being transformed to a people-focused approach (Hodges, 2016). The *process approach* to change has traditionally dominated change efforts and is in contrast to the *people approach*. The differences between the process and the people approach to change are illustrated in Table 1.1. The benefit of the latter is that it ensures that people are engaged in change and enabled to participate in the decision-making, and therefore able to influence the change interventions.

In the process approach, the power to create change comes through positional authority, whereas in the people approach power comes from relationships and the ability to influence through networks. The process approach focuses on change to achieve the mission and vision of the organization, usually this is change that is driven from the top down. In contrast, on the people side, the emphasis is on a shared purpose of the rationale and decisions for change. On the process side, change approaches are driven by

Table 1.1   Process and people approaches

Process approach	People approach
Power through position	Power through relationships
Mission and vision	Shared purpose
Making sense through logic, linear tasks	Making sense through emotions
Leadership-driven innovation	People connectivity
Traditional, based on experience	Open approaches
Transactional	Relationships
Getting things done	Capability

logical, linear tasks, whereas the people approach emphasizes the connection with the emotional aspects of change. While the passion and energy for creativity and innovation are driven by leaders on the process side, in the people approach the drive for creativity and innovation is sparked by people across the organization at different levels, often via virtual networks and social media. The process side utilizes traditional planning and improvement methodologies such as Lean, Six Sigma and TQM; the people approach focuses on the increasingly open and connected world where there are many new opportunities to share ideas, compare data and co-create novel approaches to change, such as crowd wisdom. Many of the levers for change with the process approach are transactional, such as compliance. People are accountable through transaction performance targets; instead, with the people approach, change is about commitment and ownership. People are accountable through shared commitments and to how they work together. The process approach focuses on getting things done, completing them and moving on; while on the people side the emphasis is on capabilities and building capabilities for change that will be of benefit to the organization in the longer term. Traditionally, the process approach has been used in organizational change initiatives where the focus tends to be measurement; and execution and the people and emotional dimensions of change are largely ignored. The move to a people approach means the focus is on: building a shared purpose; connectivity; innovation; relationships; empathy; and change capabilities.

The people approach to change is illustrated in the following case study by Perry Timms, Founder of PTHR and the iPractice, social media adviser and a TEDx Speaker on 'The Future of Work'.

CASE STUDY

Change through people: Talent development as a lever for change

How do you take a young organization and create change to bring about a more mature company? That was the problem I was not asked to solve at the Big Lottery Fund – the largest funder of lottery income to the charity world, providing £600 million per year to good causes. Why was I not asked that? Because most of the people who had been with the company in either of its former guises or since its inception believed it to already be a mature organization. The senior leaders did, however, recognize that there was an immaturity about creating promotion-readiness for people to step into leadership and management roles.

So Aspire and Ascend were born. These were two programmes for a small but powerful number of people to showcase their potential and get themselves into a position of success for any internal vacancies of a management nature. This was a chance to use a talent programme as a Trojan horse into culture change.

A culture change was needed for a range of reasons:

1 There was a power struggle that no one talked about openly; namely a struggle between a very large operations function and everyone else.
2 There was a fixation on being taught content in a classroom with no e-learning, no coaching and no recognition of experiential learning.
3 There was a strong feeling that HR was a support function, and not really an enabling one since HR was not exactly driving business change, innovation or creative energy.
4 People felt it was a good place to work but career advancement was not exactly top of the senior leadership priorities and consequently good people were leaving for elsewhere.

For this change, I put in place: a series of communication, engagement, involvement and participation techniques; a cross-divisional board to advise; a sponsor from a large non-HR role, with influence at board level; and a sustained approach to a project using the tired old PRINCE2 methodology. There was no nine-box grid and no psychometric tests, instead there was a selection process that allowed potential and experience to be given equal weighting. There was no unfreeze, change, refreeze model. Instead, the nearest thing to a model that I used was Morgan's metaphors – in shifting the business from a political machine model to a more organic one.

The talent programme was introduced to include people in order to allow previously unheralded stars to shine more brightly and to give people permission to take control over their own development. The real model used was people-powered change.

The following approach worked well:

● Consulting people on the design and creating a multi-divisional board, not just made up of directors but of people at different levels. This was critical in proving it was not a management initiative but something for all people, and that included membership to the cross-divisional board. Directorates had such a strong identity that this had previously been a divisive aspect of the organization. Management in each division had become a little entrenched. People at other levels had more spirited approaches to working together and this board proved that was the case.

- HR was on the board and involved in supporting it but did not chair it. It was vital to prove that it was not just a people's initiative or HR hobbyhorse. This had huge people benefits, but it was also about building a sustainable way forward for the entire organization and the people who made things happen (not to mention a subtle culture change enabler).

- Having an agile and iterative approach. Version 1 and version 2 of the programme differed slightly. Version 3 differed greatly and was literally a democratic talent programme – ie everyone had talent. It was up to managers or the organization to deploy this talent and get it firing best.

- Letting innovation thrive. It was important that the programme learned from itself and that innovation in the world of work was allowed to thrive. Democratizing talent management proved a little too tough for the business to take on board but it was regarded highly by the industry. In 2013 I attended a presentation by Stephan Thoma who described exactly this democratic talent model. So it clearly works in the right environment and with the right level of maturity across the organization.

This approach for the programme of change had one lasting impact: that people believed in their potential to improve, develop and push on. It created a centrifugal force that was present until the day I left the company and people have been accelerated into key roles through this and they have effected change in a range of areas. These talented people pushed on with all sorts of their own change and organizational-level programmes. They had appetite and guile, and they were self-directed and purposeful. People with a spark and creativity, liberated to make change happen, are the magic ingredient for success in delivering change.

In contrast the following did not work:

- Being led a little too much by operational leaders. It was run like a business programme with rigour, which helped, but was also biased towards process, certainty and operationalizing every element. It made experimentation difficult.

- This was a people programme, and at times there were too many processes. There was a mechanical orientation that made it difficult to deliver and adapt to people's needs.

- There were some interference factors on decisions and this led to some unrest and some people feeling let down by the programme. Others who were 'wild cards' were forced down a different track based on development centre results. One left and two felt very let down. This was not HR's decision but that of influential board members. Quotas on the programme were often disputed and this showed how the organization was far from united.

- Promotion rates were good and so, unfortunately, this caused some people to move to other organizations. Nothing says 'you're good' like inclusion on a talent development programme and a few people took advantage of that and left. Whilst it was disappointing that several people used the programme to move on to other organizations, it did prove that people are valued more when they are given this endorsement and support. It is a risk worth taking because many more people were fiercely loyal to the organization that was seen to invest in them.

For this change programme I learnt that inclusivity in change is key. Not by forming a massive committee but through talking to people at all levels and by involving them and letting them loose with concepts to shape the programme. Keeping the numbers tight helped the focus while it meant that we could include whoever else we wanted on the fringe. It was a test of people's willingness to adapt – if they were not selected, would they shrink and sulk or rise and take up the challenge?

I also involved other learning and change practitioners from outside the company, who created their version of this and it too changed their organization.

I had the chief executive officer (CEO) join the board for the second and third iterations of the programme when the operations director left for another role. This was a masterstroke. Bringing a CEO closer to people at all levels like this proved so powerful. Next time I will start with the CEO on the board and as part of the design process. They are never too busy for the future of their company, surely?

I would also start the process of democratizing the method sooner so that other teams and divisions could start their own change revolutions and not just rely on HR doing a corporate one. Change-related assignment work delivered huge results. More of that across the different parts of the organization would have been great to leverage more.

In summary, this was not a change programme in the traditional new product/ new markets/mergers and acquisitions type – it was what appeared to be a talent management initiative but it was secretly a culture change programme. Enabling and involving people, giving all-comers a chance to lean in and be part of a talent revolution. Confidence surged and potential created energy. Managers reminded themselves that they have talent to lead, shape and deploy. It had triple return on investment in that it returned on investment, interest and inclusivity. It really was people-powered change.

Organization development

The nature of change has a considerable impact on the people in organizations. To support people through transitions the role of OD is more relevant than ever, especially as OD uses social and behavioural science knowledge to develop interventions that help organizations and individuals change successfully (Anderson, 2012).

OD is an interdisciplinary field with diverse intellectual roots. It grew out of Kurt Lewin's (1947) pioneering work on behaviour and his development of T-groups. The T-group approach is often referred to as 'sensitivity training', because it sensitizes participants to their own behaviour. Today such an approach is often adapted and used as the first stage in teambuilding activities.

Traditionally, OD tended to focus on group issues in organizations, and promoted Lewin's approach to change in the values it espoused until the 1970s. This changed with the oil shocks of the 1970s, the economic turmoil of the 1980s and the rise of Japanese competitiveness. As a consequence, organizations became less interested in group-based change and more concerned with transformational change (Burnes, 2009). This resulted in a major broadening of the scope of OD as it began to focus on organization-wide transformation initiatives (French and Bell, 1999), resulting in it moving from its roots in group-based planned change to a far more organization-wide view of change.

There are various definitions of OD. One of the most frequently cited definitions comes from Richard Beckhard:

> Organizational development is an effort which is planned, organization-wide, and managed from the top, to increase organization effectiveness and health through planned interventions in the organization's 'processes', using behavioral science knowledge.
>
> (Beckhard, 1969: 9)

This definition describes OD as a planned approach that is initiated by senior leaders. French and Bell broaden this definition and emphasize the role of the consultant and the use of applied methodologies and tools: 'Organizational development is a long-term effort, led and supported by top management, to improve an organization's visioning, empowerment, learning, and problem-solving processes, through an ongoing, collaborative management of organizational culture... using the consultant-facilitator role' (French and Bell, 1999: 25–26).

OD is, therefore, a process of change, involving a collection of activities and techniques, facilitated by a consultant. This emphasis on the purpose of OD being about change is stressed by Warren Bennis who says that OD is 'a response to change, a complex educational strategy intended to change the beliefs, attitudes, values and structures of organisations so that they can better adapt to new technology, markets, challenges and the dizzying rate of change itself' (Bennis, 1969: 2).

Based on such definitions it would therefore seem that when organizations plan change, OD provides relevant processes and frameworks to help implement and sustain the change. As Donald Anderson (2012: 9) says, 'when organizations attempt conscious changes... OD offers relevant processes and techniques to make the change function effectively'. Anderson is, however, adamant in pointing out not just what OD is but also what it is not. It is not, he points out, just training and development nor is it the mere application of a standard procedure or toolkit.

In sum, OD is based on principles that promote and sustain change which can help develop the ability to create innovations and adaptations without creating 'toxic' consequences for people, processes and the organization's culture (Barnett and Shore, 2009). OD can provide concepts, tools, theories and techniques that help consultants in organizational change. OD can, therefore, be described as a process for initiating, implementing and sustaining change (Hodges, 2015) that can be carried out as part of consultancy. Hence the specific focus on OD interventions in this book.

OD consultants

OD consultants understand the people elements of change and can provide a valuable service. As Bradford and Burke say, 'in a world where change is constant, for organizations to be adaptive, decisions must be pushed down the hierarchy and members must be aligned around the same strategic goals. OD practitioners know how to do this' (2005: 196).

Professionals that carry out OD consultancy include a much larger group than those who hold the title of consultant. They include 'many kinds of people for whom organizational change is a priority, such as managers and executives, project managers, and organizational members in a variety of roles' (Anderson, 2012: 15).

Traditionally, OD practitioners offer help in areas such as:

- Problem solving. Helping to identify a key issue, gathering information about it and outlining decisions or action plans needed to address the issue.

- Talent management. Helping to assess the capability of the workforce, succession planning and identifying and providing development options to grow, build and retain talent.

- Business process redesign. Analysing the current way of doing a specific piece of work to determine how to improve it.

- Organizational change. Helping to identify the need and readiness for change; and identifying, planning and implementing interventions.

- Training and development. Designing and delivering development interventions to enhance capabilities.

Despite the obvious benefits of such OD activities, it is not without its critics. Based on his study of strategic change at ICI, Andrew Pettigrew rejected OD, arguing that it was too rational, linear, incremental and prescriptive, did not pay enough attention to the need to analyse and conceptualize organizational change, and failed to recognize that change processes were shaped by history, culture, context and the balance of power in organizations.

Others have criticized OD as having too much of a Western bias. For example, Adler (1997) warns that not all OD methods and techniques are transportable across national boundaries to other parts of the world or even to different ethnic groupings within single countries. According to some writers, this is particularly true with regard to the range of OD techniques for bringing about change (Senior and Fleming, 2006). In order to address such reservations about the degree to which OD approaches can be used to help to facilitate change there is a need to ensure that OD interventions are tailored to the organizational culture in which they are being applied.

In response to criticisms about traditional practices, OD practitioners have sought to develop alternative approaches. One such alternative is what has been termed 'dialogic', which focuses on an ongoing conversation, in contrast to the more traditional OD diagnostic process. Examples of dialogic OD methods include appreciative inquiry, free-space thinking (see Chapters 5 and 6 for a discussion of these approaches). In accordance with the dialogic approach Bushe and Marshak (2008) propose that OD has evolved and is now based on the following values:

- *The encouragement of facilitation of greater systems awareness.* OD works to increase the knowledge of employees about the organization, usually through facilitating events where the organization is an object of enquiry and discussion.

- *Concern for capacity building and development of the organization.* OD attempts not only to achieve a change target but also to develop the organization's efficacy and increase its capacity to survive and prosper.

- *Consultants stay out of content and focus on process.* OD practitioners emphasize their neutrality and encourage employees to decide for themselves rather than provide advice or an opinion on decisions.

The ensuing need for reinventing OD has also led to the examination of it from an emotion-based standpoint. In support of this, de Klerk (2007) writes about how emotional trauma can negatively affect performance. For instance, due to downsizing, outsourcing, mergers, restructuring and continual changes, employees may experience the emotions of aggression, anxiety, apprehension, cynicism and fear that can lead to a deterioration in their performance at work. De Klerk (2007) suggests that, to heal such trauma and improve performance, OD practitioners must acknowledge the existence of the trauma, provide a safe place for employees to discuss their feelings, symbolize the trauma and put it into perspective, and then allow for, and deal with, the emotional responses. This is an important but often neglected part of change. In my book *Managing and Leading People Through Change* (Hodges, 2016) I stress the vital need to recognize and address the emotional aspects of change rather than ignoring them.

The development of different approaches helps to emphasize that OD is not a 'one-size-fits-all' approach to organizational change or a methodical set of rigid practices and procedures. Instead, it consists of multiple methods, perspectives, approaches and values that influence how it is practised. OD is, therefore, more than a toolkit. It offers more than a procedure for moving from point A to point B. It involves being attuned to the emotional dynamics of individuals that usually require dialogue and not just a standardized set of procedures or tools. Ultimately, OD approaches have to be adapted to the organization, team and/or individuals they are aimed at, in order to embed and sustain organizational changes.

Clients

A key question for any consultant to clarify is 'Who is the client?' It is not unusual for a project to fail because the relevant client was inappropriately defined (Cummings and Worley, 2001). Schein (1997) suggests a typology that defines six types of client:

1 *Contact clients.* The contact client is the individual who first approaches the consultant (internal or external) and proposes that the consultant addresses the specific change issue.

2 *Intermediate clients*. Intermediate clients are stakeholders who become involved in the consulting project. They will attend meetings and will work with the consultant and provide data during the consultancy process.

3 *Primary clients*. The primary client is the stakeholder who identified the need for the consultancy. They are also the budget holder for any payment required for the consultancy.

4 *Unwitting clients*. Unwitting clients will be affected by the change intervention but may not know of the consultancy activity or that it will affect them.

5 *Indirect clients*. Indirect clients are individuals who will be affected by the outcome of the consultancy and who are aware that they will be affected. However, the consultant may not know them.

6 *Ultimate clients*. Ultimate clients consist of any stakeholders who will be affected by the consultancy intervention and whose interests need to be taken into account.

Recognizing these different types of clients is useful for a consultant in order to identify the real client and whether or not they are what Michael Mitchell (2010) terms a 'good' client. This, according to Mitchell, is someone who is:

- secure in their leadership and is not a control freak;
- a good manager and/or leader;
- open minded about potential change if it leads to better performance;
- neither strongly authoritarian nor laissez faire but involved;
- honest and willing to share information with employees;
- able to allow others to solve problems differently than he or she does;
- focused more on the results than the methods;
- trustworthy; and
- can partner with the consultant.

Rather than using the term 'client', which is usually preferred by external consultants, internal consultants may refer to the 'stakeholder'. Stakeholders are any individuals or group of individuals who may be affected by a change. Identifying who the stakeholders are and whether they are supporters or blockers of the change can be done effectively using stakeholder analysis (see Chapter 2 for details). Defining the client/stakeholder is important and can help frame: how the client issue is defined; what the diagnostic process should be; and what interventions are selected.

Why do we need consultancy for change?

The value of consultancy

If an organization has to change, how can consultancy help? This is dependent on the value that consultancy can bring, depending upon the type of consulting being delivered, the perspectives of both the client and consultant, the nature of the organization or managerial need (perceived) and the level of analysis (individual or system). Over the years, as consulting has morphed into many different kinds of services, there have been shifts in what is considered 'value', from the standpoint of both the seller and the buyer. The range has continued to grow, from buying answers to problems, to buying expertise, to buying processes, to buying human capital, to buying catalysts for change or developers of capacity (Jamieson and Armstrong, 2010).

The fact that consultancy can add value does not, however, mean that it always does so. Research by Source Information Services (2014) found that only 38 per cent of 900 senior executives in multinational organizations think that consultancy can add value. The report concludes that consultants have yet to find a consistent, systematic way of explaining the value they add.

In an attempt to define what value clients expect it is worth considering the reasons why clients buy consultancy services. These reasons are outlined in Table 1.2. Clients are looking for expertise, externality, extension and endorsement from consultants. Consultants can provide this through specialist capabilities that clients rarely possess (Armbruster, 2006). But being able to assess and measure this can be difficult because defining value and determining whether or not it has been achieved is highly subjective because what constitutes value for one person may be different for someone else and vary in different situations and organizations.

Table 1.2   Clients' buying reasons (adapted from Matthias 2013)

Reason	Definition
Expertise	Looking for knowledge they do not possess, be it 'knowing how' or 'knowing what'
Externality	Looking for an external perspective, be it geography or industry
Extension	Looking for an injection of extra resource
Endorsement	Looking for a decision to be legitimized or depersonalized

One way for consultants to identify how they add value is by utilizing a value management process. There are two elements to a value management process: value management and value differentiation. *Value management* is the ability to understand clearly and communicate where value is being created. Value in this sense is tangible – it is something that the client will receive benefit from. Nagle and Holden (1995) define it as the total savings or satisfaction that the client receives. Jamieson and Armstrong suggest that 'It generally involves what the consultant does or says that enables the client or client system to do or change something they were not previously able to accomplish or something desirable or beneficial gained by the client system through the consultation' (Jamieson and Armstrong 2010: 4).

Such value can emerge during a change process. For instance, clients might find value in being asked the right questions, having their concerns alleviated or their confidence improved, or from something specific they learn as the change progresses. *Value differentiation* is the difference in value between different options. For instance, it might be seen as the difference between the value of the change carried out by an external consultant, in comparison to that delivered by an internal consultant, or vice versa. The value a consultant provides is determined by the experience, skills and knowledge that they bring to what appears to be an intractable issue. The capability of the consultant does not, however, just lie in having a toolkit full of models and frameworks but in knowing which are the most appropriate to use and how to apply them within the given context. The value is also in being able to provide ideas that are possible to implement in practice and which will achieve sustainable benefits. To achieve this it is important that the consultant and client are clear as to the change that is needed and about the value to be realized.

The value of consultancy during a change process

Consultancy can add value to the process of organizational change in various ways, including:

- *Need for change.* Recognizing the drivers of, and the need for, change is a key element for competitive advantage. Consultancy can influence the need, readiness and commitment among individuals and within a team and/or organization for change.
- *Content.* Identifying the content of change – what to do – to meet the drivers for change is a key focus of consultancy. Consultants can use their knowledge and experience to diagnose the situation to help identify relevant content.

- *Process.* An important aspect of consultancy is assisting with the process of change – how to transform. Consultancy can provide an approach for how to go about the change.

- *Emotions.* Change is an emotional process and consultants can help to identify and deal with the emotional dynamics of the change process.

- *Stages.* Planned change involves initiating, dialogue, feedback, learning, implementation, engagement, evaluation, leadership as well as management. Consultants can work jointly with managers and leaders during each stage of a change process.

- *Diagnosis and analysis.* Consultancy is able to trigger the expression and extraction of knowledge that tacitly exists in organizations, frame it into a coherent case and present it to key stakeholders. Consultancy can therefore help to express, extract, distil and frame the knowledge for organizational change.

- *Capabilities.* Consultants can bring unique, different or unencumbered and innovative perspectives, knowledge, skills, attitudes, and expertise to organizational change.

- *Impact.* Through their actions and/or behaviours consultants can exercise influence and create relationships in which they achieve impact.

- *Relationships.* The client–consultant relationship is important to the effectiveness of consultancy and to the change process. Consultants will be of benefit by developing, modifying and maintaining an engaged relationship with clients.

Depending on the purpose of the consultancy project there may well be other areas where consultancy can be of benefit and add value to change.

Summary

Consultancy is based on the interaction between people; it involves guiding and influencing clients' decisions and helping them to diagnose and identify the most appropriate intervention to address an issue. This can involve transferring knowledge and expertise, and helping clients to learn and build capability. Such a definition derives primarily from an OD orientation, where there has traditionally been a focus on the client–consultant relationship, which distinguishes consultancy from other forms of helping. This is especially relevant for consultancy for change since working with and through people, by forming relationships, is an important aspect of sustaining change in organizations.

Clients need to rethink consultancy investment. Simply spending more money on consultants (whether internal or external) is not enough. To deliver a superior return on investment and gain value, clients' spending must be far more focused on and targeted at what works, with a focus on evidence and results.

The value of consultancy, like beauty, is in the eye of the beholder and is not always an absolute element. Although value might be defined as savings or satisfaction that the client receives from a change carried out by a consultant (internal or external), there are many factors that drive this satisfaction. So it is important to understand what the client perceives as value, since value must be measured, not from the consultant's perspective, but from that of the client.

References

Adler, NJ (1997) *International Dimensions of Organizational Behaviour*, 3rd edn, South-Western College Publishing, Cincinnati, OH

Anderson, D (2012) *Organization Development: The process of leading organizational change*, Sage, London

Armbruster, T (2006) *The Economics and Sociology of Management Consulting*, Cambridge University Press, Cambridge

Arygris, C (2000) *Flawed Advice and the Management Trap*, Oxford University Press, Oxford

Bamford, DR and Forrester, PL (2003) Managing planned and emergent change within an operations management environment. *International Journal of Operations and Production Management*, **23** (5), pp 546–64

Barnett, CK and Shore, B (2009) Reinventing program design: Challenges in leading sustainable institutional change, *Leadership & Organization Development Journal*, **30** (1), pp 16–35

Beckhard, R (1969) *Organization Development: Strategies and models*, Addison-Wesley, Reading, MA

Bennebroek Gravenhorst, KM, Werkman, RA and Boonstra, JJ (2003) The change capacity of organisations: General assessment and five configurations, *Applied Psychology*, **52** (1), pp 83–105

Bennis, WG (1969) *Organization Development: Its nature, origins, and prospects*, Addison-Wesley, Reading, MA

Bessant, J and Rush, H (1995) Building bridges for innovation: The role of consultants in technology transfer, *Research Policy*, **24** (1), pp 97–114

Bradford, DL and Burke, WW (eds) (2005) *Reinventing Organization Development: New approaches to change in organizations*, Wiley & Sons, London

Bradley, J, Loucks, J, Macaulay, J, Noronha, A and Wade, M (2015) *Digital Vortex: How digital disruption is redefining industries*, Global Center for Digital

Business Transformation, Global Center for Digital Business Transformation. [Online] http://www.cisco.com/c/dam/en/us/solutions/collateral/industry-solutions/digital-vortex-report.pdf

Brown, S and Eisenhardt, K (1997) The art of continuous change: Linking complexity theory and time-paced evolution in relentlessly shifting organizations, *Administrative Science Quarterly,* **42**, pp 1–34

Buchanan, D and Storey, J (1997) Role-taking and role-switching in organizational change: The four pluralities, *Innovation, Organizational Change and Technology*, pp 127–45.

Buono, AF and Jamieson, D (2010) *Consultation for Organizational Change*, Information Age Publishing, Charlotte, NC

Burke, WW (1994) Diagnostic models for organization development, *Diagnosis for organizational change: Methods and models*, pp 53–84.

Burke, WW (2002) *Organization Change: Theory and practice*, Sage, Thousand Oaks, CA

Burnes, B (2009) *Managing Change*, 5th edn, FT/Prentice Hall, Harlow

Burnes, B (2013) Looking back to forward, in *Organizational Change, Leadership and Ethics*, ed RT By and B Burnes, pp 243–58, Routledge, London

Bushe, GR and Marshak, RJ (2008) The post modern turn in OD to meaning making: From diagnosis to meaning making, *OD Practitioner*, **40** (4), pp 10–12

Christensen, CM, Wang, D and van Bever, D (2013) Consulting on the cusp of disruption, *Harvard Business Review*, **91**(10), pp 106–14

Clark, T and Fincham, R (2002) *Critical Consulting: New perspectives on the management advice industry*, Blackwell, Oxford

Clark, T and Salaman, G (1998) Telling tales: Management gurus' narratives and the construction of managerial identity, *Journal of Management studies*, **35** (2), pp 137–61

Cummings, TG and Worley, CG (2001) *Essentials of Organization Development and Change*, Cengage, Mason

Czerniawska, F (2002) *Value-Based Consulting*, Palgrave McMillan, London

Czerniawska, F and May, P (2004) *Management Consulting in Practice: A casebook of international best practice*, Kogan Page, London

Dawson, P (2003) *Organizational Change: A processual approach*, Paul Chapman, London

de Klerk, M (2007) Healing emotional trauma in organizations: An OD framework and case study, *Organization Development Journal*, **25** (2).

De Wit, B and Meyer, R (2004) *Strategy: Process, content, context – an international perspective*, Thomson, London/Connecticut

French, WL and Bell, CH (1999) *Organization Development: Behaviour science interventions for organization improvement*, 6th edn, Prentice Hall, Upper Saddle River, NJ

Gersick, C (1991) Revolutionary change theories: A multilevel exploration of the punctuated equilibrium paradigm, *Academy of Management Review*, **16**, pp 10–36

Hansen, MT (2002) Knowledge networks: Explaining effective knowledge sharing in multiunit companies, *Organization science*, **13** (3), pp 232–48

Hill, A (2015) Hybrid consulting firms feed off digital fear, *Financial Times*, 9 November

Hill, A (2016) Meeting the 'gig' consultants, *Financial Times*, 7 October

Hodges, J (2016) *Managing and Leading People Through Organizational Change: The theory and practice of sustaining change through people*, Kogan Page, London

Hodges, J and Gill, R (2015) *Sustaining Change in Organizations*. London: Sage

Jamieson, D and Armstrong, T (2010) Consulting for change, in *Consultation for Organizational Change*, ed AF Buono and D Jamieson, Information Age Publishing, Charlotte, NC, pp 3–13

Kanter, R, Stein, B and Jick, T (1992) *The Challenge of Organizational Change: How companies experience it and leaders guide it*, Free Press, New York

Kotter, J (1996) *Leading Change*, Harvard Business School Press, Boston

Kotter, J (2012) Accelerate!, *Harvard Business Review*, **90** (11), pp 44–58

Lewin, K (1947) Frontiers in group dynamics II: Channels of group life, social planning and action research, *Human Relations*, **1** (2), pp 143–53

Maister, D, Galford, R and Green, C (2002) *The Trusted Advisor*, Simon & Schuster, London

Matthias, O (2013) *Developing a Customisation Blueprint for Management Consultancies to Better Serve Their Clients*, University of Bradford School of Management

MCA (2016) *The UK Consulting Industry*, Management Consultancies Association [Online] http://www.mca.org.uk/about-us/the-consulting-industry

McCallum, E (2016) *Future of Consultancy*. [Online] http://2nl301mfq7z3k8c8z3fobjbk.wpengine.netdna-cdn.com/wp-content/uploads/2016/05/Future-of-Consulting-Survey-2016-Results.pdf

McDonald, D (2015) *The Firm: The story of McKinsey and its secret influence on American business*, OneWorld, London

Mitchell, M (2010) Whole system consulting, in *Consultation for Organizational Change*, ed AF Buono and D Jamieson, Information Age Publishing, Charlotte, NC, pp 41–78

Nadler, DA and Tushman, ML (1995) Types of organizational change: From incremental improvement to discontinuous transformation, *Discontinuous Change: Leading organizational transformation*, Jossey-Bass, San Francisco, pp 15–34

Nagle, TT and Holden, RK (1995) *The Strategy and Tactics of Pricing*, Prentice Hall, London

O'Mahoney, J and Markham, C (2013) *Management Consultancy*, Oxford University Press, Oxford

Paton, R and McCalman, J (2008) *Change Management: A guide to effective implementation*, 3rd edn, Sage, London

Pettigrew, A (1985) *The Awakening Giant*, Blackwell, Oxford

Pinault, L (2000) *Consulting Demons: Inside the unscrupulous world of global corporate consulting*, HarperBusiness, London

Plimmer, G (2016) Consultancies bypass Oxbridge in search of digital skills, *Financial Times*, 13 June

Price, D (2009) The context of change, in *The Principles and Practice of Change* ed D Price, pp 3–23, Palgrave Macmillan, Basingstoke

Salaman, G (2002) Understanding advice: Towards a sociology of management consultancy, in *Critical Consulting: New perspectives on the management advice industry*, ed T Clark and R Fincham, Blackwell, Oxford, pp 247–60

Schein, E (2002) Consulting: What should it mean?, in *Critical Consulting: New perspectives on the management advice industry*, ed T Clark and R Fincham, Blackwell, Oxford, pp 21–27

Schein, EH (1997) The concept of 'client' from a process consultation perspective: A guide for change agents, *Journal of Organizational Change Management*, **10** (3), pp 202–16

Schrage, M (2012) Are you driving too much change, too fast?, HBR Blog Network, *Harvard Business Review*, 14 November

Schwab, K (2016) *The Fourth Industrial Revolution: What it means, how to respond*, World Economic Forum. [Online] https://www.weforum.org/agenda/2016/01/the-fourth-industrial-revolution-what-it-means-and-how-to-respond/

Senior, B and Fleming, J (2006) *Organizational change*, 3rd edn, Prentice Hall/FT, London

Shaw, P (2002) *Changing Conversations in Organizations: A complexity approach to change*, Routledge, London

Sorge, A and van Witteloostuijn, A (2004) The (non) sense of organizational change: An essay about universal management hypes, sick consultancy metaphors, and healthy organization theories, *Organization Studies*, **25** (7), pp 1205–31

Sourceforconsulting.com (2011) *Management Consulting Market Report*. [Online] SourceforConsulting.com

Source Information Services (2014) The US consulting market. [Online] http://www.sourceforconsulting.com

Stern, S (2010) Strategy consultants need some new ideas, *Financial Times*, 5 April

Tadena, N (2016) PwC pushes further into design, digital business. [Online] http://www.wsj.com/articles/pwc-pushes-further-into-design-digital-business-1444192201

Tenkasi, RV and Chesmore, MC (2003) Social networks and planned organizational change: The impact of strong network ties on effective change implementation and use, *The Journal of Applied Behavioral Science*, **39** (3), pp 281–300

Tushman, M and Romanelli, E (1985) Organizational evolution: A metamorphosis model of convergence and reorientation, in *Research in Organization*

Behaviour, vol 7, ed B Staw and I Cummings, pp 171–222, JAI Press, Greenwich, CT

Weick, K (2000) Emergent change as a universal in organisations, in *Breaking the Code of Change*, ed M Beer and N Nohria, Harvard Business Review Press, Boston, MA

Weick, K and Quinn, R (1999) Organizational change and development, *Annual Review of Psychology*, 50, pp 361–86

Wylie, I (2016) MBA graduates' love affair with consultancy endures, *Financial Times*, 31 January

Roles and responsibilities of consulting

02

KEY POINTS

- It is vital to be clear about the type of consultancy that is expected, as it can be frustrating to adopt one role when the client wants or expects another. The approach expected should be clarified by contracting with the client as soon as possible at the start of an assignment, even if it changes as the work progresses and it becomes necessary to re-contract and agree a different approach.

- Consultancy for change requires a mix of consulting roles (particularly expert and facilitative) but also, as importantly, an emphasis on: building and maintaining relationships; continuous learning; and collaboration.

- There are a number of advantages and disadvantages to using internal consultants and external consultants. The main ones discussed here are: organizational insight; cost; flexibility; objectivity; dealing with organizational politics.

- Comparing the advantages and disadvantages of internal and external consultants helps to highlight the critical aspects of consultancy and can influence selection decisions concerning which type of consultant to employ.

Introduction

Consultants of one kind or another have existed for centuries. Han Fei Tzu, founder of the legalist school of ancient Chinese philosophy and adviser to the emperor, has been called the first consultant (Higdon, 1970). Much has been written about the purpose and nature of the consultant role over the years, and opinions are as varied as the people who carry out consultancy work and the different types of work they do (see, for example, Buono and Jamieson, 2010; O'Mahoney and Markham, 2013).

The aim of this chapter is to explore the roles and responsibilities of consultants. It begins by examining the nature of consultancy and provides an overview of the different types of consultancy including: reactive; proactive; expert; and process consulting. This is followed by a discussion of the different type of consultants – internal and external – and the differences between them. Claire Osborne, a Retail Manager, and Steven Paterson, Depute Director of CELCIS, share their experiences as internal consultants of implementing a transformational change programme in each of their organizations. The chapter goes on to critically evaluate the advantages and disadvantages of internal and external consultants. Practical considerations are provided as to whether internal or external consultants are the most appropriate to use for a change initiative.

Learning outcomes

By the end of this chapter you will be able to:

- differentiate between the different types of consultancy;
- critically evaluate the role of external and internal consultants in organizations;
- identify the responsibilities of a consultant;
- appreciate the advantages and disadvantages of using external and internal consultants;
- select the most appropriate consultants to use for a change process.

Types of consultancy

Traditionally, consultants were external resources, which meant that the classic roles were shaped by the employment of external consultants. The most common types of consultancy approaches were defined as 'doctor–patient' and 'service provider'.

Doctor–patient approach

The earliest consultancy firms modelled themselves on medical doctors in terms of providing diagnosis, treatment and improvement for their clients and the consultant was assumed to have more expertise regarding the specific problem than the client. The consultant was also expected to solve the problem in a relatively short period of time with minimal disruption and involvement of managers and other employees. This '*doctor–patient*' approach involved the client hiring a consultant to analyse a specific problem and prescribe a solution.

Although this is still a popular approach to consulting today, it does have a number of drawbacks. First, it tends to limit the use of consultants to times when an organization is 'sick' (McKenna, 2006) – consultants are only called in to deal with a problem. Second, the responsibility for gathering data, analysing the results, making a diagnosis and selecting an intervention is left to the consultant. For the client this approach can provide a huge sense of relief, especially knowing that someone is prepared to 'take on' their problem and sort it out for them. However, it relies on the ability of the consultant alone to accurately gather information and select the appropriate intervention based on the diagnosis. The limitation of this is that diagnosis is not something that a consultant can or should do on their own; they need input not only from the client but also from staff in the organization. According to Donald Anderson this approach frequently results in low success following implementation because 'no one other than the consultant has seen the data or believes that the diagnosis is the correct one. As a result, interventions that are completed tend to be for the consultant's benefit, not the client's, so long term change is unlikely' (Anderson, 2012: 87).

Leaving diagnosis solely to the consultant means that if something does not work out, clients have a ready-made scapegoat to protect their credibility and reputation (Kenton and Moody, 2003). Even when the problem is successfully addressed, clients are unlikely to know how to solve it themselves due to their lack of involvement in the diagnosis and solution (Schein, 1988). So the next time the issue occurs, the client will be forced to call the consultant again.

Service provider approach

The *service provider* approach means that the consultant provides temporary support for the client, which the organization desires but does not have the expertise or resources to supply on its own. The client scopes the problem and the solution, and the consultant is brought in to implement the solution that the client had already decided upon. Consultants who serve as an extra pair of hands typify this approach. An advantage of hiring service providers is that the organization does not need to employ additional internal staff; instead, selected services can be purchased, and when no longer needed the contract can be terminated (Mitchell, 2010). Moreover, experienced consultants can deliver the services provided at a high level of quality. A disadvantage of the service provider approach is that the services provided may not be in line with the client's actual needs, because in self-diagnosing the issues the client is often unaware of the root causes of the problem. A further disadvantage of this type of consultancy is that the consultant is not included in the early and important discussions and decisions about the need for change and is therefore unable to influence the approach taken for problem solving. Ultimately, working as an 'extra pair of hands' consultant means the power, influence and the responsibility lie with the client.

So neither the doctor–patient or service provider role enables the consultant to effectively engage in consultancy for change. Two other types of consultancy that offer more proactive engagement are the expert and facilitative approaches.

Expert approach

The *expert* approach involves providing knowledge to solve a problem defined by the client. The client defines the issue and asks the consultant to solve the problem. The consultant tells the client what the right answer is and solves the problem for them. With this role the consultant's currency is their expertise which the consultant can use to offer a client knowledge and/or 'off the shelf' solutions. The consultant's work is usually complete when they have provided the requested information or the recommended course of action. This type of role may be appealing to consultants for, as Naomi Raab says, 'consultancy is an anxiety producing profession. Faced with what can seem like an overwhelming problem in the client organization, plus [the] need to perform and succeed, it's no wonder consultants use the bravado of expert' (2013: 75).

The expert approach has some advantages for both the consultant and client. For the consultant it provides them with the opportunity to introduce innovative ideas or solutions, which the client may lack or have failed to consider. It is also a chance for the consultant to impress the client, which may lead to the consultant enhancing their credibility and ultimately to repeat business.

For the client it can provide a huge sense of relief to know that the consultant is prepared to take on their problem and sort it out for them quickly.

There are also a number of disadvantages to this approach. Once in this role, attempting to get the client to accept ownership and responsibility for the problem can be tricky and attempts by the consultant to release themselves from this expert role may cause anxiety for the client who has come to depend on the consultant's advice. For the client it can be challenging supervising the consultant's work since the consultant's specialized knowledge is usually greater than the client's (Freedman and Zackrison, 2001). Consequently, the client may be vulnerable to being misled (Schein, 1988).

For this role to be effective, the client must have already conducted an accurate assessment of the issues and clearly defined the problem and what they expect from the consultant (Schein, 1988).

When considering whether or not this is the most appropriate role for consultants during change, it is important to note that there is a difference between taking an expert approach to consulting and actually being an expert. It is the business of consultants to be experts in a number of areas, such as diagnosis, and knowledge and design of potential organization interventions. Such expertise is an essential part of the facilitative approach of consultancy.

Process or facilitative approach

In contrast to the expert approach, the *process or facilitative* approach involves the consultant being an expert in process consulting rather than specific content areas. In his seminal book for consultants, entitled *Process Consultation: Its role in organisational development,* Edgar Schein describes process consultancy as 'a set of activities on the part of the consultant that help the client to perceive, understand and act upon the process events that occur in the client's environment in order to improve the situation defined by the client' (1988: 11). So the process consultant helps the client to understand the management and people processes at work in a way that enables the client to deal with the problem themselves.

Compared to the expert approach, which often involves 'off the shelf' solutions that may have general validity but in fact are not the best option for the organization, process consultancy has the advantage of being by its nature customized to specific situations. Similarly, whereas the expert role will provide a toolkit of best practice methods, the process role will ensure that the tools that are employed will best fit the organization's needs.

In contrast to the doctor–patient approach, the process approach involves working in partnership. The consultant and the client recognize that each has expertise and experience that are of value and contract to work together in joint data-gathering and diagnosis. It means that the client needs to be ready to devote time, energy and the committed involvement of the appropriate people to the problem-solving process (Lippitt and Lippitt, 1986). The benefit of this approach is that it leaves clients more skilled, or more able, to solve their problems and with greater ownership than before the consultant started on the change initiative. There is also a benefit in that clients will have the opportunity to learn and grow and to be in a better position to deal with future change. This is less common with an expert consultant. Additionally, both the client and the consultant begin the consultation without a commitment to the intervention to be implemented; instead it will be determined by their joint efforts to understand the needs and solutions. This enables the real issues to be identified and the root causes addressed. The client will own the change and the outcome and so there is more chance of sustaining the change.

The disadvantage of this approach is that the client may not perceive themselves as needing to be involved in diagnosis, seeing themselves instead as directing the consultant to solve the problems that they have identified. This can occur when the client does not perceive a need for change, and/or the client does not have the appropriate diagnostic skills to engage in joint diagnosis. This approach can also take longer to diagnose and implement a solution, so it can be more expensive because of the time being invested.

In practice, consultancy for change does not usually involve adopting either an expert or a facilitative approach. Instead, it involves employing a mix of roles, with the consultant adapting their approach depending on the context in which they are working.

Consultancy for change approach

Consultancy for change requires a mix of consulting roles (particularly expert and facilitative) but also, as important, an emphasis on: building and maintaining relationships; continuous learning; and collaboration.

- *Building and maintaining relationships.* Consultancy for change is primarily about building and maintaining relationships, as ultimately clients will want to work with people they trust – whether they are internal or external. It is therefore vital that consultants spend time building trust and credibility with clients.

- *Continuous learning.* The focus of facilitative consultancy is on identifying and solving the issue. However, in a world of constant change and development, there will always be solutions that are sustained, as well as those that fail. In the consultancy for change approach there is more emphasis on learning from failure as well as success. Consultants need to ensure that they build in time for reflecting on and sharing the learning from each change initiative. External consultants should also spend time transferring their knowledge and skills internally in order to help develop the internal consultancy and change capabilities.

- *Collaboration.* The consultancy for change approach involves consultants working jointly with their clients throughout the change cycle while the client provides the knowledge of the organization's nature, business, and issues; and the consultant provides the knowledge of the techniques, ways of thinking, and practices that can provide help to solve the problem. In these ways both provide their knowledge to collaborate with each other. This helps to create shared responsibility and specifically for the client to develop ownership of the change interventions once the consultant has completed their work.

The responsibilities of this consultancy for change approach for consultants comprise:

- providing information to clients;
- helping to identify the need for change;
- jointly making a diagnosis, which may necessitate redefinition of the issue;
- making recommendations based on the diagnosis;
- assisting with the implementation of the recommended actions;
- building a consensus and commitment around the need for change and then proposing intervention/s;
- facilitating client learning;
- permanently improving organizational effectiveness;
- ensuring change is sustained and benefits are realized from it.

We will explore each of these responsibilities further in future chapters.

In sum, it is vital to be clear about the type of consultancy that is expected, as it can be frustrating to adopt one role when the client wants or expects another. The approach expected should be clarified by contracting (see Chapter 3 for a discussion on this) with the client as soon as possible at the start of an assignment, even if it changes as the work progresses, and it becomes necessary to re-contract and agree a different approach.

In the following case study Steven Paterson, Depute Director of CELCIS,[1] describes the facilitative approach for consultancy for change that he has taken as an internal consultant for two major transformations.

CASE STUDY

Wise crowds, co-production and engagement

The Centre for Excellence for Looked After Children in Scotland (CELCIS) was formally launched in September 2011 and is dedicated to making positive and lasting improvements to the well-being of children and young people living in and on the edges of care, across the whole country, and the globe. These children, through no fault of their own, are often not able to enjoy the same positive experiences and outcomes as many of their peers.

During the last five years we have gone through (and indeed are still going through) two major organizational transformations. The purpose of the first transformational change in 2011 involved an expansion in services, remit and scope alongside a 25 per cent reduction in funding over three years. Since then we have undergone incremental change and developments in the organization that reflect the interplay between incremental and transformational change and a punctuated equilibrium (as described in Chapter 1).

As I write this, we are going through our second transformational change as an organization. This change is in response to an expanded remit and scope, and increased resources, and is on the basis of our successful delivery over the past five years. It involves: the introduction of new work; a structural review; an office move; a revised vision and mission; a revision of our brand; and becoming part of a wider initiative.

In order to be able to do more than just cope with change but to be in a position to identify the right responses and implement them, it was important for us to build internal consultancy capacity and leadership to manage and lead our change processes. This led to me being 'bought out' of my substantive role as depute director to fulfil the role of internal consultant. For the duration of the change process we recruited someone to undertake the duties and tasks of my usual role to allow me to focus my time and activities on leading the change process.

When working as an internal consultant I view my role as that of a facilitator. In his book *The Skilled Facilitator*, Schwarz (2002) reminds us that *facilitate* comes from the Latin 'to make easy', an aim that I strive to deliver. Being an internal consultant facilitating a change process has both challenges and benefits. An aspect of this is reflected in the challenge and complexity of having a vested interest alongside the benefit of having the history, understanding and long-term strategic outlook and perspective associated with the organization. My understanding, from an internal perspective, allows me to appreciate the change history and experience, group dynamics, preferences in approach/ways of working and my own and others' biases in a way that would be extremely difficult for an external consultant. Schwarz recognizes the impossibility of having no opinions, whether you are an internal or third party facilitator, but refers to an approach of being substantially neutral and ensuring that you are explicit when presenting a preference as opposed to facilitating the consideration of a number of options.

Another important consideration is the ability to develop the confidence and trust of staff in the consultant role, particularly if you have a substantive post in senior management. This has been achieved by: open and two-way communication opportunities; building a culture of safe challenge; and developing a shared understanding of the change by testing my own and staff assumptions and reactions at every step of the way.

A significant part of my facilitation approach was to help the group work within the core values identified by Schwarz (2002) for all facilitation roles: providing valid information; enabling a free and informed choice; and building an internal commitment to change.

Fundamentally my approach has always included: creating opportunities for staff to contribute to the decisions about the change and also share their views on the change; communicating regularly with them; not falling into the trap of going with the obvious or easy answer – unless of course it is the right one; and making the right choices based on the right information, knowledge, experience, policy and legislation as appropriate. However, some staff felt that some of the opportunities were tokenistic and that 'decisions had already been made'. Our learning from this has been that it is critical to ensure that any engagement of staff is well planned, effective and appropriate. Furthermore, it is vital that the feedback loop is closed to ensure that staff do not feel that their engagement is tokenistic.

There were also many competing demands when undertaking change and we, like most organizations, needed to continue to deliver our business as usual. This creates a difficulty in ensuring there is sufficient time and space to lead and manage the process effectively. No matter how much time you may think is required for a change process it will undoubtedly take more. However, it could also be endless and it is important to avoid change fatigue by ensuring there is a point at which it becomes the new 'business as usual'. This has heightened my awareness of the need for a detailed plan for the change process that takes into account what we are trying to achieve, how we want to achieve it, including more effective engagement, and sufficient time, capacity and resource to deliver this plan.

In reflecting on the lessons learned it is helpful to note that although the scope and scale of change are broadly the same now as they were in 2011 my approach has changed. Figure 2.1 illustrates a comparison of the scope and scale of change undertaken in CELCIS between 2011 and 2016, while Figure 2.2 illustrates the difference in my approach to change, which reflects higher levels of co-production and more effective engagement with staff. The most significant difference in our second and current transition has been an increase in our resources. However, we would have applied this new approach even if we faced a decrease, but with additional consideration to the sensitivity and potential implications.

Learning from these change experiences has helped develop an approach to managing and leading change that has evolved and is increasingly internally led. Throughout the process we aimed to avoid any unintended consequences by continuously assessing the readiness for change and stress testing the decisions that we made. We achieved this by 'checking in' with staff through individual meetings, groups and other forums to enable us to clarify levels of understanding and concern staff are experiencing to give us the opportunity to address these before moving forward.

Figure 2.1   Scope and scale of change undertaken in CELCIS, 2011–16

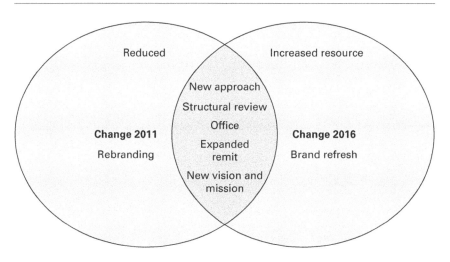

Figure 2.2 Staff engagement opportunities and approach, CELCIS, 2011–16

Change Group
Visits to the new office
Operationalizing the changes
Development of new vision and mission statements
Office Move Group
Change 2016
Co-production
Drop in sessions
Creation of change vision statements
Informal gatherings
Closing the feedback loop

Structural review survey
Formal meetings
Office move survey
Feedback on new vision and mission statements
Regular communication
Feedback

Video of the new office
Change 2011

There are five important components that form the basis of our approach to change. A commitment to:

1 *Effective engagement with staff.* We provided genuine and authentic engagement opportunities where there is a commitment to apply changes as a result of staff responses and suggestions as appropriate and closing the feedback loop.

2 *Creating the time, space and capacity to achieve the best decisions and outcomes.* We negotiated support for my 'buy out' and replacement cover and allowed sufficient time to cope with the significant transition we are going through while continuing to deliver business as usual.

3 *Closing the feedback loop.* We are ensuring that we provide feedback following engagement at each stage of the process. This includes a 'you said, we did' approach, including reference to what we did not do.

4 *Implementing and sustaining change.* We are producing a detailed plan of how things will work and what will be different. This is being developed and co-produced with staff to encourage 'buy in'. This covers new competencies, responsibilities, processes and ways of working.

5 *A lessons learned approach.* Throughout the process we have applied a lessons learned approach to ensure we continue to learn from, develop and improve the experience, process and outcomes. Apart from co-production and engagement with staff at each stage, we have formed our questions around 'what works/worked well?' (www) and 'even better if'.

So, why bother engaging with staff? They will ask difficult questions, and make suggestions you do not want to think about or do. When I talk to people about staff engagement they focus on how difficult, challenging or annoying it must be – they see it as an impossible task. Although it is not the easy option, it is the right option, and will impact on staff commitment to change. Some staff are surprised and unsure about how to respond to engagement opportunities; some have said 'I am not used to being asked,' while others said they did not feel the need to contribute as they were comfortable and confident with the process and opportunity for engagement. My response is to encourage and make it easier for everyone to take up the opportunities.

My commitment and approach to effective engagement are a belief in the contribution that our staff group can make, a point reinforced by Surowiecki (2005) in his book *The Wisdom of Crowds*. Surowiecki presents compelling evidence and examples of how, with the right conditions, groups can outperform individuals even when the individual is an expert.

The ways in which we have implemented the four conditions that characterize Wise Crowds (Surowiecki, 2005: 10) are:

1   *Diversity of opinion – each person has some private information that informs their view.* We created opportunities for staff from across the whole organization to contribute from the perspective of their role: administration, research, consultancy, learning and development and so on.

2   *Independence – people's opinions are not determined by those of others around them.* We have provided opportunities for staff to contribute individually – such as individual responses to surveys and feedback via drop-in sessions.

3   *Decentralization – people are able to specialize and draw on local knowledge.* We have recognized that due to the variety of roles that staff have in the organization they each bring their own perspective of how things work in practice from the perspective of their role.

4   *Aggregation – some mechanism exists to turn private judgements into a collective decision.* We collated and analysed all the responses to inform the outcome.

Effective staff engagement in practice should be more than a few opportunities for staff to respond to surveys, a mistake we made in the past. Meaningful engagement should underpin the whole approach. It is about being available, accessible and visible. I walked around the office, talked to staff and got a sense of how things are for them. We also established two staff groups – the Office Move Group and the Change Group – which have been invaluable in both informing the process and letting us know what it feels like for themselves and others more generally. An open door policy, drop-in sessions and support from line managers and others also form the basis of my approach. These are coupled with the creation of a range of other engagement opportunities including conversations at the copier, surveys and living infographics, which ultimately reinforces the genuine interest in what staff think and helps to ensure that they trust and value the process.

In the current change process we have been really clear about only asking about things that could be influenced and/or changed by staff feedback. There is no point in asking questions when a decision is already made. For example, if funding has already been allocated to a particular activity, there would be no point in asking how the funds could be used. Only ask if you can act, or are at least prepared to act, otherwise it risks breaking trust in the process and undermining the benefits of engaging with staff.

Throughout the process we reminded everyone that we are a diverse, skilled and knowledgeable group of staff, with a range of experiences, and as such we will not all want the same things. However, we emphasized that what we want is to get to the right and best answer for the organization so that we can have the best impact for children and their families. We have also consistently reinforced that as well as being individuals and team members we are all part of CELCIS.

Another development in our approach has been to ensure we are closing the feedback loop. We have gone back to staff and outlined 'what you said', 'what we did' and the gaps, with an explanation of why there are things that we could not or did not do. This has helped staff understand the rationale, even if the decisions and outcomes were not what individuals had wanted.

Feedback to date on the current change process has been very positive, with survey responses and individuals' feedback acknowledging the importance, value and benefit of our approach to staff engagement.

Our learning from our previous experience and our wider work supporting system change to improve services have reinforced the view that having a plan in place to operationalize the changes is critical to the success of implementing and sustaining change. This includes providing space and support for people to deal with change and loss, and ensuring there is continued engagement in how this is delivered. We are developing our plan, which will include opportunities for staff to engage in the development of job competencies, the clarification of tasks associated with various roles, and the review and the development of our revised vision and mission statements. A critical component of my role and approach as internal facilitator is to ensure that the time I am bought out allows for completion of the change process through to new business as usual. The change plan and process go beyond the physical move and restructure to the implementation of the plan and checking that it actually works in practice.

There will undoubtedly be lessons to learn from our current experience. However, the introduction of more effective engagement with staff and ensuring we close the feedback loop have been critical improvements in our process. We often frame things through the perspective of 'what worked well' and 'even better if', and have applied this throughout the whole change process. It will be an important part of our reflection and review of the process and outcomes that we do this again at the end of the process. We know there will be things we can improve upon and we want to understand how we can improve the experience and outcomes of our next change process, since, after all, change is the only constant.

Discussion questions for the case

1 What benefits are identified of being an internal consultant?

2 How might you apply the five components of change either in the organization in which you work or one you are familiar with?

3 How might you apply the four conditions of Wise Crowds to a change you are working on or one you are familiar with?

4 What key lessons can be identified from the case?

External vs internal consultancies

In developing our understanding of the nature of consultancy it is useful to compare the role of external and internal consultants as this helps to highlight critical aspects of the different approaches of consultancy.

External consultancies

The traditional view and definition of consultants are as independent experts, that is, as outsiders with new knowledge (Czerniawska, 2002). External consultants are usually employed for a fixed period to work on a specific change process. They tend to have specialist expertise and experience of change that are not present in the organization (Buono and Jamieson, 2010). As Christopher McKenna says, 'Whether in computer systems, strategic counsel, organizational design, or corporate acquisitions, consultancy firms have become, and continue to be, a crucial institutional solution to executives' ongoing need for outside information' (2006: 78). McKenna describes external consultants as '"pre-eminent knowledge brokers" on the basis of their "status as outsiders" and the "economies of knowledge" this brings compared to insiders... [they] have flourished primarily because they have remained outside the traditional boundaries of the firm' (2006: 12–16). Such a view is based on the rationale that 'the very reason why clients hire consulting firms, is the fact that consultants have the ability to gain experience, expertise, methods and tools in one industry or organization and then apply them in another, thereby saving the client the costs of developing them in-house' (Armbruster, 2006: 54). This is supported by Mark Summerfield, Chief Executive of The Co-operative Insurance company, who says that the use of external consultants provides him with access to skills in specialist areas that he does not choose to keep on the payroll on a full-time basis, as well as objectivity, rigour, insight and learning (Newing, 2015).

External consultants are therefore seen as providing a number of forms of capital that are attractive to clients, including:

- Human capital. This includes skills, experience, attitudes and motivation.
- Social capital. This consists of teams, networks and groups of individuals working together and their shared intellectual capital.
- Knowledge capital. This comprises sector and expert knowledge.
- Financial capital. This includes the ability to fund the development of ideas and learning.
- Technological capital. This includes diagnostic and analytical tools.

As long as external consultancies continue to build such capital and continue to offer expert help, combined with ever more powerful analytical tools that companies have neither the time nor skills to develop in-house, they are likely to be in demand and able to command a premium for their services.

External consultancies are, however, facing growing demands and expectations from clients. For instance, managers have become much more professional in managing external consultants due to an increase in their expectations of consultancy, especially with regard to the value and solutions provided, global delivery and technological capability required. Clients have also developed more experience of consultancy; many of them know all the large consulting firms and have a comparative perspective of them. Some might even have worked for such firms. Clients also have considerable negotiation expertise, with many having professionalized their sourcing processes with procurement departments being involved in the selection of consultants. As a result, consultancies are facing growing pressures to offer ever more compelling advice and support at negotiable rates, in order to avoid losing business to the growing internal consultancy capabilities within organizations.

Internal consultancies

Internal consultancies are becoming more common in organizations as an alternative to external consultancies (Hodges, 2017). For example, Nordstrom has formed a People Lab Science Team to define and curate changes that will attract top talent and enable the retailer to compete with tech companies such as Tableau and Microsoft. The team takes a multidisciplinary approach to designing change interventions to define and reinforce Nordstrom's culture.

The considerable cost of external consultants has led many large organizations to search for less expensive sources of organizational analysis and problem solving and to the development of internal consultancy capabilities.

Consequently, in some organizations internal consulting is established as a new function or team with staff often being recruited from external consulting firms; while in other organizations existing internal functions are sometimes renamed as internal consultancy teams, and the staff of the former functions are retained with a few additional external consultants recruited to enhance capability.

Depending on which of these approaches is taken, then, the business model of internal consulting will differ. For example, it may be organized as independent subsidiaries or as teams embedded in organizational departments; as centralized headquarters functions or as decentralized local units; or as profit centres charging market prices or as free internal services. The organizational models of internal consultancies are, therefore, heterogeneous (Armbruster, 2006).

Similarly, the business drivers for an organization setting up an internal consultancy are varied. Kenton and Moody (2003) highlight the key drivers as being:

- Strategic alignment. To improve the alignment of people management practice with business goals; and to help managers understand their people in the context of the organization's change requirements.

- Service. To provide an accessible point of contact for clients and to improve overall service levels.

- Financial. To provide improved services at no extra cost and to control burgeoning costs on externals.

A further driver for establishing an internal consulting capability, which can be added to this list, is dissatisfaction with external consulting work. For instance, some managers may feel that external consultants provide abstract solutions that do not really fit with the concrete reality and needs of their organization (Armbruster, 2006). There are, therefore, a number of drivers pushing organizations to develop an internal consultancy capability.

There are various benefits for the organization and for individuals in developing internal consultancy capabilities. For individuals, taking up a consultancy role can provide them with stretching professional development. As Meislin says, 'after many years of proficiency in a particular field, people can get stale. In-house consulting experiences can provide invaluable variety, [and] learning opportunities' (1997: 7). For the organization, internal consultancy provides the opportunity to maximize the knowledge and skills currently existing within the company. An internal consulting team can also be a source of additional revenue by offering their services externally.

Hence, internal consulting teams can be considered as competitors to external consulting firms, both for work within the organization in which they operate and sometimes, but not always, for contracts in the market.

The establishment of an internal consultancy signals aspects about an organization. It symbolizes a commitment to developing internal capability and continuous improvements without the large costs entailed in seeking external advice. It also signals to those outside that the company takes a responsible attitude to its own organization and cost structure, for internal consultancies are mostly less expensive than external ones. It also signals that the organization is not content with 'on paper only' advice but has a strong focus on implementation, which in turn signals readiness for change and organizational adaptability (Armbruster, 2006).

So, despite being characterized as the 'poor cousin' of their external counterparts (Sturdy *et al*, 2014), internal consultancies are a vital organizational resource and are becoming increasingly common, particularly in large organizations that are able to afford to employ permanent resources and have sufficient work to keep them employed (Burtonshaw-Gunn, 2009).

Questions for discussion

- Identify the drivers pushing organizations to develop an internal consultancy capability.
- What benefits might there be for the organization you work in or one you are familiar with in setting up its own internal consultancy function?

What is an internal consultant?

Internal consultants are members of the organization for which they provide advisory and support services. In comparison to an external consultant, an internal consultant already works inside part of the organization, is on the payroll and is tasked with helping the organization. While some organizations do have formal internal consultancy teams performing this role, there are often many more people fulfilling the role without the title. Such individuals may be drawn from one of the teams of professional service providers such as HR, IT or finance where there is a history of supporting internal customers with specific problems. Managers may also act internally as consultants by brokering change and exercising the facilitation skills that were once the preserve of an external consultant (Randall and Burnes,

2016). Such experience is often gained either as external consultants or from involvement as internal change agents (Sturdy *et al*, 2014).

An internal consultant's deliverables typically include some combination of recommendations for interventions for change, implementation plans that are sensitive to the sociocultural and political realities in the organization, and the ability to transfer knowledge to those who manage and/or do the work. External consultants may have similar deliverables, but the ongoing, day-to-day interactions internal consultants have with stakeholders provide them with opportunities for greater levels of access and influence and ready availability onsite to provide support (Barnes and Scott, 2012). Internal consultants tend also to play a more active role in the implementation of change than external consultants. As internal consultants are part of the organization, they have the opportunity to engage in such long-term activities, where external consultants typically have shorter interactions (Kitay and Wright, 2004). Internal consultants may also be used to commission external consultants; to brief them about the culture and context of the assignment; to ensure that they are compliant with the governance requirements of the business; and to assess if they provide value for money. They may also work alongside internal consultants to support and learn from them. Internal consultants are therefore a vital organizational resource for change initiatives.

The role of internal consultant

The role of the internal consultant is typically defined through its separation from the organization it serves in that the consultant holds neither line responsibility nor budget, nor do they tend to have direct power to make changes or implement solutions (Block, 2011). Consultants, however, may often have status and recognition (Kenton and Moody, 2003) and be in a position to have some influence over an individual, team or organization.

Given their lack of formal power to impose change, consultants need to influence the client through credibility, expertise, skills, knowledge and understanding. They can do this in a number of ways. Anthony Buono and Karthik Subbiah (2014) identify the following key roles of internal consultants: troubleshooter; sensor; researcher-analyst; coach and mentor; implementation supporter; adviser and critic. Internal consultants often play the role of *troubleshooter* of minor and major problems that an organization faces, in essence serving as an expert operational resource. Internal consultants are also *sensors* of the organization's internal and external environment, helping to identify and share issues of importance to the organization's success and survival. Working with the organization as a *researcher-analyst,* internal consultants can draw attention to non-crisis situations, which are often overlooked or ignored, and can help in the development of appropriate recommendations for improvement (van Aken, 2004). Through their roles as *coach* and *mentor*, internal consultants have the potential to impact the knowledge, ability and motivation of other employees by helping to develop and implement training and development interventions. Internal consultants can also be an *implementation supporter* by assisting managers who have functional and/or business responsibilities, helping to oversee implementation of those responsibilities, and, in general, serving as an operational resource. This also includes activities to identify the functional issues and then working with the heads and team members of those functions to eliminate or mitigate the causes of the issues through the development and joint implementation of solutions. Finally, internal consultants can act as *advisor* and *critic*, by providing a critical appraisal of solutions that might not be a good fit with the organization and also by challenging the views of managers with the intent of helping them make more robust decisions.

To be successful in such roles as troubleshooter, sensor and researcher-analyst, consultants must have in-depth knowledge of the organization and its internal and external environments. Similarly, the roles of coach and mentor, implementation supporter, and advisor-critic require trust and credibility, both of which require time, interaction and experience within the organization by the consultant. By being visible in the organization and establishing regular contact with key stakeholders, internal consultants are in a good position to successfully fulfil these roles.

Reactive and proactive role

Another way of considering internal consultancy is to examine whether the consultant is taking the lead (such as suggesting to the client that a particular situation should be examined) or following the client's lead (for example, the client gives the consultant all the work). The positioning of an internal consultant is illustrated in Figure 2.3.

The majority of internal consultants begin their consultancy careers in the lower (reactive) half of this diagram, and it is the aspiration of almost all of them to move upwards so that, at least for some of the time, they are taking the initiative and helping to move the organization forward. This is a positive strategy because it is in the 'proactive' area that they potentially offer the organization the greatest value, as they may well alert managers to

Figure 2.3   Reactive and proactive roles (adapted from Hodges, 2016)

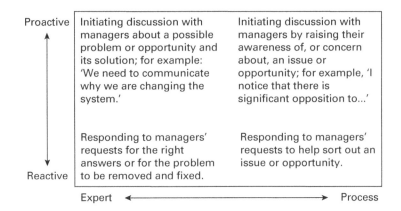

> ## Activity
>
> Using the grid in Figure 2.3 ask yourself:
>
> 1 Where do you find it most comfortable to be?
>
> 2 Where do you find it least comfortable to be?
>
> 3 Where does the organization want you to be?
>
> 4 What do you need to do to change your consulting approach to support change in the organization?

an opportunity or problem (external or internal) before anyone else does so. But it is also the area of greatest risk since to confront senior managers, and to seek to change their thinking, especially from a position lower down the hierarchy, can be uncomfortable and potentially risky. That is why internal consultants require well-developed consultancy capabilities (as outlined in Chapter 7).

Internal consultants, by fulfilling a diverse set of roles, such as those described above, can help an organization sustain successful change (Hodges, 2017). Determinants of that success, however, are embedded in a full understanding of the organization, the internal and external drivers for change, the views of employees, the organization's needs, and its political and sociocultural realities. By ensuring that staff, from senior management to frontline employees, are knowledgeable about the challenges and opportunities faced by the organization, internal consultants can help to reduce the uncertainty involved in the change process. Internal consultants can help the organization develop and deploy an approach that interweaves understanding of issues and solutions, organizational development, resource needs and infrastructure support, with interventions that provide social and emotional support for employees and a facilitative culture that supports change.

In the following case study Claire Osborne, a Retail Manager, shares her experience as an internal consultant of implementing a company-wide transformational change programme, and how she coped with individual reactions to the change.

CASE STUDY

Retail cultural change programme

A couple of years ago my previous experience of dealing with cultural change resulted in me being chosen as one of twelve company-wide internal consultants to act as a change lead to initiate the biggest cultural change programme in my organization's (a retail company) history to secure and protect their place as the leader in their field. The aim was to increase customer satisfaction in order to increase the revenue from sales. Covering over 1,400 stores and franchises and including 16,000 employees, my primary task was to instigate a behavioural change programme within the company's management teams. This involved introducing a new method of managing team performance using observation and feedback models alongside coaching techniques to maximize engagement levels with customers.

The operational team faced a task of completing the programme within a 36-month time frame, with each store having a training plan of 6–12 weeks. Tools such as Belbin Team Role theory, Insights, and Gallup engagement questionnaires provided valuable insights into the employees' learning preferences, personality and perceptions to change which enabled a tailored approach to delivering the content of the programme that would be engaging and more reflective of personalized character traits. The annual staff employee survey results provided data about each store's individual engagement and attitudes towards their management teams, which showed clear areas that needed to be addressed as part of the change programme.

Initially, within the smaller stores, which were known for having close-knit communities, resistance to change was evident as employees did not see the necessity of the change and some even strongly opposed it. Being a traditional organization with a strong sense of values engrained through decades of established and habitual rituals, some employees had operated in the same role, and in the same store, for over 40 years and had never had to be accountable for their own or others' performance management. The fear of change manifested itself in sickness, aggression, and some individuals refusing to accept the change as the way forward. In opposition to the proposed changes one employee undressed and locked themself in a nearby office, refusing to leave until the change lead left the property.

To compound the issue of the opposition to change, many employees had not previously been given or received any significant feedback in relation to their job role, performance, or indeed their attitudes. Many viewed the negative feedback from the annual employee survey, which identified the strengths and weaknesses of each management team, as personal.

The more people felt that the change was being pushed and forced onto them, the more they rebelled, and sometimes with devastating consequences. Some respected and established employees left the company, others took sick leave, while others reacted aggressively in a way that they had not done before. This had a wide impact on the change management programme, altering the way in which the programme was to be initiated in subsequent areas, and forcing the change leads to incorporate more group training sessions around engagement, managing the transition that individuals went through, leadership workshops and coaching courses.

The need to determine the root cause of resistance in order to be able to address it was vital. Techniques that we used to achieve this included the Fishbone exercise, scenario planning (see Chapters 4 and 5 for a description of these techniques) and open discussion forums, which helped to identify what aspects needed to be addressed.

No two managers or stores were alike, with each store having unique individual personalities working within it. Each change lead was issued with an organizational change manual, giving directions and examples of change management practice to assist in the implementation of change. The degree of direction given by the change manual had little or no relevance to the array of personalities shown within the stores. This resulted in many of the change leads attempting to alter the behaviour of individuals without fully considering the individuals' beliefs or values, or what was driving their behaviour. Therefore, a continuous review of the programme, in order to change and adapt it to circumstances that had not been accounted for, was necessary.

In advising any consultant embarking on a transformational change programme, I would recommend that they gain an insight into what drives the emotional and behavioural responses of the individuals within their team in order to understand how individuals and teams interpret their environment and interact with colleagues and customers. Understanding how teams and individuals react to change and why they respond in certain ways allowed me to manage the transition to new ways of working, to address conflict and to initiate negotiations. The use of empathy to build trust and understanding provided a platform to build a relationship that encouraged open dialogue regarding past experiences, feelings and emotions regarding areas of interest. This provided a significant advantage in attempting to work towards behavioural change.

In my view, the key ingredient essential for successful implementation programmes is consultants who are capable of thriving in an ever-changing environment, whose ethics and values reflect those of the organization and who create conditions in which change is not only accepted, but driven by those with the understanding that the speed of change and its necessity are at the very core of how businesses survive and prosper.

Discussion questions for the case

1 What were the key challenges faced by the change leads? How would you address them in your organization or one you are familiar with?
2 What are the best approaches for managing individuals' reactions to change?
3 If you were faced with a similar transformational change programme what would you do differently?
4 What key learning from this case could you apply in practice?

Challenges of the internal consultancy role

If the role of the consultant is to facilitate change, then particular challenges exist for the internal consultant over and above those faced by external consultants. The skills and attributes that internal consultants bring to the role are often overlooked when managers look for support to achieve change, so internal consultants can often find themselves being seen as an 'extrapair of hands' and given mundane operational tasks whilst external consultants are given the more challenging, strategic change projects. This sidelining of internal consultants is due to many factors including: the lack of understanding of the role of the internal consultant within the business; the credibility of the consultants themselves; their lack of power to action projects/proposals; and value issues connected to the use of consultancy (Kenton and Moody, 2003).

Internal consultants, therefore, have to be aware of how they are perceived and of the advantages and disadvantages associated with using them.

Advantages and disadvantages of internal and external consultants

There are a number of advantages and disadvantages to using internal as well as external consultants. The main ones that we will discuss here are: organizational insight; cost; flexibility; objectivity; and dealing with organizational politics.

Organizational insight

A key advantage of using consultants is their knowledge. Internal consultants accumulate their knowledge primarily within the boundaries of the organization in which they work, whereas external consultants are exposed to several companies a year. As a result, the type of knowledge provided by internals and externals will differ. Whereas internal consultants are more familiar with the business issues in their organization and industrial sector, external consultants accumulate knowledge from across a number of sectors and regions (Armbruster, 2006).

The advantage of internal consultants is not necessarily the amount of knowledge they possess but the type. They are likely to have an in-depth understanding of the company's culture, enabling them to understand what makes different people react in different ways to change, as well as knowledge and processes. They are also able to understand how changes in the external environment relate to potential opportunities and challenges for the organization (Sturdy et al, 2014). Being in the organization provides the internal consultant with exposure to organizational intelligence and to the organizational culture, which can help them to diagnose issues more quickly and easily. So internal consultants are well positioned to counsel their colleagues against hasty adoption of predesigned solutions, which critics suggest are often offered by external consultants (Mabey, 2008).

Internal consultants are also in a good position to research and analyse non-crisis situations, helping to generate recommendations for improvement that would otherwise be overlooked or ignored. Their role within the organization has the potential to enhance operational effectiveness and efficiency, guide strategic analysis and assessments, and conceptualize and support interventions. Internal consultants are also likely to be well socialized into the norms and beliefs of the organization and more sensitive to organizational politics and behaviours. There is, however, a word of caution here in that internal consultants may be more subjective than objective to such issues and to certain people (Kenton and Moody, 2003). So an internal consultant will have a considerable amount of knowledge, but will also have personal perspectives on the organization.

In contrast, the external consultant will not have the same quality or depth of organizational knowledge and insight. This may mean that the external consultant provides solutions that are more artificial or superficial in nature. Or, alternatively, they may well provide help that is more precisely related to the issue because they are not drawn into a myriad of irrelevant knowledge and data, or political and power dynamics. An external consultant will also be able to transfer into the organization the knowledge and expertise from the different businesses in which they have worked. They may also have extensive, comparative knowledge of change processes, contexts and interventions, as well as fresh, creative insights and ideas from their experience. There are, therefore, a number of advantages and disadvantages to using internal and external consultants in terms of their organizational knowledge and insights.

Cost

The costs of using consultants are a key advantage or disadvantage for clients when deciding whether to use internal or external consultants. Organizations have found that the costs for an internal consultant per day are lower than for external consultants (Nevo *et al*, 2007). In his book *The Economics and Sociology of Management Consulting,* Thomas Armbruster (2006) illustrates that there is a comparison of costs that clients consider when deciding whether to develop skills in house or to look externally for consultants. These are illustrated in Table 2.1.

Table 2.1   Comparison of internal versus external consultants

External costs	Internal costs
Fees	Hiring new staff
Searching for consulting firms	Training staff
Assessing their competences	Labour costs
Selecting between firms	Reallocating tasks
Negotiating, contract drafting	Monitoring staff
Monitoring consultants	Researching project
Reinforcing the contract	

According to Armbruster (2006) this comparison needs to be scaled according to the following factors:

- How often the project/task will occur. If the project/task will happen frequently then it is likely that the accumulation of fees will make the external more expensive than the interval consultant.

- The assets required. The assets required for a project may be expensive and specialized, such as implementing a customer relationship management (CRM) system, while other assets may be relatively inexpensive and general, for instance quality improvement training. The less specialized and the cheaper the assets, the more likely they can be provided by internal consultants.

- The commodification of the project. This relates to the extent to which a project can be measured and monitored. 'The higher the uncertainty of a task the more likely that an in-house solution will be more efficient' (Armbruster, 2006: 47).

Managers need to consider these factors, as well as the fixed and variable costs. The costs for external consultancy are variable, as they vary in line with the number of projects, or, more precisely, with the number of consulting days. The costs for internal consultancy, by contrast, comprise a large proportion of the fixed costs for setting up the internal consultancy (hiring, office space, holiday allowance, remuneration and so on) and maintaining it. Salaries must be paid permanently and do not vary with the number of consulting cases; however, a disadvantage of this for internal consultants is that they may be biased in favour of what their stakeholders want rather than need due to their financial dependence on the organization. So both the fixed and the variable costs need to be considered when deciding whether to use external consultants or enhance and utilize internal consultants.

Flexibility

Flexibility to respond to client needs is an important aspect when considering the use of consultants. An advantage of internal consultants is that they are more flexible since they are available more readily than external consultants. The costs of producing a speedy analysis of a problem that arises suddenly may then be lower. However, this is based on a number of conditions that do not always apply. For example, it assumes that an internal consultancy has the capacity and capability, with the result that some internal consultants can take on the task straightaway. Moreover, arguing that internal consultants are more readily at hand and thus more economical for immediate problem solving ignores the initial costs of setting up an internal consultancy. Furthermore, external consultants who enjoy already established relationships of trust with managers within an organization are often just as readily at hand as internal consultants. So the flexibility of consultants should be considered when differentiating between the use of internal and external consultancy support.

Objectivity

Providing objective help is a key advantage of consultants. The advantage of an external consultant is that they are not emotionally involved in organizational issues and can therefore be more objective and provide a critical evaluation of the issue and proposed interventions, whereas an internal consultant may be prone to being too emotionally involved in the organization, which can influence their ability to be truly objective about a transformation. The internal consultant may therefore seem to lack the independence and objectivity of the outsider. As Armstrong (1992) points out, internal consultants may have just as much expertise, although as employees it may be more difficult for them to be – or be seen to be – as independent as those from outside the organization. Internal consultants thus have to demonstrate that they are able to deliver truly objective advice.

Dealing with organizational politics

A key difference between internal and external consultants is how they are affected by the politics and power plays within an organization. Since an internal consultant tends to be immersed within an organization's political system, this enables them to have clear insights into who holds political power amongst the key stakeholders and how to manage them. However, the disadvantage of this is that they can be drawn into the political struggles and power games of the organization, resulting in the internal consultant being biased against individuals due to their own personal opinions about 'office politics' and power dynamics. As a result, they may become ethnocentric after several years of being in the role (Barnes and Scott, 2012; Sherrit, 2016).

In contrast, an external consultant is likely to be free from, or perceived to be free from, allegiances and outside the organizational politics that can get in the way of objectivity, and not caught up in the internal power plays. External consultants do, however, need to be aware of and understand the political framework and power dynamics, as they will be connected to them for the duration of the consultancy assignment.

In sum, in exploring the nature of consultancy it is useful to compare the advantages and disadvantages of internal and external consultants as this helps to highlight critical aspects of consultancy. In examining the differences between the two it is not intended to set one group against another but simply to recognize that there are key differences and that they can influence selection decisions concerning which route clients will take. You will see from Table 2.2 that some of the differences can be used to promote a case for using internal consultancy as opposed to adopting the external route, or vice versa.

Table 2.2   Advantages and disadvantages of internal and external consultants

Internal consultants	External consultants
Advantages	*Advantages*
Understand the organization's culture, history, processes, people, systems and language.	Able to transfer into the organization knowledge and expertise from the different businesses in which they have worked.
Understand what it is like to work in the current environment.	Can draw on a pool of talented individuals.
Understand the overall drivers for change in the organization better than external consultants.	Extensive, comparative knowledge of change processes, context and choices.
Are in regular contact with key stakeholders, so are able to build and maintain trust over longer period of time.	Fresh, creative insights and ideas from experience.
Existing relationship with employees in the company.	Ability to use expert status to influence views.
Perceived as having a longer-term commitment to the company.	Employees may feel more comfortable sharing confidential information with someone they do not work with.
Financially more efficient and less costly.	Credibility through brand status and previous experience.
Potentially able to generate more internal commitment to a change initiative.	Not emotionally involved in organizational issues and can therefore be more objective and critical in reviewing the proposed approach for change.
May have developed an approach or methodology for transitioning people through change that is more appropriate for organizational context.	Often invest heavily in new approaches and methodologies for organizational transformation, so they have something new to offer.

(Continued)

Table 2.2 *(Continued)*

Internal consultants	External consultants
Disadvantages	*Disadvantages*
May be blind to seeing some issues due to history with the culture.	May find it difficult to understand the culture and its issues.
May have less experience with other sectors and companies.	Limited knowledge about the organization.
Might find it hard to say 'no'.	Have to build relationships and trust in a short time.
Employees may be reluctant to share information with one of their colleagues.	May be perceived as short-term and only doing it for the money.
May be seen as agents of management.	Might not be able to follow through beyond proposing interventions.
Can be overcautious in defining the reality due to employment related concerns, career advancement.	'Off-the-shelf' approach.
Limited access to senior leaders due to position in the hierarchy.	Lack of ownership – will move on at the end of the engagement.
Change may be viewed as continually ongoing, as consultant remains with the organization and may not want to disengage	Need time to understand the people – may misinterpret actions and interpersonal dynamics.
Knows the people but may have preconceptions.	Timed, expensive, rare and rationed.
Potentially lack the apparent credibility of some external consultants	May create a sense of dependency among company's managers – 'We cannot function without you.'
Prone to being too emotionally involved in the organization, which could influence their ability to be truly objective about a transformation.	Not always required to live with the consequences of their work.
Required to live with the consequences of their advice, as they will still be around long after external consultants would have left.	

Selecting internal or external consultants

Such advantages and disadvantages as are outlined in Table 2.2 will encourage managers either to use external consultants or to develop and use internal consultants, depending on the capability required. Choosing the right type of consultant for both the organization and the specific change is vital to ensure that a transformation is sustained. The following questions are recommended as an aid for managers when considering whether to select an internal or external consultant for a change initiative:

1   Does the consultant understand this business? How do they demonstrate that understanding?

2   Can I trust them to respect confidences? How will they deal with an issue of competing loyalties?

3   What relevant experience of this kind of transformation do they have?

4   Do they have the right tools for managing change and the knowledge to use them effectively? What experience do they have?

5   What change capabilities do they have? How do these relate to this transformation?

6   Is there a gap in talent, education, and qualification between the experienced internal consultants and the experienced external consultants?

7   Do external consultants have more qualified staff?

8   Is the learning curve of external consultants steeper?

9   Do we have to engage in costly negotiations with external providers?

10 To what extent does the task require comparative knowledge across firms, industries, or regions, or does it primarily concern the collection and leverage of internal knowledge?

11 To what extent can an external provider use procedures that have been proven useful in other sectors and that the internal consultants could build up only at much greater costs?

12 Can internal or external consultants overcome sources of opposition at lower cost?

13 Do we have to search for and select external consultants or do we have trusted relations with qualified external providers that would render the search and selection costs low?

14 How high are the fees for external consultants per day and how many days would they charge us?

These questions provide a useful framework for considering the options of using internal or external consultants. Although this kind of analysis is helpful, it is also worth remembering that great synergy and mutual benefit can be achieved when internal and external consultants are selected to work in partnership and when the contract with external consultants includes the transfer of skills and knowledge to internal consultants. It is also vital to note that even from a short-term perspective and disregarding the up-front costs, the personal relations between clients and consultants (whether internal or external) will play a significant part in selecting the type of consultant with which to work.

Summary

Consultancy can be provided by either internal or external consultants, each of which has advantages and disadvantages for both the consultant and the client.

Internal consultants know the organization from the inside out – its systems, processes, people, language and culture. They will most likely have lived and breathed the products, financing, staffing issues and business strategies and be well tuned into the hopes, fears, likes and dislikes of the movers and shakers within the business (Kenton and Moody, 2003). They will also have built up relationships with different levels of staff across the organization and know who are the key influencers. Many internal consultants have also developed extensive expertise, knowledge and skills in consultancy and are able to adapt them to the organization. Internal consultancy can bring strong benefits: there is undoubted value in having 'inside' agents who understand what is going on, who have strong, established relationships, and who are skilled in the interventions applicable to the organizational context.

The reason that clients hire external consultants rather than internal consultants is based on the perceived expertise that external consultants are thought to bring to an organization in comparison to internal consultants. External consultants are often perceived as being able to provide the capabilities that are not available internally and as having varied experience from outside the organization. This means that the client can access knowledge and experience from different companies. So knowledge, skills and experience are important considerations for organizations when opting to hire external consultants.

Although there are advantages and disadvantages to both internal and external consultants, there is not necessarily one that is better than the other. Instead there is a need to consider which is the best approach to implement sustainable change.

Implications for managers and consultants

A number of practical implications for managers and consultants arise from the discussion in this chapter.

- *Consider the advantages and disadvantages when selecting consultants.*
  Managers need to evaluate the pros and cons of different types of consultants and then use the consultants that have the capabilities to work on the issue/opportunity within the organizational context.

- *Clarify the role the client expects.*
  Consultants need to clarify what role is expected of them at the start of a consulting assignment and be prepared to act as a facilitator as well as an expert. It is vital to be clear about what kind of consultant you are expected to be, as it can be frustrating to be in one role when the client wants another.

- *Work together.*
  Internal consultants should try to work closely with external consultants, who may be able to assist in reframing what is happening and so offer insight into issues such as unconscious collusion or 'cultural blindness' (Smith, 2012).

Note

1 CELCIS was created from the Scottish Institute for Residential Child Care (SIRCC). This followed a successful 10-year tenure as SIRCC and leadership of a National Residential Child Care Initiative, which promoted a closer link between all services for vulnerable children. SIRCC was originally established to support the development of the Residential Child Care workforce and services in Scotland.

References

Anderson, DL (2012) *Organization Development: The process of leading organizational change*, Sage, London

Armbruster, T (2006) *The Economics and Sociology of Management Consulting*, Cambridge University Press, Cambridge

Armstrong, M (1992) How to be an internal consultant, *Human Resources*, Winter (3), pp 26–29

Barnes, BK and Scott, B (2012) The influential internal consultant, *Industrial and Commercial Training*, **44** (7), pp 408–15

Block, P (2011) *Flawless Consulting*, 3rd edn, Jossey Bass/Pfeiffer, San Francisco

Buono, AF, and Jamieson, D (eds) (2010) *Consultation for Organizational Change*, Information Age Publishing, Charlotte, NC, pp 3–13

Buono, AF and Subbiah, K (2014) Internal consultants as change agents: Roles, responsibilities and organizational change capacity, *Organization Development Journal*, **32** (2), pp 35–53

Burtonshaw-Gunn, S (2009) *The Essential Management Toolbox: Tools, models and notes for managers and consultants*, Wiley & Sons, London

Czerniawska, F (2002) *Value-based Consulting*, Palgrave, New York

Freedman, AM and Zackrison, RE (2001) *Finding Your Way in the Consulting Jungle*, Jossey Bass/Pfeiffer, San Francisco

Higdon, H (1970) *The Business Healers*, Random House, New York

Hodges, J (2016) *Managing and Leading People Through Change*, Kogan Page, London

Hodges, J (2017) To be or not to be an internal consultant, in *Management Consultancy Insights and Real Consultancy Projects*, ed G Manville, O Matthias and J Campbell, Gower, London

Kenton, B and Moody, D (2003) *The Role of the Internal Consultant*, Roffey Park Institute, London

Kitay, J and Wright, C (2004) Take the money and run? Organisational boundaries and consultants' roles, *The Service Industries Journal*, **24** (3), pp 1–18

Lippitt, G and Lippitt, R (1986) *The Consulting Process in Action*, 2nd edn, Jossey-Bass/Pfeiffer, San Francisco

Mabey, C (2008) *The Process of Change: Building momentum*, The Open University, Milton Keynes

McKenna, C (2006) *The World's Newest Profession*, Cambridge University Press, Cambridge

Meislin, M (1997) *The Internal Consultant: Drawing on inside expertise*, Crisp Publications, Menlo Park

Mitchell, M (2010) Whole System Consulting, in *Consultation for Organizational Change*, ed AF Buono and D Jamieson, pp 41–78, Information Age Publishing, Charlotte, NC

Nevo, S, Wade, MR and Cook, WD (2007) An examination of the trade-off between internal and external IT capabilities, *Journal of Strategic Information Systems*, **16** (1), pp 5–23

Newing, R (2015) More clients question whether firms deliver value for money, *Financial Times*, 9 November

O'Mahoney, J and Markham, C (2013) *Management Consultancy*, Oxford University Press, Oxford

Raab, N (2013) Working with the client–consultant relationship: Why every step is an intervention, in *Handbook for Strategic HR: Best practices in organization development from the OD network*, ed J Vogelsang, pp 76–81, AMACOM, New York

Randall, J and Burnes, B (2016) Managers as consultants, in *Perspectives on Change: What academics, consultants and managers really think about change*, ed B Burnes and J Randall, pp 203–06, Routledge Studies in Organizational Change and Development, Routledge, London

Schein, E (1988) *Process Consultation: Its role in organization development* (Vol 1) FT Press, Upper Saddle River, NJ

Schwarz, R (2002) *The Skilled Facilitator: A comprehensive resource for consultants, facilitators, managers, trainers, and coaches*, 2nd edn, Jossey-Bass, London

Sherrit, D (2016) Is OD just a back of interventions?, in *Perspectives on Change: What academics, consultants and managers really think about change*, ed B Burnes and J Randall, pp 245–65, Routledge Studies in Organizational Change and Development, Routledge, London

Smith, V (2012) *Key concepts in counselling and psychotherapy: A critical AZ guide to theory*, McGraw-Hill Education, London

Sturdy, A, Wright, C and Wylie, N (2014) Managers as consultants: The hybridity and tensions of neo-bureaucratic management, *Organization*, 15 July. [Online] DOI: 1350508414541580

Surowiecki, J (2005) *The Wisdom of Crowds: Why the many are smarter than the few*, Abacus, London

van Aken, J (2004) Management research based on the paradigm of the design sciences: The quest for field-tested and grounded technological rules, *Journal of Management Studies*, **41** (2) pp 222–46

PART TWO
The consultancy for change cycle

Preparation and contracting

03

KEY POINTS

- The consultancy cycle for change comprises different phases: initial contact and contracting; diagnosis and analysis; intervention; implementation; evaluation; and transition. Each of the phases informs the orientation of previous and subsequent phases and will vary in length and complexity depending on the nature of the change and the client's expectations.

- Each of the phases of the consultancy for change cycle is bolted together with dialogue, feedback, the client–consultant relationship and stakeholder management.

- Initial contact and contracting are the preparatory and starting phases of the consultancy for change cycle and set the parameters for how the subsequent phases will be conducted.

- Contracting involves developing a mutually agreed contract between the consultant and the client. This is fundamental to the success of any consultancy for change cycle as it clarifies the what, how, when and why of change.

Introduction

All things being equal, people prefer to do business with people they get on with. So in any consultancy engagement, well before the change is planned, a great deal of time and effort needs to be invested by a consultant into establishing a relationship with a client, and identifying not only what needs to change but also how they will work together to achieve it. This is done in the first two phases of the consultancy for change cycle, which are (1) initial contact and (2) contracting. Although it can be tempting to move straight to solutions, skipping the early phases of the consultancy cycle can have dire consequences later on. For, as the old adage goes, 'failing to prepare is preparing to fail'. These preparatory stages help to lay the foundations for the subsequent phases of the consultancy for change cycle, which are: diagnosing and analysing; identifying and designing the change intervention; implementing the change; evaluating the impact and benefits of the change; and transitioning the work to the client.

The aim of this chapter is to provide an overview of the consultancy for change cycle, with specific focus on the initial phase of the cycle. The main focus is on identifying what needs to be done during the initial contact and contracting phases in preparation for change. The chapter begins by critically evaluating traditional linear approaches to consultancy in comparison to iterative approaches. The rest of the chapter is split between the initial contact and contracting phases. In discussing the initial contact phase the focus is on what needs to be done when preparing to consult, followed by an exploration of the key elements of contracting. The chapter highlights the importance of a consultant starting to build a collaborative relationship with the client and other key stakeholders. Attention is paid to identifying and managing stakeholders and tools for helping with this. The challenges of managing stakeholders are described in the case of a chain of German hospitals written by Ronald Graefe, Accenture Management Consultancy Manager. The chapter goes on to explore the formal and psychological contractual elements of the client–consultant relationship, including the need to clarify the issue to be addressed, agree roles, responsibilities, accountabilities and expectations, as well as how the consultant and client will work together. Luca Sabia, a consultant in the marketing and communication industry, describes his personal experience of what happened in a merger between two Italian banks when contracting was not done effectively. Key questions considered in this chapter include: What is the most effective consultancy approach to use for organizational change? How should the consultant start to build a relationship with the client? What does a consultant need to do to prepare for an initial meeting with a client? And what are the key success factors for contracting effectively with a client?

The consultancy for change cycle

Consultancy models often depict a linear, sequential approach to consulting, proposing that one stage must be completed before the next stage begins. The exact stages may vary, although they generally describe the activities that connect the initial meeting between a consultant and a potential client through to a final review. These models suggest that each step must be taken in order for the consultancy to move forward and that if one step is not completed or is not completed correctly then each subsequent step is in jeopardy as any errors, omissions or oversights will be carried through the remainder of the consultancy (Ainsworth, 2010). Such a step-by-step approach is illustrated in Figure 3.1.

In contrast, the consultancy for change cycle is iterative rather than linear, with each phase constantly informing the orientation of previous and subsequent phases. So, for instance, during the diagnosis and analysis phase the consultant may discover information that results in the original contract with the client needing to be reviewed and revised. The cycle is illustrated in Figure 3.2 and is based on the experience of the author, as well as incorporating phases identified by other authors, and has been used in practice.

Each of the phases shown in Figure 3.2 is briefly described below.

Figure 3.1 A linear consultancy process

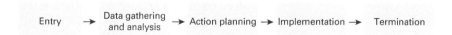

Entry → Data gathering and analysis → Action planning → Implementation → Termination

Figure 3.2   The consultancy for change cycle

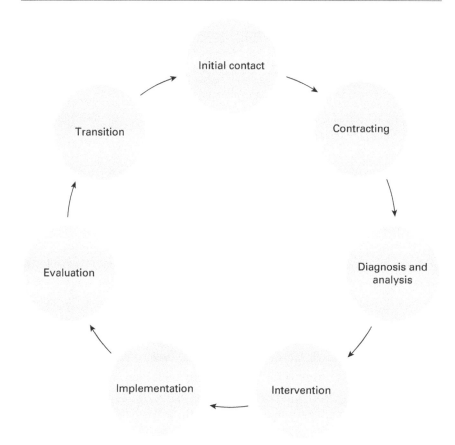

- *Initial contact.* Consultancy assignments start with an initial contact between the consultant and the client. The client usually makes the request by describing the issue (problem or opportunity) and what is driving the need for change. The outcome of this phase will be an understanding of how the client views the issue and some initial thoughts about what the client expects from the consultant and how they might work together to address the client's issue.
- *Contracting.* The initial contact phase is followed by contracting about *what* needs to be done, *how* and by *when*. The outcome of the contracting phase is that the consultant will provide a proposal about what they will do. When this is mutually agreed between the client and consultant the work can commence.
- *Diagnosis and analysis.* This phase involves joint diagnosis, by the consultant and the client, through gathering, analysing and interpreting

data in order to understand, in more depth, the key issue and the root causes of the problem. The outcome of this phase is that the consultant will present to the client the feedback from the data analysis and both will agree how to address the issues identified. This stage may be ongoing since further analysis may be required as the consultancy progresses. This can involve re-evaluating the issue that is being addressed or gathering additional data about it.

- *Intervention.* When it has been identified what needs to change, the client and consultant need to jointly agree on what change intervention would best address the issue and how the intervention will be designed.

- *Implementation.* Once the change intervention has been agreed and designed the next phase is to plan and implement it. This may require gathering and analysing further information to ensure the implementation is successful.

- *Evaluation.* This involves the client and the consultant evaluating the outcomes of the change intervention and agreeing whether or not the intervention has resulted in the desired benefits and outcomes.

- *Transition.* Once the intervention has been evaluated and the change has been operationalized the consultant needs to disengage from the work and ensure that the client is able to sustain the change in the organization. It is also an opportunity to identify potential further work with the client.

The bolts of the consultancy cycle

Each of the phases of the consultancy cycle is bolted together with *dialogue, feedback, the client–consultant relationship* and *stakeholder management,* as illustrated in Figure 3.3.

- *Dialogue.* At the heart of the consultancy for change cycle is dialogue. Creating change using dialogue is about creating organizational conversations that lead to understanding and action. Dialogue allows the consultant, client and other key stakeholders to contribute to decisions about the issue and the proposed change and to generate not only wisdom and a wealth of ideas but also engagement and commitment. It is about engaging in discussions about the why, how, what and when of change (Hodges, 2016). Knowing the *what* enables consultants to identify what needs to be changed and *how* it should be changed. Knowing the *why* allows consultants to engage with the issues of their client and work with them (Balogun, 2006), while knowing the *when* enables timescales to be agreed.

Figure 3.3   Bolts of the consultancy cycle

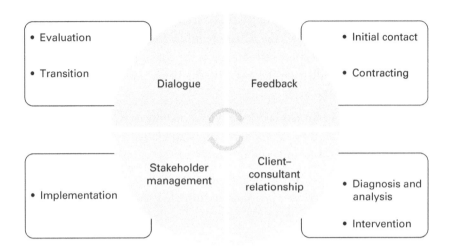

So dialogue enables: mutual understanding; an approach through which to consult effectively; and the opportunity to gain engagement and commitment to change.

- *Feedback.* Feedback runs throughout the consultancy for change cycle and should be regularly sought and, where possible, actioned. Giving and receiving feedback are essential for consultants in order to monitor whether or not the change intervention is working, and how their relationship with the client is progressing. All too often consultants fail to explicitly ask for feedback and only realize that their relationship with the client is failing or producing unintended consequences when something unexpected happens to draw their attention to it. So feedback needs to be an ongoing part of the consultancy.

- *The client–consultant relationship.* The relationship between the client and the consultant is a crucial bolt of the consultancy for change cycle as a close working relationship, mutual respect and trust between the client and consultant will carry the consultancy through the tough times as well as the good.

  The consultant needs to build rapport and gain credibility in order to win the trust of a client. Building rapport involves the consultant listening, asking questions and empathizing with the client. To gain credibility with a client, the consultant needs to have the skills, knowledge and experience (capabilities) and be ready to challenge assumptions and take action.

The consultant also needs to show an understanding of the client's industry, market sector and competitive position. This can be done, for instance, by conducting a SWOT (strengths, weaknesses, opportunities and threats) analysis of the internal and external environment in which the organization operates.

The success of the consultancy for change cycle is dependent on the ability to create a relationship of trust. Trust is, however, extremely hard to gain but amazingly easy to lose (Czerniawska and May, 2004). For consultants, the way to build and maintain trust with clients is to develop a two-way relationship that is based on joint decision-making and working together to solve the issue that the client is facing. If the relationship is only one way, with the client not making any suggestions or expressing concerns, problems may arise. For example, the consultant might be in a position in which they, rather than the client, are forced to make decisions. Alternatively, consultants might find themselves in a situation where the client agrees with the procedure that is being put in place despite not fully understanding it. This can result in what can be described as the 'nodding dog syndrome' – where the client just nods and says 'yes'. This can be the case when the consultant does not challenge the client to find out what they actually think. The client–consultant relationship therefore has to be based on trust and mutuality, and this must be maintained throughout the consultancy assignment.

- *Stakeholder management.* Key stakeholders need to be identified and managed throughout the consultancy for change cycle. A stakeholder is someone who is involved in or impacted by the consultancy for change cycle. To identify who the key stakeholders are consultants should consider the following questions:
  - Who will be affected by this change?
  - Who will be responsible for making it happen?
  - Who will be accountable for it?
  - Who will benefit from the change?
  - Who can influence the change happening, or not?
  - Who has the power to block the change?

Stakeholder management can be achieved by developing an understanding of the most important stakeholders and identifying the impact of the change on them and how they are likely to respond, so that the consultant can work out how to win their support, as well as assessing whether or not stakeholders are champions, blockers or 'sitting on the fence' (neither blockers nor supporters).

Once all the key stakeholders are identified the next step is to assess how much power and influence they have. This can be done by considering the following:

– How much influence does each stakeholder have to make the change happen, or to prevent it from happening? Is it high, low or medium?

– How much power do they have to make the change happen, or to prevent it from happening? Is it high, low or medium?

The final step of the stakeholder analysis is to agree how to manage the stakeholders. For this, the template for a stakeholder plan in Figure 3.4 can be used. Stakeholders who are not committed to the change and who can influence the consultancy for change cycle represent a potential risk. Unless they are proactively managed, project costs can escalate, timescales slip, and benefits may not be fully realized. The stakeholders who are optimistic and supportive of the change need to be engaged in the consultancy for change cycle, as they will help to ensure that the change is owned, implemented and sustained successfully. This exercise of analysing and managing stakeholders will provide consultants with a guide to where they need to devote their time and effort.

Identifying and analysing stakeholders is a continuous activity as new stakeholders may emerge during a consultancy cycle and old ones may leave the organization or move to another job where they are no longer involved or impacted by the change. As change progresses, its scope may alter and

Figure 3.4   Stakeholder management plan

	Stakeholder role	Action	Action owner	Completion date	Performance measures	Progress
Stakeholder A						
Stakeholder B						
Stakeholder C						
Stakeholder D						

some stakeholders may become less relevant or lose interest, while others may become more important. The management of stakeholders is therefore an ongoing and dynamic activity of the consultancy for change cycle.

In the following case study Ronald Graefe, Management Consultancy Manager in Accenture, describes his work with a German hospital chain that was facing increasing competition from small and independent hospitals.

CASE STUDY

The case of a German healthcare chain

The German hospital chain was aiming to improve patient turnaround times, which are measured economically as length of stay (LOS). For this task, the hospital chain approached a leading global management consultancy firm (which I worked for) to help them to implement measures to allow a better predictability of care and to address the increasingly tighter budgets in all departments of their sites. The top management support was assured and the overall project was sponsored. The expectation of top management was for a visible short-term impact. I was asked initially to conduct an assessment of the current situation and then brought in later as an external change manager.

The focus of the change was to establish an improved forecasting system by utilizing existing data and introducing system learning – the key element for switching to in-time documentation – which would have an impact on thousands of users in all departments of the hospital chain's sites. The change was planned in two steps. First, forecasting quality was increased by in-time utilization of currently available case information. The second step was to establish more in-time case data into the system, which would allow a more frequent adjustment of the LOS calculation parameters.

In preparation for the upcoming change, the individual departmental performance for two years on all sites was analysed over a four-month time span. This revealed that the average adjusted LOS of departments varied based on the German benchmarks. Although the LOS was within the acceptable range for the majority of their cases, the remaining exceptional cases (about 10 per cent) had either too low LOS (<24 hours), due to the transfer of a started case to a specialized clinic, or too high LOS, which could not be addressed by the available medical data. Besides the LOS evaluation, it was identified that clinical documentation was finalized generally after the patient was released from the hospital. This was satisfactory from a documentation point of view but caused a delay or even prevented the availability of in-time documentation.

The first assessment of the current status revealed the various concerns of stakeholders. The local site manager of each hospital also saw a need for change, and the department heads felt generally positive about the change, but felt they were being controlled or feared that low-performing departments would be identified and put on the spot while departments with great performance would be rewarded. Nurses and doctors were concerned about additional work with insufficient predictability of the calculated LOS. Some nurses felt that they might lose their job if the current utilization of beds was not as high in the future. Medical records department staff, on the other hand, were concerned that they would be blamed for the general unavailability of in-time documentation.

To address the concerns of these stakeholders five key objectives of the change were identified:

1   Increase the quality of care.

2   Support clinical decision-making.

3   Reduce errors and increase patient safety.

4   Increase patient throughput.

5   Secure people's jobs.

Given the financial impact of the change and the timeline to roll the change out within every department, there was a high rate of urgency from management to implement the change. However, it was politically challenging to propose a reduction of clinical services, at the same time, as an improvement in the balance sheet being required to prevent any further unpopular steps. There was a massive disconnect between what was happening outside the hospital and what was happening internally at all employment levels. This was a major barrier to creating a sense of urgency. Therefore, in order to create a sense of urgency external consultants were brought in to utilize internal and external data sources.

The change would impact several hundred users, whose support for the desired change was needed. Two similar initiatives at comparably sized hospitals had failed to achieve user acceptance. Users had attempted to achieve overambitious economic goals by utilizing incomplete data and insufficient tools. Therefore, the technical capabilities of the change had to be confirmed and targets defined, followed by a realistic identification of the possible impact.

A strong preference for a collaborative approach was identified for a number of reasons. First, the level of trust in external change managers was low. Second, short-term visibility of financial benefits was required. This would necessitate an overall improvement of case management, not merely by one or two departments at each site. Thus, the success of the implementation plan was highly dependent on the commitment and effort of others. Third, there was uncertainty abut the end state design – a predictable in-time calculation of LOS. This end state could only be achieved by timely contributions from all the medical personnel involved. The switch from reactive documentation to proactive documentation required a significant change in behaviour and cross-department collaboration. Resistance was identified during the first stakeholder interviews driven by concerns in the areas of activity tracking and potential additional work.

The collaborative approach was executed in four stages. First, the change potential per department was analysed, adjusted and compared with national benchmarks. During the second stage the highest LOS improvement potential by initial diagnosis per department of each site and the relevant stakeholders were identified. In the third stage all stakeholders of each site were brought together in a kick-off meeting to discuss the change potential, workflow impact, implementation timeline and responsibilities. During the fourth and final stage, the implementation was executed and results were analysed weekly to identify unforeseen obstacles, adjust workflows and measure successes.

A number of factors worked well. The vision statement was communicated repeatedly to ensure the change message reached every level of the hierarchy. The chosen collaborative step-by-step approach motivated and engaged users of the first two pilot departments. An informal benchmarking process began amongst users and later amongst departments, regardless of whether or not all relevant data was already being entered into the system on a daily basis.

Based on the lessons learned from two other initiatives that had failed user acceptance by implementing the full scope of the change at once, the staged approach of implementation helped gain acceptance. The IT department was approached early in the process for a feasibility assessment, prior to involving stakeholders. The outcome demonstrated the capabilities of the technical components and was shared with stakeholders to identify pilot departments for each site. The gradual implementation ensured a proof of concept for the pilot departments selected, because of the transparency on the benefits and drawbacks of the technical capabilities, plus the involvement of users in the decision-making process. This helped to set realistic expectations of stakeholders in and outside the pilot departments.

On the operational side, an external consultant with broad industry expertise supported by an external medical advisor was deployed to identify the economic potential of the changes. The workshops conducted by these externals with individual stakeholders proved to be very important, as people felt involved and supported as regards the proposed changes within the department.

Explaining the need to drive the project urgently paid off. Instantly, it became clear that some people wanted to actively contribute, but felt unable to do so within the established structures. Partly this was addressed by the IT department in the form of the extension of user rights or by introducing new features. A high acceptance of graphical user interface proposals was reached by useful mock-ups of realistic cases.

With hindsight, despite this approach leading to the successful implementation of the change, some aspects could have been improved and done differently. For example, uncertainty among staff was inadequately addressed by merely repeating the vision, which caused some people to disengage. This could have been addressed by being more sensitive to how people felt about the changes. Although a successful strategy in one department was transferred successfully to another department, some department heads were reluctant to constructively support the new directive. Partly this was triggered by the different incentives that senior physicians had. At other times the quality of forecasting was significantly lower and sparked doubt. Additionally, as the reliance on external resources to introduce the change grew, the more the departmental drive for the change became directed from the top down. Again, more attention needed to be paid to individual views and feelings about the change and more effort made to engage people in it.

During the alignment and kick-off meeting, some key people were out of the office, and this created a challenge in bringing all the stakeholders together. Although the hospital operated a 24-hour service, during the early stages of the change some key resource people were only available during normal office hours. The quality of documentation at nights and weekends was identified as being of a lower level. The communication did not sufficiently include guidance for off-hour shifts during the start-up phase. After the initial phase, constant retraining needs were identified with a continuous quality monitoring system.

The key lessons I learned were varied. The collaborative approach proved very valuable. The achievement of goals set within the time given, preparation, early alignment with stakeholders, and timing proved to be essential components.

The end state was not known at the beginning. This made it difficult to plan the timeline for a possible solution. The implementation of systems to achieve easy goals first helped show positive effects early on and stimulated the department motivation.

The communication of the goal for the change must be clear and tangible. Specifically, one voice and message from executives, site, department and change manager is important. Within each site and department, official and unofficial reporting lines were identified and needed to be considered. Previously scheduled meetings were utilized for department kick-offs to avoid scheduling additional sessions.

As an external consultant I was able to help drive the urgency for change. However, without the support from departmental heads it was difficult to change the behaviours of people.

Overall, gaining trust was vital. This was achieved by evaluating specific cases with responsible department heads and repeating again and again the vision to the stakeholders involved in the change.

Challenges of using the consultancy cycle approach

There are a number of aspects with the consultancy for change cycle that a consultant needs to take into account when applying it in practice. The first factor is that each of the phases of the cycle will vary in length and complexity, depending on the nature of the change and the client's expectations. At each phase, the consultant will need to decide whether to proceed or return to the previous phase(s). The tasks of each phase must, however, be sufficiently completed in order to move to the next phase. As new information emerges, there may need to be a return to previous phases to ensure that adjustments are made, before progressing further. The second factor is that each of the phases may not be used in all consultancy assignments. For instance, if the client wants to restructure their department the consultant may gather and analyse data but might not be involved in the design and delivery of a new structure. Alternatively, there may be no diagnostic phase if the client already knows what they want. The third factor is that the cycle assumes that consultants will use the diagnosis to recommend solutions that are most appropriate to the client. However, few, if any, consultants start with a blank piece of paper, designing their solution according to what would best suit the client. Instead, most consultants are solution-led, offering clients a fixed number of standardized solutions. Finally, it is increasingly rare for the same consultant to carry out the consultancy for change cycle from beginning to end. Instead, transformations are often broken up into stages where two or more consultants may conduct the work. For a large transformation, such as an acquisition, there may be a number of different consultants (internal and external) involved in the due diligence compared to those involved in the implementation.

Overall, the consultancy for change cycle is a helpful way of structuring consultancy work for organizational transformations. It provides an approach for: realizing benefits – the benefits of the change can be identified, measured and monitored (further details on benefits are in Chapter 6);

gaining commitment and engagement from clients and stakeholders – the cycle provides an approach for involving stakeholders and keeping them informed of progress; and improving the client–consultant relationship – each of the phases focuses on building and maintaining trust and a joint approach for working together.

Initial contact

The first phase of the consultancy for change cycle is the *initial contact* between the consultant and the client before the contracting process begins. The initial contact, although it is not confined to a single meeting between the consultant and the client, is the formal and structured discussion, which forms the start of a consultancy for change cycle. There may, however, be a need to have a number of initial discussions before both the client and consultant feel that they are ready to decide whether or not they can work together to address the specific issue.

The initial meeting is the first impression that a client has of how the consultancy relationship will progress. During the meeting the client will want to receive reassurance that the consultant possesses the capability to achieve the desired transformation and will be observing the consultants' behaviours, physical presence, energy and confidence, and deciding whether or not they feel that they can work with and trust the consultant. So how the consultant behaves during the initial meetings will send verbal and non-verbal signals that either assure or potentially concern the client.

From the start of the initial contact onwards consultants need to be aware of the rhetoric they use and avoid 'consultant speak', or so-called 'consul-tobabble'. In a study conducted in Italy, Cristina Crucini and Matthias Kipping (2001) found that the use of specific business jargon could create anxiety and mistrust. For instance, using the names of practices such as LEAN or TQM can create confusion and diffidence if the client is not familiar with them. Consultants need to use clear, simple language and avoid consultancy jargon.

Effective initial meetings will involve the consultant listening carefully to the client, asking questions and expressing empathy for the client's issues and requests. Questions for consultants to use during initial meetings in order to identify the help and value they can provide to the client include:

- What is the client's long-term mission or strategic direction?
- What is the client's biggest challenge and/or opportunities?

- What kind of help will the client need to face this challenge/opportunity?
- How can the consultant help the client to reach short- and long-term business objectives?
- What value-add benefits is the client expecting from the consultant?

Moving from initial contact to contracting

Moving from the initial contact to contracting phase happens when there is an agreement between the client and consultant that they can work together. During this transition there needs to be confirmation of the assumption that the relationship and work desired by the client match the consultant's capabilities and that they have the capacity to do the work. There also has to be clarity about what is really needed and wanted in order to develop a clear scope, objectives and outcomes.

The consultant and client are ready to move to contracting when the initial contact tasks and actions (as outlined in Table 3.1) have been sufficiently completed and when the client and consultant have concluded that there is a fit between each of their expectations, values and differences so that they can work together.

Table 3.1 Initial contact tasks and actions (adapted from Gallant and Rios, 2005)

Tasks	Actions
Introductions	Share and acknowledge personal and professional information for building credibility and the client–consultant relationship. Listen to what is being said and what is important to the client.
Agree the agenda	Agree the agenda at the start of the meeting. Manage the meeting effectively in terms of time, pace, outcomes, roles and responsibilities.
Identify client(s)	It is vital to identify who are the client/s and key stakeholders. Most consultancy assignments will have multiple clients, including the contracting client(s), the client making use of the consultation, and the client with the authority to control the process and implement outcomes.

(Continued)

Table 3.1   *(Continued)*

Tasks	Actions
Invite client to tell their story	Ask questions and ask for examples to understand the client's concerns and issues, what they want to change, the rationale behind their request to meet, what other change initiatives the client is leading, current and previous approaches to transformation including successes and failures. Actively listen and summarize your understanding of issues.
Ask the client about their needs, wants, expectations, hopes, and concerns	Engage in dialogue about needs, wants, expectations, hopes, concerns and risks in relation to the change.
Explore differences	Explore client–consultant differences and how they might impact on the work and relationship.
Explore values and ethics	Share values and ethical boundaries and enquire about those of the client. Identify potential conflicts or ethical dilemmas that may impact on the consultancy and explore them with the client.
Identify any potential opposition	Explore the forces that will help and hinder success. Explore potential opposition to change from key stakeholders.
Assess the client–consultant fit, and decide whether or not to proceed with the consultancy	Assess the fit between the client's and consultant's needs, values, interests, time requirements, credibility, trust, readiness and commitment to the work. If you feel that there is a mismatch in any of those that will impact on the success of the project, or that you lack the capability and/or capacity to do the work consider whether or not you want to proceed.

Contracting

The consultancy for change cycle requires some form of explicit contracting that results in an agreement between the consultant and the client on the work to be carried out (Block, 2011). The purpose of the *contracting* phase is to develop a clear, mutually agreed formal contract. Contracting must be mutual, with the client and consultant choosing to enter into a contract for working together. Unless there are mutual understanding and agreement there is a considerable risk that there will be a lack of commitment and support from either or both parties (Cummings and Worley, 2001). Mutuality must be achieved or there is no contract, and if there is no contract there is no consultancy assignment.

Contracting is a continual process and usually begins with a face-to-face meeting, although it is not confined to a single meeting. Consultants and clients may return to validate agreements and renegotiate expectations at various times during the consultancy for change cycle.

Internal consultants often overlook the need for contracting and instead make assumptions about what the client needs, and how the need will be met. This is not surprising, since the nature of contracting for the internal consultant is complex, as the boundaries of the client–consultant relationship can be less clear than for external consultants and often involve multiple contracting relationships up and across the organization. Internal consultants are also often faced with competing priorities and this, combined with a lack of perceived power and influence, can mean challenges in defining the boundaries and priorities for client work (Kenton and Moody, 2003). Despite such constraints it is essential to have some defined parameters to help establish roles and responsibilities for both consultant and client.

The contracting meeting is a predictor of how the consultancy process as a whole will proceed (Block, 2011). The client's actions during this phase can be perceived as symbolic of the working relationship to come (Anderson, 2012). Susan Gallant and Daisy Rios say that it is essential that consultants pay 'attention to words, tone, metaphors, and other linguistic differences that are peculiar to the client' (2006: 190). So consultants should see the contracting process as a time to gather data on how the client behaved, for example did they appear nervous, brusque or anxious? Did they describe the issue to be addressed as challenging, annoying, impossible to solve, typical or devastating? Did the client feel like a willing partner in trying to solve the problem, or did they need to be persuaded about joint participation in the process? Responses to such questions as well as the consultant's instinct about the proposed change can be illustrative or symbolic of how others in the organization may be feeling and can be instructive in planning the approach for the diagnostic phase, which is discussed in Chapter 4.

Areas to clarify during contracting

During the contracting phase there are several areas that will have to be identified and clarified including: who the client/s is/are; the issues to be addressed; roles, responsibilities and accountabilities; expectations; and the readiness of the client for change. Each of these is briefly examined next.

Client identification

At the start of the contracting phase it is important to establish exactly who the client is, or even if there is more than one client. It is always assumed that the client is easily identifiable, but as Edgar Schein (1997: 202) says, 'the question of who actually is the client can be ambiguous and problematical'. Schein (1997) goes on to point out that not being able to identify who the client is can potentially generate goal and role conflicts that might damage the relationship between the consultant and the client, and therefore jeopardize the change initiative. The consultant, therefore, needs to meet with the client who is initiating the change, even if they are at a very senior level in the organization, for a consultant cannot contract with a client who is out of the room (Block, 2011). If the client is not present when a consultant is contracting about an assignment then the consultant cannot assume that the client supports the need for change until they have discussed it with them. It is also important to identify if there is more than one client as, in some cases, there can be multiple clients with whom the consultant will need to contract.

Clarify the issue/s to be addressed

The client usually has a story that needs to be told and an issue to be resolved. The client's story may typically start with the issue that is causing them to consider a change. It may be specific, such as a decrease in market share or an increase in absenteeism, or the opportunity to acquire another company, or general, such as 'we need to expand' or 'we have become too complacent'. The issue may have an implied or stated solution and the client may want to move to action to solve the issue without providing the full story. For example, a client might believe that the solution is to make roles redundant. They may even state the issue in the form of a solution: 'We need to reduce our headcount.' The consultant must ensure that the client does not skip straight to solutions and omit elements from their story. For, in many cases, the issue is only a symptom of an underlying problem that needs to be explored during the diagnostic phase of the consultancy for change cycle. For example, increasing costs may result from several root causes, including ineffective new product development or manufacturing processes, or inadequate customer service policies and procedures. Alternatively, a request for a team-building event to eradicate dysfunctional team behaviour may, on further analysis, show that a controlling leadership style or unfair reward processes are the main causes. One question, in particular, that can open up dialogue and lead to new insights for the consultant and the client when asked at the right time, is 'How does the client know what the problem actually is?' This can help in understanding how the client identified the problem. Without this understanding the definition of the problem may be based on rocky foundations with no certainty that the proposed approach will be appropriate. The issue facing the client must, therefore, be clarified early in the consultancy cycle so that subsequent diagnostic and intervention activities can be designed to focus on identifying the root causes of the specific issue/s.

Agree roles, responsibilities and accountabilities

During the contracting stage the consultant needs to agree with the client what roles they will each perform, including: Who does what? With whom? And: How will the client and consultant work together? Confusion can occur when clients presume the consultant is operating in one role, such as expert, and the consultant has assumed that they in fact are working in another, such as facilitative. Of course, consultancy assignments do not usually require only one type of role, so consultants do have to be able to change between roles.

There also needs to be clarification about responsibilities and accountabilities.

The difference between responsibility and accountability is that responsibility can be shared, while accountability cannot. Being accountable not only means being responsible for something but also ultimately being answerable for the actions. For example, a consultant may be responsible for identifying the relevant change intervention, while the client will be accountable for ensuring that it is implemented, monitored and sustained successfully. No matter how convivial or trusting the relationship with the client, roles, responsibilities and accountabilities should be specified and formalized, which in turn reinforces the nature of the client–consultant relationship.

Internal consultants must not neglect the need to clarify responsibilities and accountabilities. For, unlike the external consultant who is always a third party to the process, the internal consultant may be expected to drive the project alone, or on behalf of the senior management team. As Alan Weiss (2003) says, one of the chronic and avoidable failures of internal consultancy projects is in the client's view that the consultant is responsible for the project and that in the meantime the client can simply get back to business as usual. The exact nature of the client's position and involvement must, therefore, be clarified and internal consultants must avoid having work dumped on them by managers. So there needs to be clarity on who within the organization will have what responsibilities and who will be held accountable.

During the contracting phase there also needs to be exploration about the role and responsibilities of the sponsor. A sponsor – or champion – for the transformation needs to be identified, as it is important that the consultant is not seen as the champion. Sponsorship should be at the most senior level of the organization, in order to show that there are support and commitment from the leadership team. Contracting needs to include the consultant's expectations of the sponsor, which can potentially be a difficult conversation for an internal consultant, especially if the sponsor is at a more senior level. To help with this conversation consultants need to consider what effective sponsorship should look like and how this should be demonstrated so that people throughout the organization know the work has commitment and backing at the most senior levels.

There may, at times, also be a need to re-contract during the consultancy cycle, particularly if there is an expectation of a change in the consultant's role from the client. So contracting is not a one-off activity but should be considered at each of the phases of the consultancy cycle to ensure that any changes are formally taken into account.

Confirm expectations

Identifying and managing client expectations are an important factor when working as a consultant. Consultants must assess from the first meeting with the client their level of expectation. Jukka Ojasalo (2001) identifies three types of client expectations: fuzzy, implicit and unrealistic. *Fuzzy* expectations reflect a blurred idea about the outcome of the consultancy project, in which clients do not have a precise idea of what the change should be. As Steven Stumpf and Robert Longman say, 'unlike the customer, the client is not always right, what they say they want is not necessarily what they really want' (2000: 128). These authors also point out that although clients might be unclear about what they want, they are usually amazingly clear about what they do not want. The second type of client expectation is referred to as *implicit*. This means that 'elements of the service are so self-evident that customers do not actively or consciously even think about them, or about the possibility that they will not materialize' (Ojasalo, 2001: 203). To deal with this type of expectation consultants need to adopt a proactive approach, think further ahead than their clients, and ensure that expectations are made explicit. The third type of expectations identified by Ojasalo are *unrealistic* and can occur when clients have completely unreasonable expectations and view consultants as magicians who can resolve all problems by waving their magic wands. So consultants need to be aware of these different types of expectations and decide whether or not they are achievable.

There is often a difference between what the client expects from the project and what the client expects from the consultant. The client can be very clear about what is expected from the project, for example: improved customer service; reduced overhead charges; improved employee engagement; an increase in sales revenues. However, clients may be less clear on what they expect from the consultant. To help clarify such expectations, the following questions should be addressed: What type of help is the client looking for from the consultant? And: What are the needs and wants of both the client and the consultant in the consultancy relationship? A key question for the consultant to ask in order to clarify expectations is 'What do you want from me?' The answer to this question is at the heart of the contracting process, since it is the key qualifying question to determine whether or not the client and consultant can work together.

The management of expectations is crucial in consultancy since projects can fail because of the inability of the client and consultant to articulate their expectations clearly (Schein, 1997). The needs of clients can, however, evolve throughout the consultancy cycle. It is therefore important to constantly reassess client expectations, as they may change as a project progresses.

Identify client readiness

If a client is neither actively involved nor ready to change, a consultancy engagement is unlikely to be successful. As Schein (1990) says, it is the client who owns the problem and the solution, so they need to be ready to change. A consultant can recommend, design and even introduce change, but only the client can accept, embrace, reinforce and maintain change. A consultant needs to gauge the client's readiness for change, which includes the client's willingness, motives and aims for the change. Once an assessment has been made of the client's readiness for change the consultant can consider what needs to happen next and decide whether they are willing to work on the project, especially if the client is not ready to change. The readiness for change, therefore, needs to be identified during the initial phases of the consultancy for change cycle (readiness is discussed further in Chapter 4).

Psychological contract

Contracting has both formal and psychological components. The formal contract consists of aspects that are documented in the proposal, such as the project scope, objectives, timelines and outcomes and, for an external consultant, costs. The second part of the contract is psychological and is usually not documented, but it is just as important as the formal written contract. The psychological contract is an explicit agreement about the consultancy relationship, such as expectations and the ground rules – how the client and consultant will work together and how they will communicate with each other. Donald Anderson (2012) lists some of the initial questions that form part of the psychological contract:

- How will the client be involved in the engagement?
- What expectations does the client have in terms of how to work with the consultant, such as frequency of meetings?
- How should the client and the consultant communicate – by e-mail, phone, face-to-face, Skype?
- How should they approach one another with disagreements or requests?
- What kind of confidentiality is required? How will confidentiality be handled and what information will be held confidentially, and by whom?
- How will the consultant provide feedback to the client?
- What ethical issues need to be considered?

Delivering tough messages

Regardless of the familiarity between the consultant and the client, the consultant needs to contract with the client about how to give and receive constructive feedback. This is important especially for the internal consultant because, unlike the external consultant who risks losing one of, presumably, several clients, the internal consultant can be vulnerable to client retaliation (Block, 2011). At a minimum the client can disengage with the internal consultant, or abandon the change project altogether. In the extreme, client retaliation can result in the termination of the consultant's employment contract. These risks necessitate clear, defined contracting around the delivery of tough messages (Lacey, 1995). Clear contracting around such sensitive issues can strengthen the consultant–client relationship. It also prepares the client psychologically for the possibility of hearing tough messages, and grants permission to the consultant to address issues usually avoided.

Getting stuck in contracting

Consultants must be clear about what they need in order to work with a client. These 'must haves' can include time, support or other resources from the client, and can also include relationship imperatives such as trust and honesty. When clients and consultants cannot agree on these issues, they can get stuck in contracting. When a consultant is stuck in contracting with a client, it is often because both the client and consultant feel that if they do not get their way the project will not succeed. Peter Block (2011) suggests that to get unstuck consultants may choose to give up one of their must-have factors, such as a longer time frame, or they may renegotiate the scope of the project and agree to a shorter time frame. Ultimately, if the consultant and client cannot agree on key issues during the contracting phase they must make a decision about whether or not to proceed with working together, which can lead to the consultant saying 'no' to being involved in the consultancy.

Saying 'no'

If a consultant goes ahead with a project they do not believe they can successfully contribute to, they run the risk of failure. The reason for saying 'no' is to avoid failure and a waste of resources. Saying no to a prospective client also shows that the consultant has a right to decide on what they commit to, and that they are unwilling to take on work which they have neither the capability nor the capacity to make a success.

Internal consultants may, however, find it difficult to say 'no' to work even when it is not within their area of expertise or they do not have the capacity for it. They may feel that they are taking tremendous risks if they tell the client that it would be better not to progress with the project. Despite the risk, it is in the consultant's and the client's best interests to refuse projects that do not have a reasonable chance of success.

If it is not possible to say 'no' to a client, there are other options for the consultant. An alternative way to achieve this is for the consultant to suggest that the project is postponed and to suggest that it goes ahead at a later date – such as in six months. By the time the six months is up the client may have moved on to another project. If it is not possible to postpone the project, another option is to negotiate to minimize the scope of it and the time it will require, depending on the specific situation.

The critical point for the consultant to consider is whether it is really in their best interest to go ahead with the project. It is better to be honest with the client, than to begin a project that might fail. The client may be angry and feel rejected but proceeding with a project that might fail and in the end does not go well is even worse.

To determine whether saying 'no' is the right approach and to clarify issues during contracting the questions in the box should be addressed.

Questions to ask to clarify issues during contracting

- What is the issue? How does it appear? When is the client most aware of the issue? Can the client give an example of a recent occasion when it was experienced?
- What is the impact of the issue on the organization, its customers, specific departments/teams within the organization and its employees?
- What are the internal and external drivers for change?
- What is the client's role in the problem?
- Who are the key stakeholders and what is their involvement?
- Has the issue been experienced before in the organization?
- How long has the issue been evident?
- Why is it important to address the issue, and why now?
- What will happen if nothing changes?
- What are the potential risks?
- What has been tried already?
- Is there energy/willingness to change? Is there opposition to change? Who/where/why? Does anyone benefit from the status quo?
- What is the client asking the consultant to do?
- Why is the issue important to the client?
- What is the desired outcome?
- What role will the client play in the consultancy assignment?
- What role does the client expect from the consultant?
- What responsibilities and accountabilities will the client and consultant each have?
- How will progress be evaluated during the process and at the end?
- What will success look like? What will people be saying and doing differently?

- What time pressures are there? When should the change be implemented by?
- Who else will be involved? Other employees or consultants?
- Who are the key decision-makers?
- Is the time right for change?
- What overall benefits does the client expect from the change?

In addition to these questions external consultants will also want to ask:

- What is the organization's culture like?
- What are the formal and informal norms and values?
- What are the levels of engagement and general attitude like?
- What experience does the organization have of change?
- Has the organization experienced similar change to the one being proposed?

In the following case study Luca Sabia, a consultant in the marketing and communication industry, describes his personal experience of what happened in a merger between two Italian banks when the contracting was not done effectively due to the client not being willing to listen to the consultant.

CASE STUDY

An epic fail in contracting

When my colleagues and I met the new client, a major Italian bank, in our office in Rome we could not imagine how things would end. We met the chairman and the marketing and communication directors of two local cooperative banks which, in a few months' time, were due to merge. The new venture would create a company of 1,000 employees, 16,870 members, 170,000 clients, € 300 million equity, and operations of € 2 billion.

Due to the last-minute planning, the client asked us to support them with some of the communications during the merger. In particular, they asked for an executive profiling activity (which means raising the public profile of the top executives within the business community, securing major media coverage) to raise the profile of the new chairman and the new chief executive officer (CEO) of the new company, and for communications support during the merger process to ensure compliance with legal issues while keeping investors informed. They also asked us for support with some minor local promotional activities, such as regional media engagement, to promote the new brand of the bank.

After the initial briefing session, we met the director of marketing and the director of communications in order to start designing all the activities for the executive profiling, as well as for the corporate reputation management, both at a local and a national level.

Our first task was to develop a communication plan and then to begin implementing it within a short time frame. We arranged a media briefing, introduced the new top management of the bank while carrying out interviews and liaising with the media on a regular basis. We managed to create a lot of positive traction as well as wide media coverage, thanks to our reputation and the strong relationships we already had with journalists. Externally everything seemed to be going in the right direction as we were gaining more media coverage on a daily basis. However, things were different within the two banks, where employees had started to worry about their future and to raise concerns such as: What is going to happen now? How many layoffs will there be? Will we be made redundant? Are people going to be relocated? How many people will be affected? There was a growing list of such issues that should not have been ignored. From my professional experience, internal communication plays a pivotal role in maintaining the cohesion among workers within a company, especially when faced with severe disruption, such as a merger.

To minimize staff concerns we recommended to our client that an internal communication plan should be developed and implemented as soon as possible, despite the fact that it was not in our initial contract with the client. We stressed the necessity to have consistency with the content and the process of the internal communications, in order to maintain stability and productivity. Unfortunately, the client refused our offer and rejected the rationale we provided for the importance of internal as well as external communications, so we focused only on the external communications.

The real reason for the client refusing to develop internal communications was that the manager in charge of internal communications was terrified of the potential impact the deal would have on her career so she did everything she thought was necessary to secure her role within the company after the deal, and ignored everything else. What she would not consider, nor listen to, was that as external consultants we could support her and share our experience from a number of industries, which would be of benefit. As a result of our inability to influence her thinking, disaster loomed. The evening before the full details of the merger were announced, the communications director gave us a call at 19:00, panicking, and asking what he should do, since many of the employees had started complaining about the lack of internal communications about the merger and its impact. Despite our recommendations for the need for an internal communications plan, the communications director still preferred a different approach, and the following morning an e-mail was sent to all employees announcing the deal but with other details. Complaints and unrest about the merger and its impact continued within the company until a reshuffle at managerial level was forced to take place.

Looking back at that experience, there are three main lessons I have learned. First, during the contracting phase I would ensure that the client was clear on the benefits of internal and external communications during change. Second, in order to be effective in carrying out change such as a merger, where the uncertainties of the aftermath have the potential to negatively affect the working environment as well as the well-being and productivity of employees, an internal communications plan is vital. Third, the plan has to be designed and shared, prior to the change, with the senior management as well as affected employees. Then, once implemented, the communications plan needs to be monitored and adjusted throughout the change process.

Discussion questions for the case

1 What might have been done differently by the external consultants in this case?

2 How would you contract with a client about the importance of communication for an organizational transformation?

3 What lessons from this case would you apply to a consultancy assignment you are working on?

Frameworks to use for contracting

To help gather data in preparation for contracting, and to elicit information from a client during initial meetings, consultants can use frameworks such as Future–Now, PES and COPS.

Future–Now

The *Future–Now* framework focuses on identifying what the situation is and what it should be, at an organizational, team and/or a departmental level (Hodges and Gill, 2015). This framework is illustrated in Figure 3.5. The left-hand circle (now) should be used to define the current state and the right-hand circle (future) should identify what the future state should be. Defining the current state helps to establish a baseline so that it is clear what needs to change. Defining the future state is about developing a purpose or vision of what the organization (or team/department) ought to look like in the future. Securitas Belgium, for instance, performed an analysis of its current state and desired behaviours required for its vision and from this developed a detailed, measurable change plan for 150 of its managers.

It is debatable whether the application of the framework should start with looking at the current or the future state. The benefit of starting with the current state is that all the issues (good and bad) can be aired first. However, there is also a danger that this can result in getting too bogged down in what is wrong with the current situation rather than focusing on what the future should look like.

Some of the key questions to ask when using this framework are:

- What are the key challenges today in the organization?
- What are the current areas of concern in the organization?
- What are the strengths and weaknesses of the organization?
- What opportunities and threats is the organization facing?
- What are the internal and external drivers for change?
- What will the future situation look like or what would 'better' look like? How will we know when we get there? What will it look like and feel like?
- What will hinder progress towards that future?
- What will help progress towards that future?

Figure 3.5   The Future–Now framework

Now   ⟶   Future

Figure 3.6 The PES framework

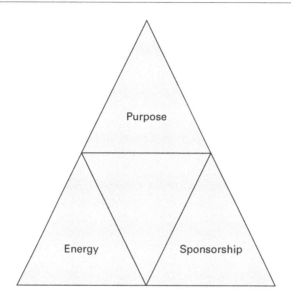

PES

During the contracting phase the purpose of the change, as well as the commitment and energy that there are for change, should be identified, including any gaps. To help with this analysis the PES framework (Figure 3.6) can be used. This framework focuses on three areas: purpose, energy and sponsorship.

Purpose This involves identifying the purpose for the change. It can be addressed by questions such as:

- What is the rationale for the change, and what is it based on?
- What is the purpose of the change?
- How clear is it?

Energy This element focuses on having sufficient energy to start the change. Questions to consider are:

- How much energy and desire to change exist in the organization?
- What other organizational changes need energy right now? Is there enough energy to do all that needs to be done?

- How will reaction to the change be influenced by the experience of previous, or other existing, change programmes?
- How will the energy be sustained throughout the change process?
- What can be done differently, if anything, to increase the amount of available energy for the change?

Sponsorship This is the commitment and support from the client and other key stakeholders for the purpose and the proposed change it will bring.
Questions to consider here are:

- How committed is the client to the change? What is the commitment to the proposed change from other stakeholders? Is there a gap between their actual commitment and what is required to drive forward the change?
- How will the change be sponsored moving forward? How involved will the client be in the whole process?

The PES framework is easy to use, in order to assess the purpose, energy and sponsorship in the organization and also to identify where there are gaps. It is important to identify where these gaps lie and what needs to be done to address them. The framework does, however, have limitations in that it can provide only a 'quick and dirty' analysis and covers only three areas. For a more detailed analysis it is worth using PES in conjunction with the COPS model.

COPS

The *COPS* framework can be used for scanning an organization internally (Wardrop-White, 2001). The four elements of the COPS framework (as illustrated in Figure 3.7) are:

C = culture (beliefs, values, artefacts, manifestations).

O = organization (structure, job roles, reporting lines).

P = people (staff, capabilities – skills, knowledge and experience).

S = systems (processes and procedures).

Questions can be designed to find out more about each of the four areas. For example, how is the culture of the organization described? What is the structure of the organization/team? What are the capabilities of staff? And how do systems connect with each other?

This framework can be used to establish the health of an organization, team or department and the relative strengths and weaknesses of each of the four elements. It can be used in conjunction with the PES and the

Future–Now model to assess what the current situation is and also what the future should look like (see Figure 3.8).

Similar to Future-Now and PES, the COPS framework can be used to do a quick high-level analysis. It does, therefore, have some limitations as well as benefits. The main limitation is that it focuses on four separate elements of an organization and ignores the nature of the interaction between those different components. The benefit of such frameworks is that they can be used quickly to provide an overview of the current and desired future state, and the gap between the two. I have used these frameworks in different consultancy situations, such as: prior to meeting a client for the first time; during an initial meeting; and as part of the diagnostic phase. If the three models are used together then they can provide a framework for gathering high-level initial data. They can be used effectively with clients, as well as with teams and groups of individuals at different levels in an organization, to gain an overview of the current situation and specify what the future should look like.

Figure 3.7   The COPS framework

Figure 3.8   Integrating the Future–Now, COPS and PES frameworks

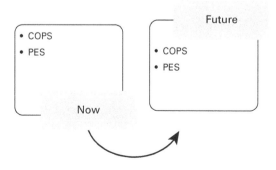

> **Activity**
>
> Apply the three frameworks to a potential consultancy assignment you have been asked to consider. Identify the strengths and gaps from your analysis.

Summary

The consultancy for change cycle is iterative and provides a route map to be used by a consultant during a transformation. However, like all conceptual frameworks it does need to be adapted to the context in which it is being applied. The consultant, whether internal or external, therefore needs to be familiar enough with the cycle to be able to use it flexibly and to revisit the different phases within it, when necessary.

Contracting is an ongoing activity throughout the consultancy for change cycle. Consultants should return to contracting discussions each time they meet with a client in order to validate progress, correct any misunderstandings and agree on what to do next. Effective contracting can address many of the issues that can occur later in an assignment, such as a lack of commitment from the client, disagreements about the consultant's role, lack of contact with the client or confusion about the objectives of the assignment. Contracting is, therefore, a critical skill for a consultant to learn, especially for internal consultants who may overlook the need for it and instead make assumptions about what the client expects and how those expectations will be met.

The outcomes of the initial contact and contracting phase are: the start of a working relationship between the client and the consultant; joint decision-making about whether to go ahead with the consultancy assignment; a proposal for the consultation; and the start of building a foundation for the remaining phases of the consultancy for change cycle. If done well, initial contact and contracting will go a long way towards helping to achieve a successful outcome with the implementation of sustainable change.

Implications for consultants

A number of practical implications for aspiring and practising consultants can be drawn from the issues raised in this chapter.

- *Prepare for the initial meeting with a client.*
  To prepare for an initial meeting with a client, a consultant should gather and review all the information they have about the organization – for example, the mission, values, philosophy, history, size, character, structure, products/services, market position, reputation, history of change and current transformations taking place. Use a framework such as Future–Now, COPS and/or PES.

- *Identify the purpose and agenda of the initial meeting.*
  Be clear about the purpose of the initial meeting, which should be to understand the context, client and the issue facing the client, in order to be able to develop the relationship, assess what kind of consultancy is needed, and propose the next step. The POGO approach can be used to help structure meetings:

  - People. Show an interest in the client, ask questions about them, such as: How long have they been in the role? What successes have they recently had? And what are their key challenges?

  - Organization. Ask questions about the organization and the client's key challenges, and other changes they are involved in.

  - Goals. Establish what the key goals are that the client wants to achieve from addressing the issue.

  - Obstacles. Identify what the client perceives as the current and potential obstacles to achieving the goals.

- *Clarify roles, responsibilities and accountabilities.*
  Clarify what the roles, responsibilities and accountabilities will be for the client and consultant and remember that a consultant can recommend, design and even introduce change, but only the client can accept, embrace, reinforce and maintain change.

- *Identify and manage key stakeholders.*
  Carry out a stakeholder analysis at the start of the consultancy and review it at each phase to ensure key stakeholders are being managed effectively.

- *Identify the 'what' and 'how'.*
  At the contracting phase, emphasis needs to be placed on both the *what* of consultancy and the *how*. The issues – *what* – as presented by the client have to be clarified, but it is equally important to discuss at an early stage *how* the consultant and client will work together.

- *Contracting is just as important for internal consultants.*
  Internal consultants need to have some form of contract with their client, as all clients and consultants will find it helpful to know what will be done and when. How a consultant achieves this will vary from client to client, but at a minimum consultants should:
  - document the terms of reference (TOR) in a written proposal, as well as the issue to be addressed, roles, responsibilities, accountabilities, timescales, resources required and costs;
  - invite the client to review and amend the proposal;
  - write a note to the client recording the joint agreement to the proposal and confirming what will happen next and who will be doing the work;
  - review the proposal at each progress meeting and record the client's agreement with the stage reached and, if necessary, their approval of any changes made.

- *Contracting is an ongoing activity.*
  A consultant may never be finished contracting, as each time they meet with the client they may have to re-contract with the client, especially if there have been developments since they last met that affect what was agreed in the initial contract. The question that every consultant should ask their client regularly is, 'What has changed since we last met?'

- *Clarify expectations.*
  A key question for the consultant to ask in order to clarify expectations is 'What do you want from me?' The answer to this question is at the heart of the contracting process, since it is the key qualifying question to determine whether or not the client and consultant can work together.

Activities – consultancy scenarios

Consider how you will approach the following scenarios

1 It is your first meeting with a potential client. During the meeting you learn that the client has not used consultants before. They seem to have a reasonable idea of what consultancy work they want you to carry out. What do you do and say at the meeting to help the consultancy proceed to the next phase?

2 You have responded to an invitation to meet a prospective client. The client has scoped out the work they wish you to do, which they show to you along with the deadline and what the client expects you to do. Your initial reaction is that the client is being unrealistic in terms of what they want carried out within the set timeline. You decide to challenge the client on this assumption. What questions will you ask?

References

Ainsworth, D (2010) Into the rabbit hole, in *Consultation for Organizational Change*, ed AF Buono and D Jamieson, pp 247–68, Information Age Publishing, Charlotte, NC

Anderson, DL (2012) *Organization Development: The process of leading organizational change*, Sage, London

Balogun, J (2006) Managing change: Steering a course between intended strategies and unanticipated outcomes, *Long Range Planning*, **39** (1), pp 29–49

Block, P (2011) *Flawless Consulting*, 3rd edn, San Francisco, Jossey Bass/Pfeiffer

Crucini, C and Kipping, M.(2001) Management consultancies as global change agents? Evidence from Italy, *Journal of Organisational Change Management*, **14** (6), pp 570–89

Cummings, TG and Worley, CG (2001) *Essentials of Organization Development and Change*, Cengage, Mason, OH

Czerniawska, F and May, P (2004) *Management Consultancy in Practice: A casebook of international best practice*, Kogan Page, London

Gallant, S and Rios, D (2006) Entry and contracting phase, in *The NTL Handbook of Organization Development and Change*, ed B Jones and M Brazzel, 171–91, Pfeiffer, San Francisco

Hodges, J (2016) *Managing and Leading People Through Change: The theory and practice of sustaining change through people*, Kogan Page, London

Hodges, J and Gill, R (2015) *Sustaining Change in Organizations*, Sage, London

Kenton, B and Moody, D (2003) *The Role of the Internal Consultant*, Roffey Park Institute, London

Lacey, MY (1995) Internal consulting: Perspectives on the process of planned change, *Journal of Organizational Change Management*, **8** (3), pp 75–84

Ojasalo, J (2001) Managing customer expectations in professional services, *Managing Service Quality*, **11** (3), pp 200–12

Schein, E (1990) A general philosophy of helping: Process consultation, *Sloan Management Review*, **31** (3), pp 57–64

Schein, E (1997) The concept of 'client' from a process consultation perspective: A guide for change agents, *Journal of Organizational Change Management*, **10** (3), pp 202–16

Stumpf, SA and Longman, RA (2000) The ultimate consultant: Building long- term, exceptional value client relationship, *Career Development International*, **5** (3), pp 124–34

Wardrop-White, D (2001) *The Crystal Bridge: A practical manual for internal consultants*, PricewaterhouseCoopers, Edinburgh

Weiss, A (2003) *Organizational consulting: How to be an effective internal change agent*, Wiley & Sons, London

Werr, A, Stjernberg, T and Docherty, P (1997) The functions of methods of change in management consulting, *Journal of Organizational Change Management*, **10** (4), pp 288–307

Diagnosing the need for change

04

KEY POINTS

- Diagnosis is a collaborative process that aims to understand an organizational issue and its root causes so that appropriate change intervention/s can be identified to address the issue.

- The diagnosis and analysis phase of the consulting for change cycle consists of a number of interrelated activities, which comprise: gathering the data; analysing and interpreting the data; selecting and prioritizing the right issues; and presenting the findings to the client.

- Clients and consultants may be tempted to skip the diagnosis phase, assuming that they already have sufficient information about an issue and its causes. This can result in assumptions being made that the issue and its causality are fully understood and can lead to actions being taken that address the symptoms and not the underlying causes of the problem.

- Diagnostic models represent simplifications of reality and focus attention on particular aspects of the organization, often to the exclusion of others, and this could result in a biased diagnosis. To avoid this, diagnostic tools must be chosen that are relevant to the context of the organization and the business issue that is being investigated.

Introduction

Business problems are, by nature, complex, messy and highly changeable. For this reason the issues that clients present to consultants in the initial contact and contracting phases usually require further clarification and exploration by both parties, so that the work that the consultant will do and the required change that needs to be implemented are clear. This is essential, especially when the client is not entirely clear what the issue is, which as Edgar Schein points out is not uncommon: 'In my experience... the person seeking help often does not know what she is looking for and indeed should not really be expected to know. All she knows is that something is not working right or some ideal is not being met, and that some kind of help is therefore needed' (Schein, 1999: 5).

The most effective way for a consultant to find out more about the client's problem is by gathering data to identify and clarify the issue and its causes. This enables the problem to be seen more clearly and, therefore, as Dale Ainsworth says, 'the crafting of solutions becomes much easier' (2010: 248). So a diagnostic process provides an organization with the systematic approach that it needs to design a set of appropriate intervention activities to improve overall organizational effectiveness (Van Tonder and Dietrichsen, 2008).

Ensuring that the right problem is identified and addressed is an essential but often fraught process (O'Mahoney and Markham, 2013). Consultants need to ensure that clients appreciate the importance of diagnosis, since clients are not always willing for time and money to be spent on data gathering and analysis. If the root causes behind any problem are not clearly understood, then there is potential for vagueness to creep into the solution. This can result in ill-defined problems ending up with ill-defined solutions. Even worse is when well-designed interventions are applied to poorly understood problems. This may explain why some consulting interventions do not accomplish their intended benefits (Cummings and Worley, 2001). So if the diagnostic phase is omitted, mistakes can occur by assuming that the issue and its causality are fully understood and this can lead to actions being taken that address the symptoms and not the causes of an issue.

The aim of this chapter is to explore how to conduct diagnosis as part of the consulting for change cycle in order to point the client and the consultant toward a set of appropriate change interventions that will improve organization effectiveness. To help achieve this the chapter discusses several key issues associated with collecting, analysing and presenting data. The chapter begins by exploring how the need for change can be identified using traditional diagnostic frameworks, such as the Seven-S (which this book extends to include a further seven elements), as well as another that is introduced here called the Eight Lenses. The advantages and disadvantages of each of these tools are critically evaluated in order to help consultants to select the most appropriate one to use in the context of their client organization. Bruce McCrea, Managing Director of Leanology, shares how he adapted a diagnostic tool to use on a consultancy assignment with a retail bank. The chapter then goes on to describe and critique the different methods of collecting qualitative and quantitative data, including methods such as surveys, interviews, observations and focus groups. The second part of the chapter discusses how to analyse the data that has been collected and then present the findings to clients and key stakeholders. Throughout the chapter the importance of joint diagnosis involving the consultant and the client is emphasized to ensure that the client owns the findings and is committed to taking appropriate action.

Learning outcomes

By the end of this chapter you will be able to:

- recognize the importance of diagnosis as part of the consulting for change cycle;
- select and apply diagnostic frameworks and techniques;
- gather, record and analyse data about specific organizational issues;
- effectively present findings on diagnosis and analysis to clients and other key stakeholders.

The importance of diagnosis

Definition of diagnosis

In the fast-pace world in which many businesses now operate, a consultant must respond more quickly than ever to the needs of clients. This may involve diagnosing 'on the run' and conducting organizational diagnosis in 'real time'. Warner Burke describes is as 'a bit like jazz music – improvising on a theme' (2010: 236). For consultants to be able to provide a diagnosis quickly they first need to understand what diagnosis is, why it is important and how to carry it out. Each of these questions will be addressed in this chapter, beginning with a definition of diagnosis.

Diagnosis is a collaborative process involving the client, key stakeholders and the consultant that enables a better understanding of an organizational issue and its causality. It involves both clients and consultants in collecting pertinent data, analysing the data, and drawing conclusions from it for potential change and improvement (Postma and van Kok, 1999). Diagnosis may be carried out at three levels – organizational, team and individual – or it may be limited to issues occurring at one particular level. Diagnosis is not only an informational activity but is also aimed at generating action (Martins and Coetzee, 2009). It provides the information needed to design appropriate change interventions intended to improve individual, team and/ or organizational performance.

The significance of diagnosis

Clients will often underestimate the importance and extent of the diagnostic phase and may propose, on the basis of their understanding of the issue, that the consultant simply fixes the problem. Consultants must avoid falling into this trap, for, just as neither a dentist nor a surgeon would begin remedial work without an X-ray, a consultant should not begin a change intervention without a diagnostic of some kind, as accurate data and careful diagnosis are an essential part of consultancy for change.

There are several reasons for gathering additional information, apart from that initially described by the client. First, the client will be looking at the issue solely from their own perspective, so gathering and analysing further data can provide more information from different perspectives and expand the knowledge of both the client and the consultant. Second, good data collection and analysis generate information about the functioning, effectiveness and health of an organization and/or team. Third, data collection and analysis can spark interest in change by bringing employees together to think about the issues affecting them and agreeing that there is a need for change. Fourth, by demonstrating empathy and capability through focusing on individuals and their perspectives, the consultant can start to build trust with key stakeholders (Nadler, 1977). Finally, it provides an opportunity to listen to the views held by individuals throughout the team/organization about opportunities for change. So gathering and analysing data from individuals are important since they provide a more holistic view of the client's issue by capturing valuable information and insights that are scattered around the organization.

The diagnostic process

The diagnosis and analysis phase involves a far more extensive assessment of the issue than occurs during the initial contact and contracting phases (see Chapter 3 for details about these phases). During diagnosis and analysis other issues that need to be addressed might be discovered, or it might lead to redefining the initial issue that the client identified. This illustrates the cyclical nature of consultancy, in that things may change as new information is gathered, and can lead to the consultant and client having to revisit the contracting phase, in order to re-contract on the objective of the consultancy. The process of diagnosis, therefore, needs to be an ongoing activity rather than a one-off event.

Diagnostic frameworks

For effective diagnosis consultants and clients need to be clear about what information needs to be collected and then select the most appropriate approach for doing so. Conceptual frameworks that people use to understand organizations are referred to as *diagnostic models*. They allow the categorization of enormous amounts of data into manageable chunks in order to understand and to change an organization. Such models can be helpful for:

- identifying what aspects of an organization are those most needing attention;
- highlighting the interconnectedness of various organizational elements, such as strategy and structure;
- providing a common language with which to discuss organizational characteristics;
- providing a guide to the sequence of actions to take as part of a change intervention (Burke, 2013).

Diagnostic models help to identify what areas to examine and what questions to ask in assessing a specific organizational issue.

Component and holistic models

There are various diagnostic models that discuss, describe and analyse how organizations function. *Holistic models* consider the organization as a whole, whereas *component models* focus on particular aspects of organizational functioning, such as motivation, decision-making, group dynamics and organizational structures. Researchers acknowledge the usefulness of component models but caution against combining them, since there are properties of the whole that cannot be understood by simply adding together the component parts (Nadler and Tushman, 1980). This can produce an incomplete or misleading view of the organization. To avoid this happening, a useful starting point is to use holistic models to provide an overall assessment before focusing attention on specific issues using a component model. Such an approach can provide a more complete view of an organizational issue.

Using the frameworks

Rather than relying on one diagnostic instrument, consultants are encouraged to 'mix and match' tools and techniques to suit the specific issue they are investigating. The following are some tried and tested frameworks to consider using.

Seven-S framework

The Seven-S is a framework that focuses on the interaction of different parts of an organization. It was initially developed by Pascale and Athos (1981) and honed by Peters and Waterman (Peters *et al*, 1982) before eventually becoming known as McKinsey's Seven-S model. The framework includes seven interconnected organizational elements: strategy, structure, systems, staff, style, shared values and skills. A brief description of each element is outlined below.

1 *Strategy.* The purpose of the business and the way the organization seeks to enhance its competitive advantage.

2 *Structure.* The division of activities, integration and coordination mechanisms and the nature of the formal and informal organization.

3 *Systems.* Formal and informal procedures and processes for aspects such as financial measurement, reward, resource allocation, health and safety, communication and resolving conflicts.

4 *Staff.* Employees' motivation, education and behaviour, as well as demographics.

5 *Style.* Typical behaviour patterns of specific groups, such as leaders, managers and frontline staff and the organization as a whole.

6 *Shared values.* Core beliefs and values, and how these influence the organization's orientation towards customers, employees, shareholders, the external community and other key stakeholders.

7 *Skills.* The core and distinct capabilities (knowledge, skills and attitudes) of employees.

The framework does, however, focus only on a limited number of internal factors and there is no focus on the external environment. In an attempt to address these limitations we suggest expanding the framework to 'Fourteen-S' by including the following elements:

8 *Stories.* These are told by employees to one another, to outsiders and to new recruits about the organization's history, events and personalities.

9 *Signals.* The rituals and routines that employees use with each another. They signal what is important and valued, such as promotion and recognition processes.

10 *Structures of power.* This is the positional and relational power held by individuals. Positional power is dependent on an individual's role or position in the organization, such as head of marketing department, whereas relational power is based on the relationships and influence of an individual.

11 *Symbols.* This includes the visual representations of an organization such as company logos, the layout and size of offices, dress codes, titles and the type of language and terminology commonly used.

12 *Stakeholder satisfaction.* The satisfaction of those people who have an interest in what the organization does, and how well it does it. It can include groups as diverse as customers, employees, shareholders, regulators and so on.

13 *Social responsibility.* The approach that the organization takes to ethical issues internally and externally, such as climate change and contributions to charity work.

14 *Situation.* The external environment in which the organization carries out its business.

To use this framework as part of the diagnostic process, questions should be devised for each of these elements in order to gather data about each one.

The additional elements provide a focus on the external as well as wider internal components of the organization. It can be used in conjunction with other tools such as PESTLE+ and SWOT (strengths, weakness, threats, and opportunities), and the Fishbone (Ishikawa) Diagram.

Fishbone (Ishikawa) Diagram

The Fishbone (Ishikawa) Diagram can be used to help understand the root causes of an issue (cause and effect). It was devised by Kaoru Ishikawa, who pioneered quality management processes in the Kawasaki shipyards in Japan. It is also known as the Fishbone Diagram because of its resemblance to the skeleton of a fish. It is applied by putting the issue (effect) being investigated at the end of the horizontal arrow (head of the fish); and the potential causes (such as systems, strategy, staff, structure (see Fourteen-S model) are then shown as labelled arrows (fish bones) entering the main arrow (spine of the fish). Each arrow may have other arrows entering it as the principal causes or factors are reduced to their sub-causes. To identify the root causes, 'Why?' (see Chapter 7 for the 'five whys' technique of questioning) or 'What else?' should be asked over and over until all possible causes are identified. For example, 'improper e-mail usage' is not a root cause, while 'failing to inform new staff of the regulations about sending personal e-mails' might be closer to a root cause. But the question can still be asked 'Why were they not informed of the regulations?' with the possible response 'There are none available.' It is a lot easier to take action against the lack of regulations than just the generic 'improper e-mail usage'. After the possible causes have been identified, gather data to confirm which causes are real or not. This provides a cause and effect analysis, which identifies the factors, or sources of variation, that lead to a specific issue/effect.

The Fishbone Diagram encourages people to think about the issues that cause the problem rather than focusing attention simply on the effects of that problem, and as such it allows people to tackle root causes rather than just the symptoms. The effectiveness of the diagram is, however, dependent on being able to accurately identify the causes of the problem, because when the causes are not properly identified this can lead to inappropriate interventions.

Eight Lenses

The *Eight Lenses* framework illustrates how the external environment affects elements in the organization. The eight areas of diagnosis (as shown in Figure 4.1) are: external environment; mission; customers; processes; management systems; organization; capabilities; and attitudes and behaviour.

Effective diagnosis must address all of these areas to establish an assessment of what needs to change. Each lens is briefly described below.

1 *External environment.* This is the external context in which the organization operates. An analysis of the external environment can be carried out using the PESTLE+ (political, economic, societal, technological, legal, environmental, and competitors and customers).

2 *Mission.* The mission of the organization is the statement of its core purpose. It is what the organization wants to accomplish. Questions can be asked in order to gather data on this such as: How clear is the mission statement of the organization to stakeholders? What are the barriers and

drivers for reinforcing a mission-orientated mindset? What are the needs of diverse stakeholders and are they being met?

3 *Customers.* This involves evaluating whether or not the organization adds value to its customers. Questions to explore customer service include: What value is added? What are the issues with customer satisfaction? How are the services/products that customers expect being delivered and communicated?

4 *Processes.* A process is a collection of related, structured activities or tasks that serve a particular goal and produce a specific service or product for a particular customer or customers. Questions to be asked in order to gather information on the processes include: How efficient and effective are the processes? Do they deliver what stakeholders want and when they want it? Where is there a need for process improvement?

5 *Management systems.* A management system is the framework of policies, processes and procedures used by an organization to ensure that it can fulfil all the tasks required to achieve its purpose and objectives. Questions should be asked to find out more about metrics, targets and performance systems. For example, what are the measures of success? How are they tracked? How transparent are they? How are issues raised and solved? How are people held accountable for measures? How does the organization respond to performance signals?

6 *Organization.* This focuses on how the organization is structured. Questions to be considered in order to gather data on this lens are: Where are the duplicate structures and how can they be eliminated? Are there any improper spans of control?

7 *Capabilities.* This includes the skills, knowledge and experience of employees. Questions to ask to find out more about capabilities include: What are the capabilities of the workforce? What are the capability gaps and how can the gaps be filled? How are capabilities built through training, coaching and problem solving?

8 *Attitudes and behaviour.* This focuses on the attitudes and behaviours of employees. Questions to consider using to explore this lens include: What are the beliefs and attitudes of frontline staff/management? What are the aspirations of individuals? What is the leadership and management style?

The relevant questions to explore the issue under investigation and also to suit the context of the organization should be identified and agreed between the consultant and client. In this way the eight lenses can be used to carry out an analysis to reveal the areas and processes where change efforts should be focused.

Figure 4.1   The Eight Lenses framework

Diagnostic models such as the Eight Lenses can be adapted to use with other tools such as SWOT, PESTLE+ and Fishbone to identify root causes and what needs to change. Different consultants will, of course, have different tools they will use depending on the organizational context. The following two case studies describe the experience of two individuals. In the first, Greg Longley, Lead Operations Manager for IRHP Redress Settlements, describes how he used the symptoms of operations diagnostic tool during his first assignment as an external consultant with Lloyds Banking Group.

CASE STUDY

Consulting at Lloyds Banking Group

My first assignment as an external consultant, after running a multi-million pound commercial operation, was with Lloyds Banking Group. The purpose was to conduct an analysis of part of the Interest Rate Hedging Products (IRHP) programme – which was set up to review mis-selling. The Financial Conduct

Authority (FCA) had instructed UK banks to carry out a review of IRHP sales and had initiated a Section 166 (Skilled Person Review). There was a huge amount of pressure on banks to quickly determine the outcomes (decisions following the review of alleged mis-selling cases) for customers, communicate those outcomes to customers, and then pay any compensation due. The aim of my consultancy assignment was to set up the redress settlements function and deliver redress to customers.

The senior manager (my client) and I agreed that there was a need to address the problem urgently given the demand internally from the board and the external pressure from the FCA. The approach we agreed was that I would carry out a number of interviews. The structure I used for the interviews was based on the *symptoms of operation* – a tool I had previously used in assessing 'business as usual' operations. The six symptoms are leadership, people, customer, culture, communication and management information. The questions I used to find out more about each symptom were:

1 Leadership

How did staff/contractors feel about leadership in their team, function and programme?

Were there clear direction and expectation setting?

How was their personal morale?

How did they assess the morale of the team, function and programme?

What did there need to be less of?

What was needed that was lacking?

What should continue?

2 People

How did staff/contractors feel about the value attached to their contribution?

How was their personal morale?

How was the morale of the team, function, programme?

What did there need to be less of?

What was needed that was lacking?

What should continue?

3 Customer

What mattered to the customer?

Did they think we were meeting customer expectations?

What kind of language did we use in talking about the customer?

What did there need to be less of?

What was needed that was lacking?

What should continue?

4 Culture

How would they define the culture of their team, function and programme?

What did there need to be less of?

What was needed that was lacking?

What should continue?

5 Communication

How effective was the communication on the programme?

Were they getting clear messages from those higher up in the programme?

Did they feel they could feed comments/opinions/improvements to those higher up in the chain?

Did they feel that they were listened to by those higher up in the programme?

What did there need to be less of?

What was needed that was lacking?

What should continue?

6 Management information (MI)

What MI did they produce?

What MI were they managed against?

How accurate was that MI?

Did they understand the MI?

Was MI used mainly to reward or reprimand?

What did there need to be less of?

What was needed that was lacking?

What should continue?

These questions proved to be valuable in getting 'under the skin' of the programme and in understanding the key issues. They helped to: identify the gaps; build relationships; understand the individual/team/programme power plays; identify key stakeholders; identify and analyse the key MI and its qualities/shortfalls; and identify some easy, quick wins that could make a positive difference.

As soon as I started, I employed a tactic of mass information gathering and stakeholder liaison, in order to build up my knowledge of the programme. I spoke to the heads of relevant departments and at least two members of each team in the programme. My approach with the interviewees was informal as opposed to a heavily scripted checklist of questions. It was, however, essential that I remained as objective as possible. It would have been of little use to me, or anyone else, if I had attempted to draft a symptom review based on my prejudice, or because I was looking for a particular outcome to be influenced as a result. Building trust was critical in engaging interviewees and to successfully gain their cooperation.

Once the analysis of the interviews was complete I reviewed the data with the senior manager. The findings identified a key gap in the compensation settlement part of the programme process that involved paying customers compensation following the communication of their case outcomes. To address this it was agreed that I would take on the task of setting up the compensation settlement function, and appointing a support team.

It also meant that I had to manage key stakeholders. This involved ensuring visibility of performance and operational transparency. Key to this was the production of regular progress reports to the board. I also implemented regular team huddles, SSC sessions (what we should stop, start, continue) and regular progress updates, including collation and publishing of customer feedback.

There was a huge amount of pressure both at and from board level to deliver a certain number of compensation payments quickly to customers whilst ensuring accuracy and good governance. The new compensation settlement function managed to increase the rate of compensation payments to customers from zero to 42 per cent above the board's target in just over a month. It also managed to achieve a 100 per cent success score in quality checks. After four months I ensured that the process was successfully transferred to a subject matter expert team.

As an external consultant it is imperative that you get up to speed very quickly in order to deliver results as soon as possible. The *symptoms of operation* enabled me to do just that and led to improvements in the overall process of fact-finding, evaluation and identification of gaps. It also enabled me to gain a holistic understanding of the context within which I was operating and the key issues the company was facing. All of this was at pace, which was essential in order to start delivering as soon as possible.

It also taught me that 'the basics' of a business as usual (BAU) operation can be applied to a programme /project, ie establishing an operating rhythm, team huddles, SSC sessions. These are some of the things that help ensure the smooth running of BAU that are often overlooked in consultancy projects.

MI, and more specifically, (and importantly!) the right MI can be a valuable weapon in proving competence and gaining trust from key stakeholders early on, if it is used correctly. I learned also that if you have reliable MI, don't wait until someone senior asks you for it. Make sure you understand it first, but then use it to demonstrate that you understand your operation and its challenges. I also learned that it is important to communicate the actions you are taking to influence performance and implement the change.

All in all, the overarching lesson is to not wait for information to come to you, but proactively seek to build your own picture of the environment you are in. I have used the *symptoms of operation* approach several times over now and it has proved invaluable every time.

In the next case study Bruce McCrea, Managing Director of Leanology, describes his personal experience of how he adapted a framework to use with a retail bank.

CASE STUDY

Operational diagnostic within the role of a consultant

In my most recent experience, acting as an internal consultant within a retail bank on a project designed to identify ways to improve operational excellence, I developed a diagnostic tool to meet the needs of the business and the project. This model is illustrated in Figure 4.2 and has four areas: contribution; colleagues; customers; and core processes.

Within each of the four areas, a number of questions were asked:

1 Contribution

Does the organization articulate its purpose clearly across the organization?

Are all colleagues clear on how they contribute to the overall purpose of the organization?

Is the organization structured in the optimal way to allow this purpose to be achieved?

Is there a level of consistency across answers given during this exercise?

Figure 4.2   Proposed areas of focus within an operational diagnostic

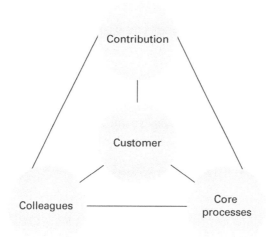

2 Colleagues

Are colleagues clear on their day-to-day roles and responsibilities?

Do colleagues have a good understanding of the work required to meet customer demand?

Are colleagues engaged and do they feel empowered to drive improvements?

Do colleagues have a good understanding of how the customers feel about the service/product?

Do colleagues communicate well with each other?

Are colleagues sufficiently skilled to be able to carry out their job and be fully utilized?

3 Customers

How do customers rate the customer journey? (Promoter of brand, easiness, satisfaction)

How do customer demands vary?

How can we delight the customer?

How can we add more value for the customer?

4 Core processes

Are processes free of rework and full of value?

Are the processes designed with the customer and colleague in mind?

Do the daily processes help colleagues contribute to the overall purpose?

Does the reward and performance system encourage colleagues in the right way?

Are processes designed to deal with the level of variation present?

When things are on track or go wrong, is it highly visible?

Within each of the four areas further probing questions and observations were used to get to the root cause of issues. For example, to consider an assessment on how clear a colleague's contribution to the organization was, these are the questions and evidence we used in the retail bank:

Tell me a bit about your objectives for this year.

What is the key objectives for the organization this year?

How do you contribute to what the organization is trying to achieve?

What is your team responsible for within the organization?

Observe whether there is team purpose or whether there are value statements, and are they visible?

Observe if all colleagues have the same understanding regarding the above.

Such questions can be ranked on a five-point Likert scale, ranging from 1 = 'no evidence at all' to 5 = 'evident in all parts of the organization'.

In summary, I found this to be an effective analytical tool to provide a picture of the current operation, and to identify the most pressing areas for improvement. Its flexible structure allows it to be customized to suit different scenarios. Although the magnitude and balance of benefits will vary by application, the main benefits of this approach include: improved employee engagement and awareness; a greater willingness from colleagues to proactively improve; and improved customer focus.

Activities

1 Consider the diagnostic tools outlined by Greg and Bruce, and identify the similarities and differences.

2 Design your own diagnostic tool using elements from both of the tools described above. Justify why you have chosen these elements. What other elements would you add to your tool?

Joint diagnosis

The success of the diagnostic phase tends to be greater when clients and consultants jointly agree upon a diagnosis strategy (Cummings and Worley, 2001). The client and any other relevant key stakeholders need to be involved in the preliminary planning of the diagnosis phase since it is vital that stakeholders are clear about the objectives of the data-gathering exercise and the level of analysis (organization, team and/or individual). Key stakeholders must, in effect, approve the proposed diagnostic approach. This is an important initial step in clients gaining ownership of the data and in ensuring that the right issues are investigated and addressed during the diagnostic phase.

The active participation of key stakeholders is necessary to ensure that once the consultant transitions out of the consultancy engagement, the change will be owned and sustained. Without the client's active participation, the results are likely to be short-lived. As Edgar Schein says, 'unless clients learn to see problems for themselves and think through their own remedies, they will be less likely to implement the solution and less likely to learn how to fix such problems should they recur' (1999: 18). The client as well as other key stakeholders, therefore, has a significant role to play in understanding and making sense of the problem.

Collecting data

Identifying the most appropriate approach to use

Data gathering involves collecting information on a specific issue. The process begins by agreeing with the client which issue needs to be investigated and then choosing the most appropriate data-collection method/s. Based on the client's description of the issue, the consultant should determine what data should be collected and why. Selecting the most appropriate method to use occurs in four stages: conceptualization; development; implementation; and analysis.

1 *Conceptualization.* The conceptualization stage involves determining: the purpose of the data to be gathered; what information is needed and why is it needed; and who can provide it. This stage also includes developing a plan for gathering the data, including a timeline as well as the estimated resources required.

2 *Development.* This stage involves developing the questions to be asked for collecting the data. Questions should be carefully planned using one

or more of the diagnostic frameworks described earlier in this chapter, and be systematically prepared and arranged in logical sequence. It is always worth piloting (testing) the questions in order to get feedback on whether or not they make sense.

3 *Implementation.* The client and other managers should explain to employees what data is being gathered, by whom, how, and for what purposes. Employees who will be involved in the data-gathering exercise should be identified, contacted, and informed of the process, timelines, and confidentiality. The data should then be collected using the appropriate methods.

4 *Analysis.* The final stage involves analysing the data using the most appropriate method and the findings should then be presented to the client and other key stakeholders.

This approach can vary depending on the data-gathering method used (as outlined in the next section) as each method will require a different length of time, number of participants and type of analysis.

Methods for collecting data

Through the use of data-collection methods the consultant can extract raw data and reduce it into meaningful information with orderly, logical facts and then present them to the client. Methods of collecting data include (but are not limited to) surveys, interviews, focus groups, observations, ethnography and secondary sources. Each of these methods is discussed next.

Surveys

One of the most efficient ways to collect data is through *surveys* or questionnaires. Surveys are quick and easy to administer, and since they typically contain fixed-response questions about various features of an organization they can also be administered to large numbers of people simultaneously (Bryman and Bell, 2015; Lewis *et al*, 2007). For example, the software company SAS has identified trust as a critical organizational attribute and regularly surveys its employees on elements of trust: communication, respect, transparency and being treated as a human being.

There are various free or inexpensive online survey tools, such as Survey Monkey or Google Forms, that make it easy to survey a large number of participants quickly.

When designing a survey it is important to begin by determining the reason for the survey and identifying who will complete it (De Vaus, 2013). The overall design should be considered in three parts: beginning, core and end.

- *Beginning.* The key features of the beginning of any survey are: the statement of the purpose of the survey; confirmation of confidentiality and anonymity; instructions for completion; advice on approximately how long it will take to complete; instructions as to what to do with the completed questionnaire; and the closing date for completion.

- *Core.* The core of the survey should have a mix of closed questions, based on a Likert type scale (Typically this comprises five options: 1 = agree strongly; 2 = agree; 3 = uncertain; 4 = disagree; 5 = disagree strongly) and open-ended questions. The latter allow participants to add any additional comments. The length of the survey is also important. If the survey is too long participants may not complete it. If it is too short, it might not provide enough information to act upon (Smith, 2003).

The most common mistakes in surveys relate to the types of questions used. To ensure that questions are appropriate Donald Anderson (2012) suggests the following:

- Avoid questions that indicate bias toward or against a particular group of people, such as race, gender, religion or any level or role of employees.

- Avoid questions that could be answered in multiple ways. For example, a question that says, 'I am satisfied with the recognition and financial reward I receive', could be answered 'strongly agree' and 'strongly disagree' if the respondent is very satisfied with the recognition they received but very dissatisfied with their financial reward.

- Keep in mind the need to translate or localize questions for respondents across global boundaries. Avoid idioms or slang that may not be applicable to employees.

- Clarify important terms. For instance, phrases such as 'senior leadership' or 'current practices' may need to be clarified.

- *End.* At the end of the survey there should be questions to obtain biographical data from the participant, such as their job title, age, gender, location, length of service and any other specifics required. There should also be a section for the participant to add any further comments that they think will be of help. Finally, the survey should end with a brief note of thanks to participants for taking the time to complete it and who to contact if they have any queries.

It is worth piloting/testing the survey with a small group of employees to determine whether or not the questions are clear and if there is any ambiguity about them.

Surveys do, however, have a number of drawbacks that need to be taken into account when deciding whether or not they are the most appropriate approach to use. For example, responses are limited to the questions asked and there is little opportunity to probe for additional data or to ask for points of clarification. A further disadvantage of surveys is that they are open to self-report biases, such as respondents' tendency to give socially desirable answers rather than honest opinions. These disadvantages need to be weighed against the advantage of being able to gather data from a large number of people relatively quickly and cost-effectively.

Interviews

Interviews are an invaluable and powerful method for gathering data (Gray, 2013). Using semi-structured probing interviews to collect data has numerous advantages. First, they allow the consultant to understand better how employees interpret a situation and the attitudes and beliefs they have about it. As Seidman says, 'at the root of in-depth interviewing is an interest in understanding the lived experience of other people and the meaning they make of that experience' (2006: 9). Second, interviews provide the researcher with the opportunity to establish relationships with the participants, in order to encourage the development of a sense of trust and cooperation that is often needed to probe sensitive areas. Third, the probing interview helps participants to interpret the questions appropriately. Fourth, the semi-structured probing interview allows flexibility in determining the wording and sequence of the questions asked, as such an interview setting allows for personal interaction and the opportunity to follow up on incomplete or vague responses (Bryman and Bell, 2015; Lewis *et al*, 2007).

Data-gathering through interviews does, however, rely heavily on the cooperation of individuals who may not be willing to open up and discuss serious issues if they do not trust the interviewer (Seidman, 2006). A significant amount of time is also required to conduct, transcribe and analyse interviews. So before starting interviews consider: What is the purpose of the interviews? Who should be interviewed? And how many interviews are enough?

Like surveys, interviews are subject to the self-report biases of respondents and, perhaps more importantly, to the biases of the interviewer. The nature of the questions and the interactions between the interviewer and the respondent may discourage or encourage certain kinds of responses. For instance, interviewees may feel defensive if they are personally involved in a problem and may therefore be motivated to stretch the truth to present themselves in a positive light (Anderson, 2012). Consultants need to ensure that they avoid biases or a wish to talk about certain facts that may not be relevant to the issue being explored. Interviewers must also be aware of their own biases, listen and establish empathy with respondents, and probe issues that are raised during the course of the interview. It therefore takes considerable skill to gather valid data through interviews. To provide some guidance, the following tips are suggested for interviewers:

- Listening actively is critical. The interviewer should listen for emotion as well as content as this can suggest areas for follow-up probing questions, such as 'You seem hesitant to talk about the performance management system. Can you say more about your thoughts on it or how you feel about it?' (Anderson, 2012), 'Tell me more about...', 'What example can you provide...?'

- Avoid agreeing or disagreeing with the interviewee, or suggesting that their response is similar to, or different from other interviewees. Seidman (2006) recommends that only rarely should the interviewer share their own experiences that are similar to an interviewee's, since this can result in the interviewer becoming the focus of the conversation and potentially alters the direction of the interview.

- Interviewers should also be comfortable with silence and not be tempted to fill the silence with more questions or their own responses.

- Interviewers should empathize rather than sympathize. This means responding with 'I understand...' or 'I appreciate...' rather than 'I completely agree that is...'.

- Interviews should be recorded if possible rather than taking notes, to ensure that nothing is missed. The taped interviews should then be transcribed as soon as possible after they have finished.

Focus groups

Focus groups are a powerful method for establishing a shared sense of an issue, as well as its impact and the solutions required (Krueger and Casey, 2014). Focus groups comprise a small number of individuals (usually 6–10) facilitated by a consultant who asks questions and then facilitates the group discussion. The main purpose of a focus group is to elicit from participants their attitudes, feelings, beliefs, experiences and reactions in a way that is not feasible using other methods, such as surveys.

Interaction is the crucial feature of focus groups as it highlights participants' views of the team/department and/or organization, the language they use about an issue and their values and beliefs about it. Interaction also enables participants to ask questions of each other, as well as to re-evaluate and reconsider their own understanding of their specific experiences of the issue that is being explored (Kitzinger, 1995).

During a focus group the role of the consultant or facilitator becomes crucial, especially in terms of providing a clear explanation of the purpose of the group, helping people feel at ease and facilitating interaction between participants. At the start of the focus group the facilitator should propose ground rules for participation, including confidentiality and anonymity, and the need for everyone to participate equally. The group may also want to agree on other ground rules.

During the focus group the facilitator will need to promote discussion by asking open questions. They may also need to challenge participants, especially to draw out different opinions and to clarify the diverse range of meanings on the issue under discussion, as well as ensuring that everyone participates and gets an opportunity to speak. They should also keep the session focused and so they may have to deliberately steer the discussion back on track, when it has drifted or stopped. At the same time, facilitators should avoid showing too much approval, so as not to favour particular participants, and should not give personal opinions, so as not to influence participants towards any particular position or opinion (Stewart and Shamdasani, 2015). The role of the facilitator is a demanding and challenging one, and facilitators will need to possess good interpersonal skills, including listening and empathy, in order to build trust with participants and increase the likelihood of open, interactive dialogue.

The degree of control and direction imposed by facilitators will depend upon the objectives of the focus group as well as on their preferred facilitative style. If two or more facilitators are involved, agreement needs to be reached as to how much input or direction each will give. There also needs to be consistency across focus groups, so careful preparation with regard to roles and responsibilities is required (Krueger and Casey, 2014). As with interviews, discussions in focus groups should, with agreement from participants, be recorded to ensure all essential points are captured and the recordings then transcribed as soon as possible after the focus group is finished.

Focus groups have a number of benefits. One major advantage is that they can elicit information in a way that allows consultants to find out why an issue is salient, as well as what is salient about it. As a result, the gap between what people say and what they do can be better understood. This also enables consultants to interact directly with participants, which provides them with opportunities for clarification, follow-up questions and/ or probing. Focus groups also provide data more quickly and at a lower cost than some other methods of data collection (Kamberelis and Dimitriadis, 2013; Krueger and Casey, 2014).

There are, however, a number of limitations to focus groups that need to be considered. First, the consultant has less control over the data produced than in either surveys or interviews. The participants have to be allowed to talk to each other, ask questions and express doubts and opinions, which can result in the consultant having very little control over the interaction other than generally keeping participants focused on the topic. The format of a focus group discussion may also discourage some people from trusting others with sensitive or personal information, since focus groups are not fully confidential or anonymous, because the material is shared with the others in the group (Acocella, 2012). To address such issues, the use of another method of data collection, such as interviews, alongside focus groups may be appropriate.

Observations

One of the more direct ways of collecting data is simply to observe individuals in their work environment. This allows the consultant to obtain first-hand information (Silverman, 2006). The process can range from complete participant observation, in which the consultant becomes a member of the team being observed, to more detached observation, in which the observer is clearly not part of the team or situation itself and may use a camera or other methods to record individual behaviours (Corbetta, 2003).

Observations have a number of advantages. A key benefit is that they are free of the biases inherent in self-report data as the consultant can observe what people actually do or say, rather than what they say they do (Marshall and Rossman, 2014). This is an important consideration since individuals are not always willing to write their true views on a survey or say what they really think during an interview or focus group. A further advantage of observations is that they are conducted in real time, allowing the consultant access to the context and meaning surrounding what people say and do. This puts the consultant directly in touch with the issue being investigated, without having to rely on others' perceptions and avoids the distortions that invariably arise when people are asked to recollect issues, events, behaviours and so on.

There are, however, a number of disadvantages with observational methods. An important one relates to the role of the observer and what effect they have on the people and situations observed. This can lead the participants to alter their behaviour in order to look good in the eyes of the observer. Observations are also susceptible to observer biases, such as the observer seeing what they want to see rather than what is really there. Another problem concerns sampling, as observers not only must decide which people to observe, they must also choose the time periods, location and events in which to make those observations. Failure to attend to these sampling issues can result in highly biased samples of observational data. Observation can be very time consuming and there is the additional limitation of being unable to take notes as an observer when immersed in a situation. Observations are also open to the ethical dilemmas inherent in observing real-life situations for data collection. It is, therefore, important to take into account such limitations when considering the use of observations.

Ethnography

Ethnography is 'a description and interpretation of the culture and social structure of a social group' (Robson, 2002: 186). It is a method that requires complete immersion in the everyday life of the people who are affected by the issue that is being explored, and involves working with these people, usually in the same role. By immersing themselves in the cultural practice of the organization, a consultant can get a deeper understanding of the values, assumptions and attitudes of employees (Silverman, 2013). Ainsworth (2010) describes this approach as 'jumping into the rabbit hole' to get first-hand experience of the environment in which individuals live and work. An important characteristic of ethnography is that it provides data that is free from imposed external constraints and ideas (Robson, 2002). This means that the consultant can produce descriptions of the work environment from an insider's view.

Ethnography is open to the same limitations as observations. In addition, there is the risk of the consultant 'going native' – that is, losing their objectivity and sympathizing with the employees they are working with. It is, however, an alternative approach to using diagnostic frameworks and can allow a consultant to live and breathe the issues faced in the organization.

Secondary sources

In contrast to the primary sources of collecting data outlined above, *secondary sources* of data do not require the consultant to intrude in the working life of employees. Secondary data is valuable and may contradict or substantiate data gathered through primary methods. For example, Starbucks analysed thousands of social media entries to gain an objective view of the company through the eyes of its employees and to take specific actions to reinforce its strengths and address weaknesses. There is a wide variety of secondary sources that can be useful to consultants, including: company records; archives; databases; management information systems; internet sites and social media. For instance, if the issue being explored is the high number of customer complaints then archival data can be used in the preliminary analysis to identify those teams with high numbers of customer complaints. Then interviews can be conducted or observations made in those teams, in order to discover the underlying causes of the problems. Conversely, secondary data can be used to cross-check data gathered by other methods. For example, if a survey reveals that employees in a department are dissatisfied with their jobs, company records might show whether that discontent is manifested in poor customer service.

There are a number of advantages and disadvantages of using secondary data. The advantages include that it is free from the personal biases of individuals. It also tends to be quantified and reported at periodic intervals, permitting statistical analysis of behaviours occurring over time. The main disadvantages are in the collection of secondary data and drawing valid conclusions from it. Collecting secondary data can be resource intensive (Saunders *et al*, 2012) and consultants need to be careful not to overgeneralize from examples that represent only one occurrence of a phenomenon. For instance, one customer complaint may not represent the view of all customers. Despite such limitations, it is beneficial to use secondary sources along with primary methods of data collection.

Selecting a method for gathering data

There are several criteria to consider when selecting the most appropriate method for collecting data, including:

- Resources required. Consideration needs to be given to the time and cost of each method. Interviews, for instance, take time to gather data, whereas surveys can produce vast amounts of data in a relatively short timescale.

- Access. Consideration needs to be given as to how practical it is to use a specific method. For instance, it may not be possible to interview every stakeholder due to shift patterns or holidays.

- Relevance to the issue. Some methods of collecting data are more relevant to particular issues; for example, secondary sources are unlikely to provide data on how an individual feels about an issue. So the method needs to be relevant to the issue being investigated.

- Accuracy. Some methods are more prone to participant and consultant bias than others. For instance, during observations a consultant's own bias may affect what they observe.

- Flexibility. Some methods allow the consultant greater flexibility in terms of being able to follow up on particular questions of interest or items that crop up during the course of data-gathering. Interviews tend to allow this flexibility since consultants can ask follow-up questions to explore an issue further. Whereas a survey, for instance, can be inflexible because once it is designed and administered it is not possible to add subsequent follow-up questions.

When selecting the most appropriate approach it is a good idea to use a mix of methods in order to obtain more in-depth and valid data. As Richard Swanson says, 'in almost all instances, using more than one data collection method is necessary to ensure valid conclusions about the trends, factors, and causes of organizational process, team, and individual performances' (2007: 122). For example, a survey could be sent out then followed up by a sample of interviews to prove further specific results from the findings of the survey. Alternatively, focus groups could be used to gather ideas about what should be included in a survey. Mixing methods can provide more valid and in-depth data. So, wherever possible, more than one method should be used to collect diagnostic data in order to ensure the validity of the findings.

Sampling

Before we discuss how to analyse data, it is worth briefly considering sampling. *Sampling* is not an issue when the consultant is able to collect interview or survey data from all members of the organization, department and/or team. If this is not possible then the sample size needs to be considered, or how many people, events or records are required to carry out the diagnosis. This question has no simple answer. The necessary sample size depends on the total numbers involved, the confidence desired in the quality of the data and the resources available for data collection (Cummings and Worley, 2001).

Purposive sampling is a non-probability sampling procedure which is based on the probability of the unknown of any particular member of the population being chosen (Struwig and Stead, 2001). Purposive sampling

occurs when participants are selected who fit the criteria of 'desirable participants' - a diverse and representative sample of employees. Alternatively a
random sample can be selected in which each member, behaviour, or record
has an equal chance of being selected (Saunders *et al*, 2012). For example, if the consultant wants to select 100 people randomly out of the 500
employees at a retail company, using a complete list of all 500 employees,
the consultant can generate a random sample, such as selecting every fifth
name (500/100=5) starting anywhere in the list.

If the population is complex, or many subgroups need to be repre-
sented in the sample, a stratified sample may be more appropriate than a
random one (Saunders *et al*, 2012). In a stratified sample, the population
of members, events, or records is segregated into a number of mutually
exclusive sub-populations and a random sample is taken from each sub-
population. For example, members of an organization might be divided into
three groups such as leaders, managers, and frontline staff and a random
sample of members, behaviours, or records can be selected from each grouping to reach diagnostic conclusions about each of the groups.

Whichever approach to sampling is chosen, consultants need to ensure
that they have an adequate sample as this is critical to gathering valid diagnostic data.

Making sense of data

Once the data has been gathered it then needs to be analysed. *Data analysis*
involves organizing and examining the data to make clear the underlying
causes of the issue and identifying what needs to change and how. The
process of data analysis must be systematic, verifiable and identified prior
to the data being gathered, such as during the contracting phase. How the
data is analysed will depend on whether it is qualitative (interviews, focus
groups, observations) or quantitative (surveys).

It is not the aim here to go into any depth about data analysis, since
there are several good resources on the subject including Bryman (2015) and
Saunders *et al* (2015), but instead to provide a brief overview.

Qualitative and quantitative data analysis

Qualitative data can be analysed using content analysis. A content analysis can reduce comments or behaviour into meaningful categories and then
into themes that effectively summarize the issues or attitudes of a group

of respondents (Bryman, 2015). For example, in answering the question 'What do you like most about your job?' different respondents might list their colleagues, their supervisors, the new database and a good computer. The first two answers concern the social aspects of work, and the second two address the resources available for doing the work. The respondents' answers to a question are then placed into one of the categories. The categories are then analysed to identify the themes that are most often mentioned. This analysis can be done manually using a highlighter pen or using a software package such as NVIVO.

Methods for analysing quantitative data range from simple descriptive statistics of cross-tabulations to more sophisticated, multivariate analysis (Saunders *et al*, 2015). The most common forms of analysis are: means, standard deviations and frequency distributions; scatter grams and correlation coefficients; and difference tests. Analysis can be produced by statistical software packages, such as EXCEL or SPSS.

Methods for analysing the data will therefore depend on the type of data collected.

Feedback of findings to clients

An important step in the diagnosis and analysis phase is discussing the findings from the data analysis with the client. Although the data may have been collected with the client's help, the consultant is likely to have analysed the data and to have responsibility for presenting the findings to the client and other key stakeholders, in a way that engages them. If the feedback engages the client then they are more likely to feel ownership of it and be energized to take action. To achieve this the data needs to be relevant, understandable, descriptive, verifiable, timely, limited, significant, comparative, and unfinalized (Golembiewski, 2000). These are explained below.

- Relevant. Clients are likely to use the findings for problem solving when they find the information meaningful. Including the client and other key stakeholders in the initial data-collection activities can increase the relevance of the data.

- Understandable. Findings must be presented to stakeholders in a form that can be readily interpreted. Statistical data, for example, can be made understandable through the use of graphs and charts.

- Descriptive. Findings need to be illustrated with examples in order to have meaning and gain the attention of clients.

- Verifiable. Findings should be valid and accurate if they are to inform interventions. The information should allow the client to verify whether the findings really describe the organization. For example, survey data might include information about the sample of respondents as well as frequency distributions for each question.

- Timely. Data should be fed back as quickly as possible after being collected and analysed. This will help ensure that the information is still valid and is linked to the client's motivations to examine it.

- Limited. The findings should be limited to what the client can realistically process at one time and not overload them with too much information.

- Significant. Findings should be limited to those problems that the client can do something about since this will help to energize them and to direct their efforts toward sustainable change.

- Comparative. If possible, data from comparative groups should be provided to give the client a benchmark as to how their organization compares to others.

- Unfinalized. Feedback is primarily a stimulus for action and thus should spur further diagnosis and analysis. Clients should be encouraged, for example, to use the data as a starting point for more in-depth discussions of the issue.

Characteristics of the feedback process

In addition to providing effective feedback data, it is also important to define the process by which findings will be fed back to participants and other employees. Feedback meetings can provide a forum for discussing the data, identifying conclusions and agreeing preliminary action plans. Some people will be energized by the findings and see them as an opportunity to identify solutions and implement changes as a result. Since the findings might include sensitive material and evaluations about employees' behaviour, other people may come to the meeting with considerable anxiety and fear about receiving the feedback. This anxiety can result in defensive behaviours and denial of the accuracy of the findings. The consultant should empathize with individuals' feelings and ask them what concerns they have about the findings. Objections to the findings and opposition to taking action is a natural reaction and will need to be acknowledged and addressed by the consultant.

Client ownership of data

The most important objective of the feedback process is to ensure that the client owns the data. Ownership is about the client being willing to take responsibility for the findings, their meaning, and the consequences of using them to devise appropriate change interventions. If the feedback session results in a rejection of the findings as invalid or useless, then the motivation to change is lost and there will be difficulty in engaging in any meaningful change. Consultants therefore need to manage the feedback process so that constructive dialogue and problem solving occur, which engage the client in owning the findings and energize them to take action.

Activity

In groups or individually, consider how you would deal with the following.

1 Your client has suggested that you spend some time talking to all staff in the organization (of which there are 20). Very early into the first of the discussions with the members of staff you sense reluctance by individuals to participate in the meeting and talk frankly. How do you proceed?

2 You are having an initial meeting with a client about some possible consulting work. The meeting has gone well and you feel you have started to build rapport with the client. But then at the end of the meeting the client says she is surprised that you had not planned a SWOT (strengths, weaknesses, opportunities, threats) analysis for the project, saying that in her experience it is the most valuable framework for pulling together information. How do you respond to this comment?

3 You have just finished your presentation to the client about the findings from the diagnosis and analysis. The client's response is, 'Well, you have not told us anything we did not already know.' What do you say or do next?

Summary

No surgeon would start operating on a patient before conducting tests and reaching a diagnosis. And when excising a tumour, they would be careful to avoid removing healthy tissue. So should it be with a change intervention. However, this step is often missed, which means that change has at best no impact and at worst undermines existing strengths. Diagnosis is an important phase of the consulting for change cycle and it should not be skipped, nor should it be a one-off activity but instead it needs to be an ongoing process of gathering and analysing data.

There is a variety of frameworks for diagnosis and the ones a consultant selects are dependent upon the issue to be explored. Consultants should, however, develop a healthy scepticism towards the usefulness of different frameworks and constantly reassess which are the most appropriate to use, since all frameworks are simplifications of the factors internal and external to an organization. The usefulness of any particular framework, in the context of consulting for change, needs to be judged in terms of whether or not it provides a helpful analytical framework for the organizational context and the issue to be investigated.

Once the data about the cause and effect of a specific problem has been collected, interpreted, discussed and evaluated then the client and consultant can begin to consider an appropriate change intervention.

Implications for consultants

There are several practical implications for practising and aspiring consultants that arise from the issues discussed in this chapter.

- *Focus on the client's issue.*
  In order to select the most relevant method for gathering data consider the client's issue, the possible reason for it and what data is needed to provide useful information on the issue and its root causes. This should all be done in consultation with the client.
- *Use a mix of empirical tools.*
  A combination of diagnostic frameworks, such as the Eight Lenses, is helpful in providing more in-depth data on a specific issue. It is also recommended to use at least two methods for gathering data, such as surveys and interviews, so that you can get some cross-validation of your results.
- *Customize tools to meet the needs of the organizational context.*
  Whichever frameworks are chosen they should be customized to meet the needs of the client and the organization.

- *Diagnosis should be a joint effort.*
  Success with the diagnosis requires the client and other key stakeholders to play a strong and highly visible role throughout the process. They need to be much more than cheerleaders; they need to be jointly involved, supporting the value of the diagnosis and analysis phase.

References

Acocella, I (2012) The focus groups in social research: Advantages and disadvantages, *Quality and Quantity*, **46** (4), pp 1125–36

Ainsworth, D (2010) Into the rabbit hole, in *Consultation for Organizational Change*, ed AF Buono and D Jamieson, pp 247–68, Information Age Publishing, Charlotte, NC

Anderson, DL (2012) *Organization Development: The process of leading organizational change*, Sage, London

Bryman, A (2015) *Social Research Methods*, 5th edn, Oxford University Press, Oxford

Bryman, A and Bell, E (2015) *Business Research Methods*, Oxford University Press, New York

Burke, WW (2010) Consulting in the fast lane, in *Consultation for Organizational Change*, ed AF Buono and D Jamieson, pp 233–46, Information Age Publishing, Charlotte, NC

Burke, WW (2013) *Organization Change: Theory and practice*, 3rd edn, Sage, Thousand Oaks, CA

Corbetta, P (2003) *Social Research: Theory, methods and techniques* Sage, Thousand Oaks, CA

Cummings, TG and Worley, CG (2001) *Essentials of Organization Development and Change*, Cengage, Mason, OH

De Vaus, D (2013) *Surveys in Social Research*, Routledge, London

Golembiewski, R (2000) Features of energizing data, in *Handbook of organizational consultation*, 2nd edn, ed R Golembiewski, pp 453–56, Dekker, New York

Gray, DE (2013) *Doing Research in the Real World*, Sage, London

Johnson, G, Scholes, K and Whittington, R (2008) *Exploring Corporate Strategy: Text and cases*, Pearson Education, London

Kamberelis, G and Dimitriadis, G (2013) *Focus Groups: From structured interviews to collective conversations*, Routledge, London

Kitzinger, J (1995) Qualitative research: Introducing focus groups. *BMJ: British Medical Journal*, **311** (7000), p 299

Krueger, RA and Casey, MA (2014) *Focus Groups: A practical guide for applied research*, Sage, London

Lewin, K (1947) Frontiers in group dynamics II: Channels of group life – social planning and action research, *Human relations*, **1** (2), pp 143–53

Lewis, P, Thornhill, A and Saunders, M (2007) *Research Methods for Business Students*, Pearson Education, London

Marshall, C and Rossman, GB (2014) *Designing Qualitative Research*, Sage, London

Martins, N and Coetzee, M (2009) Applying the Burke–Litwin model as a diagnostic framework for assessing organizational effectiveness, *SA Journal of Human Resource Management*, **7** (1), doi: 10.4102/sajhrm.v7i1.177

Nadler, DA (1977) *Feedback and Organization Development: Using data-based methods*, Addison-Wesley Longman, Boston, MA

Nadler, DA and Tushman, ML (1980) A model for diagnosing organizational behaviour, *Organization Dynamics*, **9**, pp 35–51

O'Mahoney, J and Markham, C (2013) *Management Consultancy*, Oxford University Press, Oxford

Pascale, RT and Athos, AG (1981) The art of Japanese management, *Business Horizons*, **24** (6), pp 83–85.

Peters, TJ, Waterman, RH and Jones, I (1982) *In Search of Excellence: Lessons from America's best-run companies*, Harper Row, New York

Postma, T and van Kok, R (1999) Organizational diagnosis in practice: A cross-classification analysis using the DEL-technique, *European Management Journal*, **17** (6), pp 584–97

Robson, C (2002) *Real World Research: A resource for social scientists and practitioner-researchers*, Blackwell Publishers, Hoboken, NJ

Saunders, M, Lewis, P and Lewis, P (2012) *Doing Research in Business and Management: An essential guide to planning your project*, 6th edn, Financial Times Prentice Hall, Harlow

Saunders, M, Lewis, P and Thornhill, A (2015) *Research Methods for Business Students*, 7th edn, Pearson/FT, London

Schein, E (1999) *Process Consultation Revisited: Building the helping relationship*, Addison-Wesley, Reading, MA

Seidman, I (2006) *Interviewing as Qualitative Research*, 3rd edn, Teachers College, New York

Silverman, D (2006) *Interpreting Qualitative Data: Methods for analyzing talk, text and interaction*, 2nd edn, Sage, London

Silverman, D (2013) *Doing Qualitative Research: A practical handbook*, 4th edn, Sage, London

Smith, F (2003). *Organizational Surveys: The diagnosis and betterment of organizations through their members*, Laurence Erlbaum, Mahwah, NJ

Stewart, DW and Shamdasani, PN (2015) *Focus Groups: Theory and practice*, 3rd edn, Sage, London

Struwig, FW and Stead, GB (2001) *The Psychology and Management of Workplace Diversity*, Blackwell, Malden

Swanson, R (2007) *Analysis for Improving Performance: Tools for diagnosing organizations and documenting workplace expertise*, Berrett-Koehler Publishers, San Francisco

Van Tonder, C and Dietrichsen, P (2008) The art of diagnosis, in *Organization Development: Theory and practice*, ed CL van Tonder and G Roodt, pp 133–66, Van Schaik, Pretoria

Designing and delivering interventions

05

KEY POINTS

- An intervention is a sequence of activities, actions, and events intended to help an organization improve its performance and effectiveness.

- The selection and design of appropriate interventions derive from careful diagnosis and aim to resolve specific issues and to improve particular areas of organizational performance.

- Since interventions may function differently in different organizations, so flexibility in the application of any intervention is necessary.

- Understanding readiness to change is an important part of planning and implementing an intervention.

- The consultant and the client need to agree their ownership of the intervention, so that both are clear about how the consultant will help the client achieve the objectives of the intervention.

- An intervention should be structured as an opportunity for learning, giving clients and consultants the chance to reflect on their learning and apply lessons learned to future changes.

Introduction

The intervention phase of the consulting for change cycle is solution and action orientated. Intervention is the point at which change becomes the overt objective. First, it involves identifying and developing a solution based on sound data and careful analysis (Mabey, 2008), drawing on business necessity and logical arguments (Kerber and Buono, 2005). Second, it is about how to make the change happen. This means understanding the approach to how the intervention will be managed, appreciating if the organization is ready for change and engaging people to be committed and involved in the transformation process at an individual and an emotional level (Hodges, 2016).

This chapter explores how to identify and design appropriate change interventions based on evidence from the diagnosis (as outlined in Chapter 4). In particular it focuses on organizational development (OD) interventions that are aimed at individuals, teams and/or the whole organization. Such interventions include a wide variety of activities that range from organization design to team building, to mentoring and coaching. The chapter begins by considering ways to identify relevant interventions, such as using appreciative inquiry or scenario planning. Dr Simon Haslam shares how he engaged a group of people in exploring scenarios and making recommendations for the strategy of a major financial services firm. The chapter then considers the challenges of designing and delivering OD interventions. Attention is paid to the factors that consultants need to consider as they select an intervention strategy, matched to the data from the diagnosis, and how they can structure the intervention to maximize the likelihood that it will be successful and sustainable. Lindsey Agness, Founder and Managing Director of The Change Corporation, shares her experience of designing and implementing development interventions. And Fiona Sweeney, a people and organizational Change Consultant, describes how she implemented an OD approach in a consultancy assignment for a health and fitness club chain in South Africa.

The emphasis in this chapter is not so much on a theoretical perspective but on the practical side through the inclusion of tools and techniques.

Learning outcomes

By the end of this chapter you will be able to:

- define OD in the context of the consultancy for change cycle;
- identify appropriate OD interventions and their strengths and limitations;
- select, implement and review OD interventions to help facilitate sustainable change.

Interventions

What is an OD intervention?

The term intervention refers to a set of sequenced planned actions or events intended to help an organization increase its performance and productivity (Argyris, 1970). Donald Anderson (2012) says that there are three points to stress about interventions. First, an intervention enters into the ordinary and continuous stream of organizational life and, as such, it is influenced by all of the complexities inherent in organizations, such as politics, power, goals, workload, the physical environment and interpersonal relationships. Second, interventions come between or deliberately interrupt existing processes, thinking, people, teams and relationships. They often try to unsettle current practices and may be uncomfortable for people who are not ready to change. Third, the purpose of interventions is to help or improve the effectiveness of organizations, groups, teams and individuals. Interventions therefore purposely disrupt the status quo; they are deliberate attempts to implement change.

There are a number of criteria that define an effective intervention. The first criterion concerns the extent to which the intervention is relevant to the organization and its members. Appropriate interventions are based on valid information about how the organization functions. They provide employees with opportunities to make free and informed choices and they gain individuals' commitment to those choices. The second criterion of an effective intervention involves knowledge of outcomes. Since interventions are intended to produce specific results, they must be based on valid knowledge that those outcomes actually can be produced, otherwise there is no factual basis for designing an effective intervention. The third criterion of an effective intervention involves the extent to which it enhances the organization's capacity to manage change. From active participation in designing and implementing an intervention, organizational members gain knowledge and skills to be able to carry out planned change activities on their own (Cummings and Worley, 2009). Such criteria therefore need to be considered when selecting change interventions.

Intervention strategy and activities

Interventions consist of two interrelated activities: (i) identifying and designing an appropriate intervention to address the client's issue; and (ii) implementing the chosen intervention(s) by structuring it to be the most appropriate for the individual, team or organization. An intervention can be as small as a single meeting, event or workshop, or it can be a series of events that progressively help to transform individuals, teams or organizations. The latter is an intervention strategy and the former are intervention activities or events. An intervention strategy may consist of a number of different intervention events, such as a strategic planning workshop, an executive team building event and one-to-one coaching, or process mapping and quality improvement workshops. While there are some standard approaches and ways of conducting interventions, no two applications of an intervention are the same. Depending on the organizational culture, structure, processes, systems, history, technology, readiness for change and ability to adapt, what has worked for one organization or team may not work for another.

OD interventions can occur at three levels: individual, team and/or the whole organization. Interventions at each of these levels include a wide variety of activities that range from the redesign of an organization's structure to team building activities to individual mentoring and coaching. OD interventions, therefore, integrate a collection of planned change interventions, aimed at improving organizational effectiveness and employees' well-being (Robbins, 2005).

The failure of interventions

It has been estimated, but without any valid empirical evidence to back it up, that up to 70 per cent of change interventions fail (Burnes and Jackson, 2011). The wide circulation of such statistics has created a view that organizational change has an undeniable tendency to fail based on the notion that for every successful corporate transformation, there is at least one equally prominent failure (Sorge and Van Witteloostuijn, 2004).

The apparent high level of failure has been described as 'carnage with wasted resources and burned-out, scared, or frustrated employees' (Kotter, 1995: 4). Talking and writing about why change fails have been described as an organizational taboo (Carnall, 2007). This seems rather short-sighted since learning from the success and failure of change is vital in order to ensure future improvements. There is a need to understand and appreciate the factors that can affect the failure, as well as the success of change interventions.

Factors that can affect intervention success

There are several factors that can affect the success of an intervention including: matching the intervention to evidence-based data and diagnosis;

the readiness for change; and the cultural context. Such factors need to be taken into account when designing an intervention.

Matching the intervention to evidence-based data and diagnosis

The importance of selecting the right intervention and managing it effectively cannot be overestimated. One of the most important criteria for selecting an intervention is what Bowers and colleagues call the 'principle of congruence', that is where 'change activities must be matched appropriately with the nature of the problem and their cases and with the nature of the organizational units under consideration' (1975: 406). An intervention needs to be matched to the diagnosis and designed to address the need for change.

Clients and consultants need to consider what type of method is suited to the particular issue. A common challenge is that the consultant and client together may generate too many options and may be uncertain which one/s to select. To address this they must always ask themselves 'Is this intervention appropriate or relevant to the issue being addressed, or is it just one of my favourite interventions?' An intervention is likely to be well matched to the diagnosis if it results in a high probability that the issue will be solved with the least probable recurrence (Argyris, 1970). In other words, the intervention should solve the business issue.

Readiness for change

Intervention success depends heavily on the organization and the individuals within it being ready for change. Readiness for change is the beliefs, attitudes and intentions of employees regarding the extent to which changes are needed, their capacity to undertake change successfully and that change will have positive outcomes for the job they do and their working environment (Stevens, 2013; Rafferty et al, 2013). Readiness encompasses the extent to which employees have positive views about the need for change and believe that these changes have positive implications for themselves and the wider organization (Goh et al, 2006). In other words, readiness denotes employees' belief that the organization can initiate a change and also engage in practices that lead to it being successfully implemented. If an individual, team or organization is not ready or willing to change, then any intervention is less likely to be successful.

The psychological bonding between an employee and his or her organization – their identification with the organization – has a significant positive effect on readiness for organizational change (Hameed et al, 2013). To facilitate effective change consultants need to focus on ensuring that there is a strong attachment between employees and the organization (Cherim, 2002). This includes communicating effectively, dealing with uncertainty, involving employees in decision-making and reassuring employees of their value to the organization. This can lead to an increase in organizational identification and, in turn, to an increase in individuals' readiness for change (Madsen *et al*, 2005). Consequently, this may result in employees supporting rather than opposing the change. Change readiness is, therefore, a function of the psychological bonding, shared beliefs and emotional responses of individuals. It is created through a culture of openness, trust and flexibility that influence the degree to which employees are adaptable and open to change.

Identifying the level of employees' readiness for change allows a consultant to tailor intervention efforts to make success more likely. The indicators of an individual's readiness for change comprise: people understanding the need for change; believing that the proposed change is the right change to make; believing that they can accomplish the change; and having an answer for the 'What's in it for me?' question (Armenakis *et al*, 1993). At an organizational level Judge and Douglas (2009) propose the following eight dimensions as measures for assessing the readiness for change:

1 Trustworthy leadership – the ability of senior executives to earn the trust and credibility of others.

2 Trusting followers – the ability of stakeholders to willingly support the change.

3 Capable champions – the ability of the organization to attract and retain capable champions for change.

4 Involved middle managers – the ability of middle managers to effectively link the change proposed by leaders to the rest of the organization and communicate it to employees.

5 Innovative culture – the ability of the organization to establish norms of innovation and encourage innovative interventions.

6 Accountable culture – the ability of the organization to carefully steward resources and successfully meet deadlines.

7 Effective communication – the ability of the organization to effectively communicate with stakeholders.

8 Systems thinking – the ability of the organization to focus on root causes and recognize interdependencies inside and outside the organization's structural boundaries.

Along with such lists there are a number of generic approaches to readiness assessment that organizations can use singly, in concert or in multiple combinations. Such approaches, which help gauge the readiness for change, are:

- Being aware of employees' behaviour that will reveal their reactions to proposed change, including any unusual behaviour associated with denial or opposition to change, as well as being attentive to rumours and increases in absenteeism and turnover.
- Discussing with employees how they feel about the change, either one-to-one or in teams/groups.
- Conducting a survey consisting of responses to Likert-style items and open questions (such as 'what…?', 'why…?' or 'how…?') about what people think and feel about the change.

When selecting interventions it is therefore important to assess the readiness for change.

Cultural context

The culture within which an organization is embedded can exert a powerful influence on members' reactions to change, so the design of interventions must take into account the values, assumptions, manifestations and artefacts that make up the organization's culture (Schein, 1997). Interventions need to be modified to fit the culture, particularly when they have been developed for one organization and are applied to another organization or another part of an organization. For example, a team building intervention designed for senior executives at the American subsidiary of a global pharmaceutical company may need to be modified when applied to the company's European subsidiaries. As interventions may function differently in different cultures, so adapting any intervention to the cultural context in which it will be applied is vital.

Identifying interventions

Identifying the types of interventions required can effectively be conducted through engaging organizational members in generating their own ideas. One way of doing this is through the use of Appreciative Inquiry.

Appreciative Inquiry

The essence of Appreciative Inquiry (AI) is the generation of a potential intervention through a collective process of inquiry into the best of 'what is' and what the future would be like if the best of 'what is' becomes the norm. (Cooperrider *et al*, 2008). By understanding what has worked in the past, an organization can choose to focus on these positive elements and build on the strengths of their past successes to identify interventions. To do this, AI uses a 'Four-D' model that comprises: discovery; dream; design; and destiny.

1 Discovery. During this initial stage participants reflect on and discuss the best of 'what is' concerning the subject of inquiry. Participants are interviewed by other participants about their own 'best of' stories, and asked questions, such as 'Tell me about the time the company most inspired loyalty in you.' The issue to be addressed needs to be defined in a way that focuses attention on the positive rather than the negative aspects of people's experience. For example, if the issue is a high turnover of staff, rather than focusing on why people leave the organization the inquiry should focus on why people choose to stay.

2 Dream. This involves drawing on the themes identified in discovery and envisioning what the future would look like if the best of 'what is' becomes the norm. Participants are asked to imagine their team and/or organization at its best in relation to the issue being discussed. An attempt is made to identify the common aspirations and to symbolize this in some way. One method of achieving this is by having employees draw pictures of what they feel about the situation and then having them explain their drawings to one another, as this allows employees to express emotions they may not be able to put into words (de Klerk, 2007).

3 Design. The dream (vision) is then translated into 'provocative propositions'. These are statements of intent – what might be – which challenge the status quo and current assumptions and create design principles to be used to identify what needs to change to deliver the dream. The output is that participants develop proposals for interventions.

4 Destiny. Destiny is about identifying how the organization moves towards the desired future state (the design). Widespread agreement for the proposed interventions is sought during this stage. This is often by participants committing to take action that will help bring the design to fruition.

AI can be used in a wide range of different situations. John Hayes (2014) describes how AI was used by Médecins Sans Frontières (MSF) where eight working groups were set up to look at how the organization functioned and identify what MSF was best at doing in order to consolidate successes as a basis for leveraging further development. The working groups collected information through interviews and surveys throughout the organization in order to ensure that everybody had the chance to contribute to defining best practice (discovery), defining what the future organization should look like and developing ideas (dream) about how to evolve new practices and procedures that would enable MSF to respond to new challenges (design). Finally, it was agreed what would be changed and who would be involved in the implementation (destiny). AI enables a wide number of organizational members to be involved in defining interventions. It does, however, have some limitations.

The main concern that tends to be voiced about AI is whether or not it really is any different from other change techniques and whether, if it does not focus on problems, this means that they do not exist. Despite such criticisms AI is appealing because it provides a proactive and optimistic approach to change by accentuating the positive and thereby what the organization is good at and can build upon. It can also create energy that is positive and synergistic, since it enables participants to develop a sense of commitment, confidence and affirmation that they can be successful.

A less structured approach than AI is Free-Space Thinking.

Free-Space Thinking

Free-Space Thinking (FST) involves a broad cross-section of stakeholders meeting over a short period of time to develop agreements and action plans to address specific issues. These techniques were pioneered by Emery and Purser (1996), with others proposing additional variations on, or applications of, the same concept (Weisbord and Janoff, 2010).

FST is most distinctive for its initial lack of an agenda. In different ways and to varying degrees, consultants convening free-space meetings acknowledge that they personally do not have the answer to whatever complex, urgent and important issue(s) must be addressed, and they put out a call – an invitation – to anyone in the organization who cares enough to attend a meeting and try to create a solution. In this way an FST meeting will attract those who are most concerned about the issue and who are also willing to participate in contributing to and identifying potential solutions.

Involving multiple stakeholder groups is an important feature of FST, for two reasons. First, involvement leads to better input and better decisions. When participants share what they know, every participant learns something about another stakeholder group (their opinions, goals and problems) that they may not have realized if they had just examined the issue from their perspective. This helps to build new relationships. Second, involvement means that implementation is more likely because solutions already have built-in commitment from the people who developed them.

Typically, an FST meeting will begin with short introductions by the consultant or facilitator that clarify the purpose, and explain the 'self-organizing' process. Throughout the meeting, the facilitator allows the participants to self-organize rather than managing or directing discussions. Instead of the facilitator leading the data gathering and interpretation process, people interact, collect and interpret their own data.

An FST involves few or no presentations, training or speeches by senior management or others. By self-organizing, participants take responsibility for managing their own content and group process. This may be done, for example, by individuals posting their issues in bulletin-board style (using Post-it notes on a flipchart or wall).

If at any time during the meeting participants find themselves in a situation where they are not able contribute, they are free to leave. In this way, all participants are given both the right and the responsibility to maximize their own contribution, which only they can ultimately judge and control. An FST does not work well when sceptical participants are coerced to participate, when there are significant differences in underlying values or when mixed stakeholder groups are intentionally not included because they are distrusted.

An FST is designed for participants to hold a broad dialogue about an issue and identify how to address it. In a relatively short time, it can be an excellent way to encourage individuals from different perspectives to engage with identifying and developing interventions.

Scenario planning

In more structured settings a tool that can help identify interventions and inform decision-making is scenario planning. Scenario planning starts by painting a picture of the future and works backwards, asking what would have to happen to make this future scenario a reality and what could be done (Schwartz, 1996). Scenario planning thus encourages the consideration of several likely possible future states, to consider which of those is most likely, and then to develop interventions that could account for a number of possible future situations. In this way scenario planning 'embraces uncertainty by identifying those unknowns that matter most in shaping the future of a focal issue' (Steil and Gibbons-Carr, 2005: 17). It works best when there are a number of possible options and there is a high level of uncertainty about which options are likely to pan out.

Similar to other methods of forecasting, scenario planning involves gathering data to forecast possible future conditions. However, 'scenario planning simplifies the avalanche of data into a limited number of possible states' (Schoemaker, 1995: 26) that allow organizational members to consider and to address. Thus, it is in contrast with strategic planning, in which an organization develops its own plans for its future, and also with risk mitigation or contingency planning, in which an organization plans for a single future event that may or may not happen (for example, the computer backup system may crash).

While there are many variations of scenario planning, one recommended approach by Ralston and Wilson (2006) consists broadly of four major activities:

1 Getting started. The group should agree on the process and outcomes of the effort.

2 Laying the foundation. Group members gather data about facts and trends and views of the future from organizational members.

3 Creating the scenarios. The data is analysed and compared for its predictability and influence on the organization. Three to five storylines or scenarios are written that capture the majority of the extreme future alternatives.

4 Moving from scenarios to a decision. The group makes decisions about what actions to take and agrees on metrics and processes for communicating and monitoring the actions.

Good scenarios, according to Lindgren and Bandhold (2003), have the following characteristics:

- Decision-making power. The scenario provides enough detail so that decisions can be made based on the scenario coming true.

- Plausibility. The scenario must be realistic and believable.

- Alternatives. Scenarios should include options and choices, each of which could be a likely future state.

- Consistency. A scenario should be consistent in its own story.

- Differentiation. Scenarios must be sufficiently different from one another so that they describe genuinely alternative situations.

- Memorability. Scenarios should be limited in number, and each should provide dramatic narrative for ease of recall.

- Challenge. The scenarios should confront what the organization currently believes about future events.

An advantage of scenario planning is it is a simple model to explain and enables individuals to raise and test various 'what-if' scenarios, in a non-threatening, hypothetical environment before they decide on a certain course of action. However, although it is simple to explain in concept, scenario planning can be difficult to facilitate. Facilitating a group through a scenario planning exercise requires members to have 'patience, respect for others, a sense of humour, a reservoir of knowledge and experience, [and] the ability to listen closely to what others have to say' (Ogilvy, 2002: 180). It can involve not only creative thinking about uncertain and unknown events but also can require the ability to thoughtfully consider ideas and future events that are opposed to one another and, therefore, be of benefit in identifying suitable solutions for different scenarios.

In the following case study Dr Simon Haslam, a strategy consultant, academic Fellow of the International Council of Management Consultancy Institutes and Strategy Programme Lead for the Institute of Directors, describes how he engaged a group of people in exploring scenarios and making recommendations for the strategy of a major financial services firm.

CASE STUDY

Consulting and strategic change

'We could probably sort out the strategy between the two of us, if we shut ourselves in the office for an afternoon.' The voice was that of my client at our very first meeting.

As a strategy consultant I had just been engaged by a major financial services firm to support their strategy process. My primary client, who was a national CEO, one tier below board level, had been tasked with the new global strategy for the organization's second biggest product line. His line manager was the group CEO.

My first meeting with the client was at the start of the journey during which a new strategy was to be crafted. The process was not to be a brief, intense dialogue between my client and his immediate superior, but a more fulsome approach involving a core group of 40 people and a duration of half a year, branded as '2020 Foresight'. The people were chosen from around the organization on the basis of diversity of nationality, demography, function and perspective. This group was brought together over six months on three separate occasions for two-day workshops. The aim of these workshops was to explore aspects of change in the world and play through the possible implications for the firm's strategy. Between these workshops group members took themes of interest back into the organization for additional research. These themes included: the impact of technology; millennials; age and life expectancy; the benefits gap; and middle classes in developing nations. The purpose of this was to immerse the organization more thoroughly into the flows of its markets, with the aim of enriching the ideas and possibilities that might form part of the eventual strategy.

Three different cities (London, New York and Lisbon) were chosen as the venues for the workshops, enabling the participants to feel the distinctions between some of the geographies first hand. The evenings between each of the two workshop days were devoted to social activities for the group – including a karaoke session when the group came together at the initial workshop. The national CEO sang first, and by the end of the evening everyone had taken part (I was commended for effort, having bludgeoned my way through songs from Spandau Ballet and The Who).

Overall, the strategy process had a rhythm to it akin to breathing. It shifted from concentrated discussions in the three workshops to interactions with wider stakeholder groups between the workshops. My consulting input was focused on three areas – process design, the facilitation of the workshops and contributing to the analysis and creation of the slide deck with the recommendations to the firm's board. Within the workshops themselves, my facilitation role was as a guide and strategy specialist helping stimulate discussion in potentially productive places.

The group of 40 people working on this project was clearly too large to be an effective decision-making unit and the group members also lacked the organizational seniority to make the necessary calls on resources and priorities. The group's remit was to explore scenarios and make recommendations for the organization's board. The outputs from the strategy project formed a presentation to the board, with the purpose of getting the strategy accepted and the resources necessary for its implementation identified. The culture of this client organization favours visual presentation, while written reports are very much a support act.

The links between the strategy project and the board helped both the representation of the strategy to the board and also the rolling out of the strategy to the wider organization after decisions were made. The board project sponsor engaged with the group at each of the three workshops via a sixty-minute Webex slot. The data generation process involved some members of the group interviewing main board directors and the national CEO leading the project made pre-presentations on the proposed strategy and recommendations to the group CEO ahead of the main presentation. The socializing of the ideas in advance of the board decision was mirrored by the communication channels provided by the project group members in supporting the strategy at roll-out stage.

The organization has in place formal information dissemination processes, using a cascade model. The conduits that each of the group members provided into their respective functions and geographies also helped provide informal support. The implementation of the strategic recommendations was further bolstered by some of the initiatives being headed by people from the strategy project, thus linking the evolution of the ideas with their translation into action.

In the context of change, it could be easy to see this project as an incremental endeavour. The client organization was punching at its weight in the sector and its current strategy was widely viewed as effective. But there are three factors that need to be considered (they apply to this organization, but also to many others). First, the organization is massive and the coordination of any change across continents and large teams of people is not a trivial task. Second, its previous strategy was launched five years ago and lacked current ownership as its architects were now either in different positions in the organization, or had left it. Third was the threat of the 'Uber' moment – it would be complacent to believe that the success of any business model would be immune from attack, especially in this era of market disruption.

This strategy project was supported by a substantial five-figure budget, around 15 per cent of which was allocated to consulting support. The return on investment appeared straightforward for an enterprise of this scale. You do not need to move the needle much to generate payback. My role fitted into the formal project management system applied by the organization on this and all its change initiatives. The project had a board sponsor and a project secretariat with responsibility for the Gantt charts and budgets (the bulk of which was devoted to workshop staging costs and the travel/accommodation costs for workshop participants).

Whilst the process could not be considered perfect, it incorporated ingredients of effective change management and the use of consultants, that are worthy of reflection. The change programme was planned, with a clear deliverable in mind. It was resourced and managed in a way that encouraged creativity and the socialization of ideas within the organization. The investment in the cohesion of the team members on the project was particularly noteworthy. As an external consultant, I knew the terms of reference for my contribution and was able to focus my input accordingly (as process guide rather than domain expert). The project management used by the client, with its devoted secretariat, provided strong communication with all significant stakeholders throughout the project, which helped maintain the project's alignment with the main organization changes and evolution over the half year.

Design of interventions

Designing OD interventions requires the identification of the cause and effect of a specific issue through diagnosis and the crafting of a change solution that will both address the problem and also be applicable to the context of the organization and the expected benefits. Interventions must be designed to apply to specific organizational levels, address the possibility of cross-level effects and integrate interventions affecting different levels to achieve overall success. For example, an intervention to create self-managed work teams may need to be linked to organization-level changes in measurement and reward systems to promote team-based work.

Many interventions have a secondary impact since interventions aimed at one kind of organizational issue will invariably cause repercussions on other kinds of issues. For example, a restructure at the organization level will have an impact at team and individual levels because it will set the broad parameters for the design of team and individual jobs. Careful systemic thinking about how interventions affect the different kinds of issues and how they might be integrated to bring about a broader and more coherent impact on organizational functioning is, therefore, critical to the effective design of interventions.

Input to impact

At the start of designing an intervention it is important to identify the desired impact. This can be done by linking the input – 'What is done' – to the impact – 'What is different' – of the intervention (as illustrated in Figure 5.1).

- Input – what is done. This is the action surrounding an intervention. It includes the method and tools used, such as workshops.

- Output – what is produced. These are the deliverables from an intervention.

- Outcome – what happened. This is the effect or consequence of the intervention, such as a new system being operational.

- Impact – what is now different. This is the visible, defined and sustainable change that occurs as result of an intervention.

The sequence of events

An intervention strategy consists of a number of separate events or activities, which need to be sequenced in order to realize benefits. The following

Figure 5.1   Input impact model

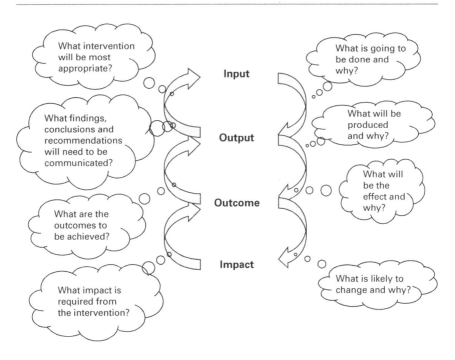

are considerations for how interventions should be sequenced as part of an intervention strategy (Beer, 1980):

- Maximize diagnostic data. Interventions that provide data about the organization should be conducted first to allow better customization for those that follow.

- Maximize effectiveness. Initial interventions should build enthusiasm for change and confidence in success so that later interventions can be more effective.

- Maximize efficiency. Interventions should conserve time, energy and money as much as possible.

- Maximize speed. Interventions should be constructed so that they do not interrupt the desire for the pace of change in the organization.

- Maximize relevance. Choose interventions so that the primary problem is addressed first.

- Minimize psychological and organizational strain. Early interventions should be safer and produce minimal anxiety.

Identifying the possible interventions and analysing them against such considerations will help identify which interventions are the most appropriate. Regardless of which intervention is selected, it is important to be conscious of the sequence of events that form the intervention strategy.

Types of OD interventions

Interventions can be designed and implemented at an individual, team or organizational level. Some of the different types of interventions at each of these levels are discussed briefly below.

Individual interventions

Individual interventions are focused on one individual at a time and can be influential in changing the behaviour and attitudes of people. Such interventions include (but are not limited to) coaching, mentoring and career development.

Coaching and mentoring

Coaching is a one-to-one intervention in which an individual works with a coach to improve a specific behaviour or skill and to take action to reach a desired goal. Coaching is a highly interpersonal activity. The role of the coach is to use questioning to enable an individual (coachee) to identify for themselves what they need to do differently, rather than merely telling them. A helpful framework to use in a coaching situation is the GROW (goals, reality, options, will) model (Landsberg, 1996). This involves using a series of questions to address each of the GROW areas, for example:

- Goal – what do you want to do differently?
- Reality – what is happening now?
- Options – what options do you have?
- Will – what options will you choose?

Along with this model, multi-rater feedback (often known as 360 degree feedback) can be used to provide individuals with feedback from a wide range of people including their manager, peers, subordinates and customers/clients, as well as self-appraisal from the individual themselves. Anonymous feedback for this purpose is usually gathered by questionnaires. The data is then analysed and fed back to an individual. Such feedback can be a powerful source for reflection and for identifying areas for personal change. It can be followed up with coaching, to address individual development needs.

Coaching involves letting the coachee figure things out for themselves (Thorne, 2004) and in this way they are more likely to be committed to making changes to their behaviours. In contrast, mentoring involves a relationship between a protégé (mentee) and a skilled and knowledgeable expert (mentor) who can provide guidance. Mentoring differs from coaching in that, unlike a coach, mentors may provide explicit advice or direction rather than wait for a mentee to find the answer themselves through self-discovery (Stone, 2004). For example, for the Master of Business Administration (MBA) students at Durham University Business School there is a mentoring scheme that matches students to mentors who can help them with expanding their network and identifying potential career opportunities.

Career development

Career development programmes aim to motivate, develop, promote and retain individuals. Such programmes are a balance between what employees want for their own career and personal development, and what organizations need from individuals to achieve organizational performance and productivity. Although the primary responsibility for career growth and development rests with the individual, it makes sense for organizations to provide career planning and development support for their employees, since this can help in developing organizational capabilities, retaining talent and increasing organizational commitment, especially during organizational change (Anderson, 2012).

Individual interventions are not, however, on their own sufficient to achieve change because organizations comprise many processes and systems, as well as teams with strong values and beliefs. So individual interventions need to be supported with team-based and/or organization-level interventions.

Team interventions

The effective functioning of teams is central to the performance of organizations. Very few organizations or consulting situations involve only people working on their own or with one other person. The great majority of organizational life consists of people working in teams. Team interventions aim to improve different aspects of a team's performance, such as how individuals in the team work together and how they make decisions and solve problems. Any team intervention needs to be aware of the life cycle of the team, which traditionally comprises five stages: forming (when the team gets together and members are polite to each other); storming (members begin to challenge each other); norming (members' commitment and involvement to the team and to each other have developed); performing (members work together as a team); and adjourning (the team breaks up) (Tuckman, 1964). To these five stages can be a sixth stage – dorming or coasting (the team is easily delivering what the organization needs and no longer being stretched in what they are doing). Any change of membership or leadership in a team can result in it going back to 'forming' and recreating the team with new norms built on fresh storms to reflect the different dynamics that the change in membership has created. Team interventions should, therefore, take into account where a team is in its evolution.

Team development

Interventions to enhance team effectiveness proactively encourage teams to develop and perform in a positive manner. They are opportunities to allow teams to identify more effective ways of working. Team interventions often employ an approach that helps to clarify the role and identity of the teams and the individuals within it and address obstacles and constraints to performance. This usually involves activities where members of the team have to work together to solve a specific issue. Many of these interventions are known generally as 'team building' and aim to improve a team's effectiveness, relationships among its members and the team's contribution to the performance of the wider organization.

There does need to be a word of caution about 'team building' events, since it is possible for considerable energy, emotion, time and money to be spent on trying to build a team with a collection of people who neither need, nor want, to be a 'team'. Teams that recognize that they have a need to improve their performance will respond better to team building activities than teams that feel that they are forced to do such activities. Before embarking on team building, consultants should therefore ask 'Why does this group of people need to be a team?' What is the thing that they can only do, or make, by working interdependently and with synergy? If the consultant and client cannot answer these questions then they may be trying to turn a tortoise into a hare, instead of a very fast tortoise.

Team psychometrics

As part of team interventions psychometrics can be used to create a better understanding of team members. In simple terms a psychometric test is a standardized activity or questionnaire that helps individuals to understand themselves and others better. For instance, feedback from a psychometric questionnaire might say that Peter is creative and sociable and works best when working with others while Tanya is disciplined and analytical, preferring to be set a task and left alone to get on with it until she has completed the work.

There is a multitude of psychometric tests that measure a variety of characteristics, many of which are underpinned by established theories of the characteristics they purport to measure (such as MBTI). Many are stand-alone tests or based on wider theories that seek to explain personality, attitudes, motivation, behaviour, learning styles (such as Kolb's learning styles model), preferred ways of working (such as Insights or TMS) and social interaction styles (such as transactional analysis) as well as cognitive and practical skills and abilities, such as verbal reasoning, creative thinking and critical thinking. Understanding individual work preferences is a critical component in developing individual and team performance and can be used as part of a team intervention.

Some people are understandably hesitant about psychometric tools. It is therefore recommended that only accredited experts facilitate such tools and use them alongside other intervention activities.

Inter-team interventions

Teams tend not to operate in isolation. Usually they interact with other teams inside and outside the organization. At such times, dysfunctional conflict may exist between teams. One OD method for addressing inter-team conflict is a technique that enables two teams to confront issues that they are facing and seeks to change the attitudes, stereotypes and perceptions that teams have of each other (Blake *et al*, 1965). It involves each team meeting independently, developing lists of the perceptions it has of itself and the other team and how it believes the other team perceives it. Lists might include, for example, the complaints 'we' have against 'them' and the complaints 'we' think 'they' would have about 'us'. Two characteristics often emerge from such lists. First, some of the complaints can be addressed fairly quickly, as they may be the result of simple misunderstandings or lack of communication. Second, the lists of both teams often show a surprising degree of similarity, in other words 'we' know what they think about 'us' and 'they' know what 'we' think about 'them'. The lists form the basis for further discussion and exploration of how conflict can be resolved and more positive working relationships established. This intervention can be used in conjunction with the Thomas–Kilmann (1974) framework, which assesses an individual's typical behaviour in conflict situations and describes it along two dimensions: assertiveness and cooperativeness. It identifies five different conflict-handling modes, or styles: competing; accommodating; avoiding; collaborating; and compromising.

- Competing is assertive and uncooperative – an individual pursues his own concerns at the other person's expense. Competing means an individual defends a position that they believe is correct, or simply try to win.

- Accommodating is unassertive and cooperative – the complete opposite of competing. When accommodating, an individual neglects their own concerns to satisfy the concerns of the other person.

- Avoiding is unassertive and uncooperative – an individual neither pursues their own concerns nor those of the other individual. They do not deal with the conflict.

- Collaborating is both assertive and cooperative – the complete opposite of avoiding. Collaborating involves an attempt to work with others to find some solution that fully satisfies their concerns.

- Compromising is moderate in both assertiveness and cooperativeness. The objective is to find some expedient, mutually acceptable solution that partially satisfies both parties.

Each individual is capable of using all five conflict-handling modes, although some individuals may use some of the styles more effectively than others and, therefore, rely more heavily on them.

To conclude, team interventions need to take into account the life cycle of the team – where it is in its development – how individuals within it interact with each other and how as a team it interacts with other teams.

Organizational interventions

Organizational interventions are designed to make significant transformations in the character and performance of an organization. The character of an organization includes the pattern of exchanges between the organization and its environment and the design of the organization includes internal structures, processes and procedures that produce products and services. The performance of the organization is measured by its productivity, market share, return on investment, and employee satisfaction and retention (Cummings and Worley, 2009). Organizational interventions can be used to address various issues such as: reducing costs; increasing productivity; speeding up the cycle time of product and service development; clarifying direction; improving morale; and meeting the expectations of stakeholders.

Interventions that target a whole organization rarely consist of a single intervention activity; rather, they often involve multiple activities over a longer period. The traditional top-down model of organizational change, where decisions are announced by senior executives, who expect subordinates to accept them and carry them out, will often create little buy-in from those lower in the hierarchy forced to adapt. To increase the commitment and participation in organizational change, interventions need to involve multiple stakeholders at various levels of an organization (Hodges, 2016).

Organizational interventions may involve sizeable groups, with hundreds or even thousands of participants. Some of the most common OD organizational interventions are restructuring, downsizing, organization design and development programmes.

Organization restructuring

To address issues identified during diagnosis may result in reorganization or restructure. Few reorganizations are, however, entirely successful. According to a McKinsey survey, more than 80 per cent fail to deliver value and 10 per cent cause real damage to the organization. McKinsey consultants Stephen Heidari-Robinson and Suzanne Heywood (2016) say that this occurs because leaders of reorganizations do not specify their objectives clearly enough, miss some of the key actions, such as forgetting process and people in their focus on reporting lines, or do things in the wrong order. Yet the problems they encounter are common and predictable. In his book *Inside Story*, Greg Dyke, the former Director-General of the BBC, writes that 'there is no perfect organizational structure and constant rethinking is healthy for any organization' (2010: 162). In contrast, Mullins (2007: 648) points out that 'Organizations cannot, without difficulty, change their formal structure at too frequent an interval.' Mullins may have a point, as a restructure can be difficult for all who are affected by it. There are almost always employee morale issues to deal with as a result of a restructure. Being aware of the impact of the change on the individuals and responding to concerns is a crucial element of a restructure, as people will be concerned about the impact on their job. To address such issues, *how* consultants go about a reorganization is as important (if not sometimes more important) than *what* they do.

Downsizing

Downsizing refers to interventions aimed at reducing the size of the organization. This typically is accomplished by decreasing the number of employees through redundancies, attrition, redeployment or early retirement, or by reducing the number of business units or management layers through divestiture or outsourcing. The reasons for organizations undertaking this type of restructure are varied and include the closing or selling of part of the business, increased productivity through greater efficiency and effectiveness, coping with external pressures, such as economic recessions and downturns, technological change and increased competitive pressures.

A planned downsizing tends to follow several stages (Cummings and Worley, 2009):

Stage 1: The rationale for downsizing is agreed and communicated. At this initial stage employees should be given opportunities to voice their concerns, share ideas and ask questions.

Stage 2: The options for downsizing are identified and assessed. Specific areas of inefficiency and high cost need to be identified and targeted. Often the obvious solutions, such as redundancies, will be chosen because they can be implemented quickly. This action tends to create a climate of uncertainty and fear as staff focus on whose roles will be made redundant and who will leave the organization. Rather than choosing the most obvious and quick option, leaders should involve employees in the decision-making process, and consider other ways of addressing the issues. This can help create a sense of commitment for identifying and implementing solutions. Participation will also provide employees with a clearer understanding of the rationale for the downsizing and increase the likelihood that whatever choices are made they will be perceived as fair.

Stage 3: Implement the changes. This stage involves implementing the methods for reducing the size of the organization. Employees need to be reminded consistently that downsizing activities are part of a plan to improve the performance of the organization. Communication is also needed to keep people informed and to help to lower their uncertainty and anxiety levels about the downsizing.

Stage 4: Address the needs of those staying and those leaving the organization. Time and attention need to be given to those staff who are staying with the organization – the survivors – as they may feel concerned about seeing their colleagues leave the company, the security of their own job and the increased workload they might have to take on as a result of fewer employees. For staff who are leaving the organization, it is important that they have outplacement support to help them find another job.

Stage 5: Follow through with growth plans. The final stage of downsizing involves implementing a process of organizational renewal and growth. Failure to move quickly to implement growth plans is a key cause of ineffective downsizing. Leaders and managers must ensure that employees understand the renewal strategy and their new roles in it. Employees also need reassurance that, although the organization has been through a tough time, their efforts and commitment will help move it forward.

Ultimately, reorganizing a company's structure is a little like turning an oil tanker into a cruise ship while being at sea: it is disruptive and complex. So restructures should not be done unless the benefits outweigh the real costs of disruption (Hodges and Gill, 2015).

Organization design

Structural changes such as downsizing often fail to achieve their desired outcomes when a restructuring is a knee-jerk reaction to other problems or the organizational structure is altered without considering fully the implications. To avoid failure, restructuring an organization involves making well-considered choices from the various alternatives available. *Organizational design* is the process of making these choices. It is a decision process to bring about coherence between the goals or purposes for which the organization exists, the patterns of division of labour and inter-unit coordination and the people who will do the work (Galbraith, 2011). This implies that the organization must be clear about its strategy and objectives. It may be the case that a strategic intervention is necessary first if the strategy cannot be clearly articulated. Indeed, Galbraith (2011) recommends that the design process always begins with reviewing the strategy.

There are times when organizational design genuinely needs to be addressed. The organization may have outgrown its previous model due to size, complexity and/or departmental barriers that might be inhibiting process effectiveness and causing the organization to no longer be serving its customers well; or employees may be frustrated at the internal obstacles to getting their work done (Ashkenas *et al*, 2015). Such challenges can be addressed when a design perspective (as opposed to a restructure) is taken between the organization's strategy, goals and structure.

Organizational design has several components, all of which must be in alignment and must support one another to produce a capable, effective organization. These elements combine into what Galbraith terms the Star Model (Galbraith, 1977: 2011). The first element is *strategy*, which determines direction. The second is *structure*, which determines the location of decision-making power. The third is *processes*, which have to do with the flow of information. The fourth is *rewards*, which influence the motivation of people to perform and achieve organizational goals. The fifth element of the model is made up of *policies* relating to *people*, which influence and frequently define the employees' mind-sets and skills.

There are a number of implications of the Star Model, which Galbraith highlights. The first is that organizational design relates to more than just structure. Most design efforts invest far too much time drawing the organization chart and far too little on processes and rewards. Structure is usually overemphasized because it affects status and power, and a change to it is most likely to be reported in the business press and announced throughout the company. The second implication is that different strategies lead to different organizations. Although this seems obvious, it has ramifications that are often overlooked. There is no one-size-fits-all organization design that all companies, regardless of their particular strategy needs, should subscribe to. There will always be a current design that has become fashionable. But no matter what the fashionable design is, whether it is the matrix design or the virtual corporation, trendiness is not a sufficient reason to adopt an organization design. All designs have merit but not for all companies in all circumstances. The design, or combination of designs, that should be chosen is the one that best meets the criteria derived from the strategy. A third implication of the Star Model is that for an organization to be effective, all the policies must be aligned and interacting harmoniously with one another. An alignment of all the policies will communicate a clear, consistent message to the company's employees. The Star Model provides a guiding framework for organizational design. It shows the levers that can be controlled and as a result can help create an effective design.

New types of design

A new organizational design is on the rise: *a network of teams* in which companies build and empower teams to work on specific business projects and challenges. These networks are aligned and coordinated with operations and information centres similar to command centres in the military. Indeed, in some ways, businesses are becoming more like Hollywood movie production teams and less like traditional corporations, with people coming together to tackle projects, then disbanding and moving on to new assignments once the project is complete (Deloitte, 2016).

A team-based organization structure can itself enable transformational change. For example, in each new city into which it expands, Uber relies on a three-pronged leadership model consisting of a city general manager, a community manager and a driver operations manager (Heffelfinger, nd). The rest of the organization is based on the unique needs of the city. Similarly, Cisco, the technology company, uses a team-based organizational model (Blenko *et al*, 2010).

To decide on the design of the organization consultants can take one of two approaches. They can change the entire organizational model – for example, organizing by customer segments instead of along geographical lines. That approach is best if your organization is completely broken or is facing a fundamental market shift that cannot be navigated under the current model. Alternatively, consultants can change only those elements that do not work, for example altering the senior board process for approvals for acquisitions, removing a layer of middle management or increasing the span of control of frontline employees while leaving the rest of the organization unchanged. That approach is best when the overall organization works well or the focus is on cutting costs. The diagnosis will help identify the right option.

Since any type of reorganization has significant implications for performance management, learning and career development, consultants need to ensure that the design is tested.

Tests of a good design

Given the complexities involved in changing a structure, what should a consultant consider when evaluating a proposed new design? Michael Goold and Andrew Campbell (2003) list several tests that can be used to appraise a design to see whether it is appropriate.

1 *The market advantage test.* Does the structure match how the organization intends to serve its markets? If the organization serves customer segments differently in different geographies, then having geographic divisions makes sense. In order to provide maximum focus, no customer segment should be missed and no segment ideally should be served by multiple divisions.

2 *The parenting advantage test.* Is the parent company organized in a way that allows it to provide the most value to the rest of the organization? If innovation is a key value of the parent company, has it organized in ways that maximize innovation throughout the organization?

3 *The people test.* Does the design support the skills and energy of the people in the organization? If the design requires that the head of engineering also manages finances, and finding a single replacement for those

dual specialized skills is unlikely if the current leader were to leave, the design may be a risk. In addition, the design may be risky if it will frustrate valuable employees who may lose status in the new structure.

4 *The feasibility test.* Will the design require a major cultural shift, such as a matrix design in a culture very comfortable with rules and hierarchy? Will information technology systems require drastic, expensive changes to report performance by customer industry versus geography?

5 *The specialist cultures test.* Is there a need for some organizational units to maintain different subcultures? For example, a group focused on the company's core products may think of innovation as a gradual series of incremental improvements to existing products, but a new products division may need rapid innovation for products that have a short life cycle. Combining research and development from both divisions may result in a dangerous culture clash.

6 *The difficult-links test.* How will divisions in the new structure develop links between them, and who will have authority when conflicts arise? If each division has a separate training function, how will they coordinate the use of resources such as classrooms and trainers?

7 *The redundant hierarchy test.* To what extent are layers of management necessary to provide focus, direction or coordination for the units in their scope?

8 *The flexibility test.* How will the new organization react when a new product is to be designed? Is it clear how the organization would work if the strategy were to change? Does the design actually obstruct and confuse rather than streamline and clarify?

Few designs will achieve all of these criteria. Goold and Campbell (2003) say that as a design fails one test, it should be revised and consultants should run through the list of tests once more. In this way, organization design needs to be an iterative process of planning and testing.

Development programmes

Development programmes are interventions that aim to build the capabilities of individuals. In the initial stages of planning a development programme consultants and clients should ask 'What is the programme for?' If the answer is, for example, to support an acquisition-led growth strategy then the organization will need individuals with ideas who are capable of devising strategies for acquiring other businesses. Alternatively, if the answer is to grow through organic opportunities, the organization will want individuals who are good at developing existing business. Once the question has been answered then the capabilities to be developed need to be identified as well as the type of development intervention.

Development interventions range from workshops delivered by internal OD specialists to off-site programmes run by external providers, such as business schools, that offer participants time to step back and escape the pressing demands of a day job. The challenge with the latter approach is that participants often struggle to transfer even the most powerful off-site experiences into changed behaviour in the workplace. Alternatively, development can be tied to on-the-job projects that have a business impact. However, it can be a challenge to create opportunities that simultaneously address high-priority needs and provide personal development opportunities. To help to achieve this, development interventions need to:

- *Provide time for reflection.* The ability to develop initiatives that enable participants to reflect, while also giving them real work experiences to apply new approaches and hone their capabilities, is a skill. Ideally, every major business project should be made into a development opportunity and development components should be integrated into the projects themselves.

- *Take individuals out of their comfort zone.* Development programmes often focus on helping participants to change their behaviour, which for some individuals can be uncomfortable. However, if there is not a significant degree of discomfort, the chances are that an individual's behaviour will not change significantly. For, just as a coach would view an athlete's muscle ache as a response to training, individuals who are stretching themselves should also feel some discomfort as they struggle to change their behaviour.

- *Track progress.* Development interventions need follow-up to track progress, for instance review meetings between the individual and their manager to discuss development objectives, or one-to-one coaching and/ or mentoring. Whatever the type of intervention selected, individuals will need time to apply their learning in practice, to receive feedback on what they are doing well and to reflect on what they have learned and what they need to improve upon.

Leadership development

One specific type of development that consultants are often asked to address is leadership development. In 2015 companies spent nearly $31 billion on leadership programmes (Deloitte, 2016). Yet, as Barbara Kellerman of Harvard University in her book *The End of Leadership* (2012) and Jeffrey Pfeffer of Stanford University in his book *Leadership BS* (2015) point out, the leadership world continues to be dominated by stories, myths and fads, often promoting superficial solutions that appear effective but fail to address the issue of helping leaders to learn and that do not deliver measurable impact and results. Results from Deloitte's (2016) Global Trends Survey highlight that only 40 per cent of executives believe that their current leadership programmes provide only some value, with even less (24 per cent) reporting that they provide little to no value. To address this, Macquarie Group Limited, a global investment banking and diversified financial services group, re-evaluated the company's leadership development programme to ensure that it builds capability. The revised programme provided leaders with a strong mental framework as well as easily digestible and readily applicable tools for their day-to-day work. The cornerstone of the programme's success was not to give participants a set of generic answers, but instead to teach leaders a set of questions they could ask themselves to help solve their own unique challenges. Participants were not taught how to behave, but how to think. The programme's catchphrase was 'Think. Lead. Act' and built around core capabilities such as setting direction, inspirational leadership, and collaboration. This flexible and innovative approach to learning enabled the company to identify and take advantage of new opportunities in a complex and rapidly evolving market (Deloitte, 2016).

Consultants need to think systematically about development interventions. A portfolio approach that simply assembles a selection of offerings is unlikely to promote consistency in leadership development or to ensure that future leaders receive the training they need. A far more rigorous process is required, using diagnostics to develop a comprehensive leadership system, not simply a collection of training packages, that can: effectively assess talent across the organization; focus training on high-potential employees; and provide opportunities for younger leaders to gain the skills, experiences and insights they need to thrive in leadership roles. The Australian telecommunications company Telstra has implemented an approach to engaging individuals in this way through *design thinking* (Telstra, 2015). The process used included:

- Focusing questions. Discovery interviews with leaders were conducted to frame the challenge and set objectives for the change.
- Ethnographic research. Interviews and focus group sessions with employees, HR and managers to explore challenges.

- Synthesis. Comparing insights from the ethnographic research with demographic and turnover data to identify key transition points and work task areas that could be dramatically improved to 'delight' employees.

- Prototyping. Developing tools and solutions that were tested and refined multiple times to allow for fast failure and the integration of lessons learned.

- Visualization. Using personal-based blueprints that describe the on-boarding journey in an engaging way, allowing leaders and others to emulate the project team's journey and increase engagement in the design (Deloitte, 2016).

In this way interventions can be systematically identified using design thinking.

Leadership development interventions need to have: pre- and post-programme assessments to measure effectiveness; research-driven content; and blended learning programmes with stretch assignments, coaching and continuous opportunities for development—all relying heavily on evidence-based data. Ultimately, development interventions should embed the learning in real work and support individuals in making sustainable changes in their behaviour.

In the following case study Lindsey Agness, Founder and Managing Director of The Change Corporation (www.thechangecorporation.com), shares her personal experience of a consultancy assignment where she designed and implemented development interventions.

CASE STUDY

Developing an army of change agents for a company going through significant change

This case is based on a project for the insurance business of an international bank, which has a strong presence in many European countries. Our consultancy team was based in Amsterdam and consisted of myself and one other consultant who was an associate working with my company. The case for change was driven by the requirement from the EU that the bank's insurance business should be divested – this was in line with the EU demands to split the group's banking and insurance operations as a condition of the Dutch state aid in 2008. This divestment was finally completed in April 2016. There was recognition that this required major transformation to get the organization into a state of 'readiness' for the transition. The purpose of our work was to build a team of internal change agents who could help to facilitate the transition at all levels of the bank.

From the start, our assignment was to design and implement a cost-effective development programme for internal change agents. In terms of our methodology, we used a blended approach to build a customized change management programme for the organization. Our bespoke method included the stages and tools outlined in Table 5.1.

The design

We developed a range of change management learning interventions featuring our bespoke change management methodology for different audiences as illustrated in Table 5.2.

Our aim was to train a team of HR professionals in the six-day programme, train key stakeholders in the business in the four-day programme, hold

Table 5.1   Stages of change management and tools used

Change Management Stage	Toolkit
Envisioning and planning the change	Creating the 'burning platform' (this was all about creating a consistent message about why the change was necessary, as seen through a staff member's eyes)
	Developing the change approach and change plan
Building commitment to the change	Identifying and mapping stakeholders
	Developing a communications strategy and plan
Building capability to manage the change	Undertaking a development needs analysis
	Designing and delivering consistent learning packages
Developing a culture aligned with strategy	Undertaking a culture survey
	Developing mission, vision, values and behaviours
Creating an organization design fit for purpose	Researching different options for reporting lines, role design, performance measures and work group design
	Developing integrating mechanisms
Developing leaders to sponsor and lead the change	Undertaking 360° assessments and feedback
	Using behavioural change tools including coaching

Table 5.2 Development Interventions

Programme	Audience	Aims	Topics
6-day change management practitioner programme	HR professionals	Develop change agents across the business who could work alongside change sponsors and leaders to deliver successful outcomes in their regions	Module one (2 days): Manage the programme and deliver benefits Plan the change Module two (2 days): Build commitment Build capability Module three (2 days): Change culture Develop leaders Organization design Pulling it all together
4-day change management business practitioner programme	Business owners of the change programmes	Develop business champions who have a clear understanding of the return on investment of change management in the business and promote its application to other stakeholders	4 days – a shortened version of the programme detailed above
1-day project manager programme	Potential project managers identified by the business	'Sell' project managers the advantages of using the change management framework and how to integrate with existing project management processes	Session 1: Understand why it is vital to have change management integrated into all projects Session 2: Help project teams understand the benefits of using change management and the risks of not having it

| | | | Session 3: Give project teams an overview of the change management framework
Session 4: Help them know what resources and tools are available to them
Session 5: Become champions of these processes with others in their region |
| Half-day personal change programme | Staff members going through change | Learn new personal development tools to make it easier to let go and move on
To feel positive about the future | Session 1: Introduction
Session 2: Ice-breaker about the impact of change
Session 3: The stages of change
Session 4: Sphere of influence
Emotional loop
Session 5: Final reflections |

various events based around our personal change event and build the project management capability in the organization.

In addition, we designed a Train the Trainer approach that upskilled a subset of the HR professionals to not only become agents of change but to also be able to offer the suite of programmes themselves. Specifically, Train the Trainer was designed to upskill HR staff to be able to:

- facilitate and present the range of change management learning interventions;
- have a thorough understanding of the bank's change management framework and the application of all the tools therein;
- be able to identify opportunities in their localities to run this suite of programmes;
- be able to explain the benefits of these programmes to their local stakeholders;
- actively contribute to change projects in their countries; and
- be motivated to champion these processes with others in their region.

We trained over 40 HR professionals in the six-day change management practitioner programme and we ran the Train the Trainer programme once for a group of 12. We also delivered the four-day business change management course in different countries and trained 25 sales people in Hungary and the Netherlands. In addition, we ran the half-day personal change module several times and gave over 100 people support to undertake the challenges ahead. This involved them attending the half-day personal change programme and then having access to the new change management champions in their regions.

In an organization where personal development was not a priority, these programmes proved to be highly popular as staff were learning pragmatic and transferable skills. This was helped by the HR professionals who started in earnest to encourage, motivate and build awareness in local teams about what they could expect, and to begin to engage with colleagues about the process of change.

Our key learning points focus on follow-up and support. A year into our contract the CEO, our main sponsor, left and was replaced by someone who was unwilling to continue to support the budget for the development programmes. This was, in part, due to the lag time between delivery of the practitioner and business programmes and the emergence of measurable benefits. As a result there are two major learning points that we would do differently next time. First, we would ensure that we had a scorecard in place from the start to measure impact and quick wins. This would have made us more influential with the new CEO. Second, we would implement a more robust process to support the 65+ people we had already trained – for example, giving 'on the ground' support in the use of the methodology and guidance on how to adapt it to different country cultures in which the bank operated. Instead we expected the group of champions to be able to largely support each other after the training. In reality they needed more of our help than we had factored into our planning and budget.

Discussion questions for the case

1 Consider how you might apply the learning highlighted in this case to the design and delivery of development interventions for an organization you are working with, or one you are familiar with.

2 What measures need to be agreed with a client for tracking progress of the development event highlighted in this case?

3 How would you ensure that the outcomes from the interventions highlighted in the case were sustained?

Changing cultures

Consultants are often engaged by clients to help them to refine their cultures. There is a variety of culture assessment tools that enable an organization's culture to be diagnosed, including well-established models, such as the culture web, which was developed by Gerry Johnson (1992). Yet, despite the prevalence of such tools, fewer than 12 per cent of companies believe they truly understand their culture (Deloitte, 2016). That is where consultants can help. Consultants can help clients to understand and improve their culture.

To effectively understand an organization's culture, consultants at Deloitte's (2016) suggest that clients and consultants must collaborate to answer questions such as:

● How do we create more high-impact customer and employee experience moments and ensure that we deliver them consistently?

● How well does our performance management or compensation system reinforce or improve our culture?

● Are we willing to reduce productivity temporarily to invest the time it takes to build a culture of learning?

- What cultural issues lie behind problems such as fraud, loss, or compliance issues? Are punishing the offenders and reinforcing good behaviour enough, or does supporting ethical conduct require changing cultural norms that enable or even encourage bad behaviour?

- In merger and acquisition situations, how can cultural barriers to integration be identified and addressed before they become problematic?

- How does our culture affect our employment brand and ability to attract, hire, and retain top talent?

To monitor and reinforce culture involves regularly assessing the behaviour of organizational members and reviewing performance management, reward systems and business practices in all areas of the organization.

In the following case study Fiona Sweeney, People and Organizational Change Consultant, outlines how she implemented an OD approach in an attempt to change the culture of a health and fitness club chain in South Africa.

CASE STUDY

Building capability for change in a health club chain

This case is about a health and fitness club chain that has 109 clubs across South Africa. Following a redefinition of their strategy by the board and a diagnosis exercise across the whole organization by an external consultancy organization, it was identified that changes, particularly in the organizational structure, sales and marketing processes and systems, were required to the way the organization did business and to transform the performance of the business over a three to four year period. I was engaged as an independent external consultant to support the organization through the change management process.

Although the health and fitness chain was customer focused in its intent, it was not optimally organized to be a leading customer-centric organization. There was a high attrition rate among members with key gaps around customer insights, proposition and innovation, as well as inconsistent operational delivery of the customer promise. Regional managers were not always aware of what was going on within the 'functional silos' within the clubs, thus resulting in contradictory communications. There was disagreement on who was accountable for what within each club, which led to the club managers being reluctant to take full responsibility for decisions and deferring to regional managers. There was also a lack of commercial skills amongst club managers, which limited their ability to attract customers and drive business performance at a local level.

The existing business model suffered from a number of issues including: silo working at regional and club level, which resulted in inefficient decision-making; unclear responsibilities, which caused confusion; career development and capability gaps, which created performance issues; and inconsistencies in management style, which led to employee disengagement.

The sales team had approximately 600 sales consultants in addition to a sales manager in each club, which meant that the majority of the sales resources were based within the clubs and there was little sales activity driven centrally. There was also a significant disparity in the performance of the club sales consultants and a high turnover amongst them, which limited potential for improvements. Much of the administration was being carried out at club level and was driven by sales, customer administration and back office processes. At a regional and club level, it was felt that the high level of administration that has to be done had a negative impact on the experience of members as it resulted in key staff spending less time on the gym floor.

To ensure the strategic targets were achieved, a project was launched to deliver a fit-for-purpose, customer-centric and highly commercial business. The objectives of the project were to have: more satisfied members who would stay longer; a sales force selling more effectively; a lower cost base, and an enduring competitive advantage. In addition, it was imperative to re-enforce a strong cost culture across the business and particularly at club level.

The vision for the future business was that a customer centric and commercial mindset would permeate the organization supported by data-driven decision-making and unbeatable execution and that the main functions across marketing, sales, and operations would work collaboratively to deliver excellent service for the members.

The proposed structural changes aimed to strengthen the regional operations, deliver clearer accountabilities, and enable the club managers to take greater ownership.

It was important from the outset of the project that there was an integrated approach to developing individual capability across the business. Therefore, in order to support the project, I developed a change management strategy that aimed to:

- position the project initiatives strategically around customer-centricity;
- minimize resistance from stakeholders to the changes;
- facilitate uniform leadership commitment to the project;
- support the transition of the club, regional and head office employees to the new structures and ways of working;
- enable employees to use the new processes and technologies;

Figure 5.2 Building capability model

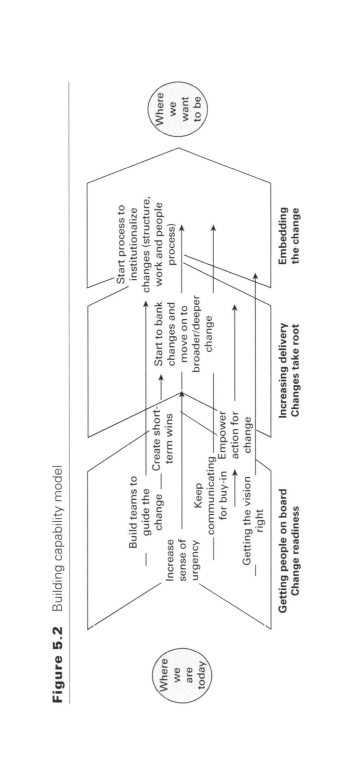

- measure readiness to transition to the new structure and ways of working and develop interventions if necessary;
- align the people strategy and business strategy for culture change;
- integrate the strategy with IT projects.

In my role as consultant I used the model illustrated in Figure 5.2. I have adapted this model over the years from other change models, to structure the strategy around and subsequently develop a change plan. I have found the model to be a useful tool to start the conversations with stakeholders in order to aid their understanding and manage their expectations around the change process. In particular, it was important, in the current case, to highlight the need to take the business through each stage in order to build sustainable capability within it. The reality check was that the transition needed to be phased over time in order to allow the organization to adapt to new requirements and put key enablers in place.

The model is helpful in illustrating that managing change is not a linear process since a lot of changes can run concurrently with the health and fitness club chain. There was a lot of upfront positioning of the project through communications in order to build awareness and understanding around customer-centricity and how it would take the business to the next level of growth. Communications were designed to build commitment to the changes and to 'paint the big picture', outlining the need for the change and preparing the organization for the changes ahead. It was important not to leave it to chance that employees would connect the dots for themselves, but make the connection for them and paint the change journey story so that it did not come across as just another initiative but a continuation of the journey the business was already on.

It was also important to ensure that the overall people strategy was aligned to the business strategy and that the people aspects from the project were incorporated into each stage of the employee life cycle. People initiatives were identified for the short, medium and long term, in order to build sustainable capability. Focus was also placed on an improved performance management process and reinforcement of required behaviours through feedback and key performance indicators (KPIs). A major emphasis was placed on talent identification and succession for lynchpin roles so that there would be a pipeline of talent for current and future roles.

Principles were developed to underpin the redesign of the business model and included: increasing the club managers' accountabilities by making them accountable for all aspects of club performance; reducing hierarchy and cost; creating manageable career steps; enabling customer-centric decision-making; and scaling for future growth. The club manager at a regional level was identified as a key role for executing this strategy.

Core competencies were identified and the club manager's job description was redesigned to take account of what was a 'good' club manager. The club manager recruitment criteria were refined to ensure the next generation of managers had commercial capabilities. There was also an initiative for up-skilling existing club managers in order to drive increased accountability, particularly in relation to sales. In order to ensure that the club managers were well positioned for future challenges, the organization needed to evaluate the strengths and development needs of each club manager. To this end, a custom-designed development centre was designed to give an indication of the bench strength of existing club managers and address development gaps through training.

Roles and responsibilities were also redesigned across sales and marketing, with the sales function being incorporated into the marketing department. Core competencies were identified for the sales force and were incorporated into the sales recruitment process and training programmes. Further local sales force effectiveness opportunities were achieved through better on-the-job training and coaching from the club and sales managers. To help with staff retention, the basic salary and commission structure for sales staff was revised.

In the annual people survey, six months after the implementation of the changes, the findings indicated a healthy working environment with an employee engagement score of 88 per cent, which was the same as the previous year. With all the changes there was an expectation that this would have been much lower. Scores were relatively high across all dimensions that were measured, including: clarity of roles; leadership and direction; and values. In the subsequent two people surveys the engagement score still remained high. There were some clubs where the results were low but this was mainly down to poor management and leadership on the part of the club manager and action plans were put in place to address these through active coaching, performance management and training.

I believe that aligning the people and business strategies and having an integrated approach to managing the changes contributed to building long-lasting capability within the business.

Discussion questions for the case

1 Conduct a stakeholder analysis for key stakeholders identified in this case, then map out an action plan for managing them.

2 What were the key challenges faced by the consultant in this case, and how were they addressed?

3 What would you do differently if you were the main consultant working with the health and fitness chain?

4 What key lessons can be learned from this case that you can apply in practice to an organization you are working with or one you are familiar with?

Implementing the intervention

The role of the consultant during the implementation of the intervention needs to be negotiated between the consultant and client. Decisions need to be made about whether or not the consultant will be an active participant in the intervention, or more of an expert/adviser (Stroh and Johnson, 2006). Among the roles which a consultant can take on during implementation, Golembiewski (2001) suggests the following, each of which can vary in the amount of involvement from the consultant:

- Facilitative. This involves helping a client attain their desired outcomes by clarifying alternatives, processes and decisions.
- Gatekeeping. This is acting as a boundary spanner between teams or between managers and teams, negotiating between them and providing constructive feedback.
- Diagnostic. This involves pointing out what has been seen, heard or learned to enhance team or individual awareness.
- Mobilizing. This is advocating a particular approach or perspective.

To conclude, the right role and the desired level of engagement from the consultant need to be agreed with the client to avoid too little or too much ownership by the consultant during implementation. It is also vital to build into the initial planning ways of implementing the change, rather than leaving it as an afterthought. This should include the measuring, monitoring and reviewing of the key objectives, benefits and risks of interventions (see Chapter 6 for further details on each of these).

Summary

The purpose of interventions is to help or improve the effectiveness of organizations, teams and individuals. An intervention strategy consists of activities that are effectively sequenced for maximum benefit. Such activities range from the redesign of an organization's structure to team events to individual mentoring and coaching. Time must be spent selecting the most appropriate intervention as failed interventions cause significant costs in time, money and motivation of organizational members. There is, therefore, a need for interventions to be properly selected, defined, tailored and managed within the context of the organization.

The ownership of the intervention has to be clarified so that the client and consultant are clear on how the consultant will help the client achieve the objectives of the intervention. While the consultant might also be involved during the implementation of the intervention, eventually they will need to disengage, as the responsibility for sustaining the change needs to be transferred to the client.

Implications for consultants

There are several practical implications for practising and aspiring consultants that arise from the issues discussed in this chapter.

- *Develop a profit and loss statement.*
  Start by defining the benefits, the costs, and the time to deliver. The costs include not just those of consultants and employees involved but also the human cost of change and the disruption it can create.

- *Select the right level of intervention.*
  Successful interventions are those that are directed at the right level to address the root cause of an issue. For example, it may not be productive to intervene at a team level when the root cause of team dysfunction lies at the level of a specific individual member of the team; in such cases, an intervention with the relevant individual may reap greater benefits. Rigorous analysis and evidence should inform every step of the development process of an intervention.

- *Involve organizational members in identifying potential interventions.*
  For the right intervention to be selected, organizational members need to be involved in identifying potential solutions (this can be done using techniques such as AI, FST or scenario planning). Extend engagement to involve a cross-section of staff at an early stage of the design of an intervention.

- *Implement, learn and correct.*
  No matter how much thought and preparation go into a change intervention, it is unrealistic to expect that it will work perfectly from the start.

Clients will have to live with it and embed it and work with consultants to correct any issues that may arise. Employees need to be encouraged to point out any issues, openly debate solutions and implement the appropriate fixes as soon as possible.

- *Understanding readiness to change is an important part of identifying interventions.*
  People must be ready to change, especially as interventions come between or deliberately disrupt existing processes, thinking, people, groups and relationships.

References

Anderson, D (2012) *Organization Development: The process of leading organizational change*, 2nd edn, Sage, London

Argyris, C (1970) *Intervention Theory and Method: A behavioural science view*, Addison-Wesley, Reading, MA

Armenakis, A, Harris, S and Mossholder, KW (1993) Creating readiness for organizational change, *Human Relations*, **46** (6), pp 681–703

Ashkenas, R, Ulrich, D, Jick, T and Kerr, S (2015) *The Boundaryless Organization: Breaking the chains of organizational structure*, Wiley and Sons, London

Beer, M (1980) *Organization Change and Development: A systems view*, Goodyear, Santa Monica, CA

Blake, R, Mouton, J and Sloma, R (1965) The union–management intergroup laboratory: Strategy for resolving intergroup conflict, *The Journal of Applied Behavioral Science*, **1** (1), pp 25–57

Blenko, MW, Mankins, MC and Rogers, P (2010) The decision-driven organization, *Harvard Business Review*, **88** (6), pp 54–62

Bowers, D, Franklin, J and Pecorella, P (1975) Matching problems, precursors, and interventions in OD: A systemic approach, *The Journal of Applied Behavioral Science*, **11** (4), pp 391–409

Burnes, B and Jackson, P (2011) Success and failure in organizational change: An exploration of the role of values, *Journal of Change Management*, **11** (2), pp 133–62

Carnall, C (2007) *Managing Change in Organizations*, 5th edn, Pearson Education Limited, London

Cherim, S (2002) Influencing organizational identification during major change: A communication based perspective, *Human Relations*, **55**, pp 1117–37

Cooperrider, DL, Whitney, D and Stravros, JM (2008) *Appreciative Inquiry Handbook*, Crown, Brunswick, OH

Cummings, T and Worley, C (2009) *Organization Development and Change*, 9th edn, South-Western Cengage Learning, Mason, OH de Klerk, M (2007) Healing emotional trauma in organizations: An OD framework and case study, *Organization Development Journal*, **25** (2)

Deloitte (2016) *Global Human Capital Trends*. [Online] https://www2. deloitte.com/content/dam/Deloitte/co/Documents/human-capital/Design per cent20thinking per cent20Crafting per cent20the per cent20employee per cent-20experience.pdf

Dyke, G (2010) *Greg Dyke: Inside story*, HarperCollins, London

Emery, M and Purser, RE (1996) *The Search Conference: A powerful method for planning organizational change and community action*, Jossey-Bass, San Francisco

Galbraith, JR (1977) *Organization Design*, Addison Wesley, London

Galbraith, JR (2011) *Designing the Customer-Centric Organization: A guide to strategy, structure, and process*, Wiley and Sons, London

Goh, S, Cousins, J and Elliott, C (2006) Organizational learning capacity, evaluative inquiry and readiness for change in schools: Views and perceptions of educators, *Journal of Educational Change*, **7**, pp 286–318

Golembiewski, RT (2001) *Handbook of Organizational Behavior, Revised and Expanded*, Decker, Hamilton

Goold, M and Campbell, A (2003) Structured networks: Towards the well-designed matrix, *Long Range Planning*, **36** (5), 427–39

Hameed, I, Roques, O and Arain, G (2013) Nonlinear moderating effect of tenure on organizational identifications (OID) and the subsequent role of OID in fostering readiness for change, *Group and Organization Management*, **38** (1): 101–27

Hayes, J (2014) *The Theory and Practice of Change Management*, 4th edn, Palgrave Macmillan, Basingstoke

Heffelfinger, H (nd) Uber and why it will continue to succeed, Stanford University. [Online] https://novoed.com/venture1-2014-2/reports/255020

Heidari-Robinson, S and Heywood, S (2016) *Reorgs: How to get them right*, Harvard Business Review, Cambridge, MA

Hodges, J (2016) *Managing and Leading People through Change*, Kogan Page, London

Hodges, J and Gill, R (2015) *Sustaining Change in Organizations*, Sage, London

Johnson, G (1992) Managing strategic change: strategy, culture and action, *Long Range Planning*, **25**(1), pp 28–36

Judge, W and Douglas, T (2009) Organizational change capacity: The systematic development of a change, *Journal of Organizational Change Management*, **22** (6), pp 635–49

Kellerman, B (2012) *The End of Leadership*, Harper Collins, London

Kerber, K and Buono, A (2005) Rethinking organizational change: Reframing the challenge of change management, *Organization Development Journal*, **23** (3), 23

Kotter, J (1995) Leading change: Why transformation efforts fail, *Harvard Business Review*, May–June, pp 11–16

Landsberg, M (1996) *Tao of Coaching: Boost Your effectiveness at work by inspiring and developing those around you*, HarperCollins, London

Lindgren, M and Bandhold, H (2003) *Scenario Planning*, Palgrave, London

Mabey, C (2008) *The Process Of Change: Building momentum*, The Open University, Milton Keynes

Madsen, SR, Miller, D and John, CR (2005) Readiness for organizational change: Do organizational commitment and social relationships in the workplace make a difference?, *Human Resource Development Quarterly*, **16**, 213–33

Mullins, LJ (2007) *Management and Organisational Behaviour*, Pearson, London

Ogilvy, JA (2002) *Creating Better Futures: Scenario planning as a tool for a better tomorrow*, Oxford University Press: Oxford

Pfeffer, J. (2015) *Leadership BS: Fixing workplaces and careers one truth at a time*, HarperCollins, London

Rafferty, A, Jimmieson, N and Armenakis, A (2013) Change readiness: A multilevel review, *Journal of Management*, **39** (1), pp 110–35

Ralston, B and Wilson, I (2006) *The Scenario Planning Handbook*, Texere, Mason, OH

Robbins, SP (2005) *Organizational Behaviour*, 11th edn, Prentice Hall, Englewood Cliffs, NJ

Schein, E (1997) *Organizational Culture and Leadership*, 3rd edn, Jossey-Bass, San Francisco

Schoemaker, PJ (1995) Scenario planning: A tool for strategic thinking, *Sloan Management Review*, **36** (2), p 25

Schwartz, P (1996) *The Art of the Long View: Paths to strategic insight for yourself and your company*, Crown Business

Sorge, A and Van Witteloostuijn, A (2004) The (non)sense of organizational change: An essay about universal management hypes, sick consultancy metaphors and healthy organizational thoeries, *Organizational Studies*, **25** (7), pp 1205–31

Steil, G and Gibbons-Carr, M (2005) Large group scenario planning scenario planning with the whole system in the room, *The Journal of Applied Behavioral Science*, **41** (1), pp 15–29

Stevens, G (2013) Toward a process-based approach to conceptualizing change readiness, *The Journal of Applied Behavioural Science*, **49** (3), pp 333–60

Stone, F (2004) *The Mentoring Advantage: Creating the next generation of leaders*, Dearborn Trade Publishing, Chicago

Stroh, L and Johnson, H (2006) *The Basic Principles of Effective Consulting*, Lawrence Erlbaum, New Jersey

Telstra (2015) Custom design: Creative and customer-focused design thinking is helping Telstra to improve its services and develop products based on customers' needs. [Online] https://insight.telstra.com.au/t5/Reimagining-Change/Custom-design/ba-p/2607

Thomas, K and Kilmann, R (1974) *Thomas–Kilmann Conflict Mode Instrument*, Xicom, Inc, Tuxedo, NY

Thorne, K (2004) *Coaching for Change: Practical strategies for transforming performance*, Kogan Page, London

Tuckman, B (1964) Personality structure, group composition, and group functioning, *Sociometry*, pp 469–87

Weisbord, M and Janoff, S (2010) *Future Search: Getting the whole system in the room for vision, commitment, and action*, Berrett-Koehler Publishers, Oakland, CA

Transition

06

KEY POINTS

- Attention to the ending or transition of a consultancy assignment is necessary because otherwise the change project will languish unproductively or end abruptly without adequate evaluation or follow-up.

- The transition phase is an opportunity to reflect, to learn and to identify what went well and what could be done differently.

- Being clear about the boundaries of the consultancy work and the correct time to withdraw is essential. Disengaging becomes much easier and clearer when the contracting process has been done effectively. If the consultant's role and the client's expectations about the outcomes for the piece of work have been clarified, the transition will be both appropriate and timely.

- Knowing what influences and determines the sustainability of change is a key part of the transition phase. Determining whether or not change has been sustained will involve measurement of the benefits achieved, as well as management of the risks associated with the change.

Introduction

Consulting engagements are by definition temporary relationships, and consultants must at some point transition full ownership of the intervention over to the client.

Attention to the ending or transition phase is necessary because too many change projects may 'linger unproductively or may end abruptly and without adequate follow-up' (Van Eron and Burke, 1995: 395). Even if the client identifies additional work or another issue to be addressed by the consultant, the current engagement as defined during the initial contracting phase still needs to come to an end and be formally closed. So, just as it is important to formally kick off a consultancy engagement with an initial contracting meeting (see Chapter 3 for further discussion on contracting), it is also important to successfully transition the change to the client/operations. As Judith Benson says, 'the ability to skilfully enable healthy closure is particularly important because of the rapid pace of 21st century change' (2010: 270). The value of having a planned transition is in leveraging all of the information and experience gathered throughout the consultancy cycle and ensuring that the change will be sustained.

The aim of this chapter is to examine how consultants can transition effectively from an engagement and transfer full ownership of an intervention to the client so that it becomes operational and business as usual. The chapter begins by examining the need for transition and the issues that have to be addressed during the transition phase of the consultancy cycle. It goes on to discuss the importance of evaluation, focusing on the measurement and monitoring of objectives and benefits, and engaging people in the change. Colin Campbell, Senior CRM Consultant, shares the importance of involving people in change and maintaining their engagement throughout the process. And Dinah Bennett, Director of International Consultants for Entrepreneurship and Enterprise (ICE) Ltd, shares her experience of how to implement and sustain change in order to ensure that it achieves a positive impact. Consideration is also given in this chapter to how accountability and responsibility should be transitioned from consultant to client. The chapter concludes by exploring what clients and consultants can do to influence the ongoing sustainability of change.

Learning outcomes

By the end of this chapter you will be able to:

- manage the key activities to be addressed during the transition phase of the consultancy cycle;
- effectively hand over full ownership of the transformation to managers;
- review and evaluate a change initiative;
- identify how the benefits from change can be realized and sustained.

The need for transition

Transition is the phase of the consultancy cycle when ownership of the change is transferred to managers so that it becomes operational, and as a result the consultancy assignment is formally closed. It is also a time when the client and the consultant can look back over the project and their working relationship in order to establish if objectives have been met, what worked well and what did not, and what the next steps are following termination of their current contractual agreement.

The transition and exit of the consultant from the consulting assignment need to be managed carefully. An external consultant should not just assume that it is all right to ask for the money and leave, nor should an internal consultant assume that they should just keep working on the transformation until told to stop. Although it can be tougher to disengage as an internal consultant, it is nonetheless important. Often the transition happens without any planning or forethought to disengagement. For instance, it may occur when the consultant and client run out of agenda items for their regular meetings, or when the client lacks information or motivation to take another action and tells the consultant to wait a few weeks until the situation becomes clear, but never gets back to them. If the transition phase is not formally recognized and managed then eventually both the client and consultant will find other change initiatives to work on and the transformation they were working on together will lose importance.

Failure to manage the closure process can lead to disaster. Lessons from a range of projects indicate that a failure to address the transition phase properly and professionally will lead to bigger problems, which are the 'ones that will come back to bite [consultants] in the longer run' (Cope, 2010: 346). The failure to close an engagement effectively is identified by Mike Cope (2010) as one of the primary reasons for the poor brand reputation of the consultancy industry, which he says will 'eventually lead to its destruction' (2010: 336). So, when transitioning from an engagement, consultants must avoid the natural urge to disengage on the assumption that everything will be all right because the change has been implemented and appears to have achieved its objectives.

Without a clear and agreed closure consultants run the risk of: being regarded as a permanent fixture in support of the transformation; being considered accountable, rather than the client and their employees, for the long-term sustainability of the change; or 'scope creep' occurring, which will involve the consultant being asked to work on related issues which are not part of the agreed initial contract (Weiss, 2003). Being clear about the boundaries of the consultancy work and the time to withdraw is, therefore, essential.

During contracting it should be agreed between the consultant and client when disengagement will begin. According to Alan Weiss, this should be about 80 per cent of the way through a transformation because, as he says, 'the worst thing you can do is show up in the [client's] office and say, "What weather? And by the way, we're done"' (2003: 179). To avoid this rather blunt approach the consultant should begin to move to transition by:

- referring to the date when the engagement will be complete (as agreed in the proposal) and when consultancy involvement will no longer be required;
- reviewing the progress of objectives and benefits towards the agreed outcome;
- confirming that the client is prepared to take full ownership and that all accountabilities and responsibilities for sustaining the transformation are agreed.

Usually the disengagement of the consultant from the transformation will be by mutual agreement and be evident when the objectives and benefits have been achieved. There may, however, be reasons for either the consultant or client ending the engagement earlier, especially if the transformation is not progressing successfully (Rothwell and Sullivan, 2005). Signs that there is a need to end an engagement earlier than anticipated include: the client putting things off; agreements that have been made are disregarded by either the client or consultant; the consultant appears to have a higher emotional stake in the outcomes than the client does; or the client is doing better and really does not need the consultant's help (Weisbord, 2012). Whether or not the engagement ends on time or earlier than initially expected, the closure should be done explicitly and with planning rather than being allowed to just fade away.

Transition activities

During the transition phase there are a number of activities that the consultant needs to perform in order to ensure that their disengagement is recognized and agreed by the client. Such activities include: transitioning any ongoing activities to the client; identifying the value of the consultancy support; facilitating client learning; and letting go.

Transitioning any ongoing activities to the client

Ownership of the transformation should be handed to the client so that there are no loose ends still to be tied up or ongoing client expectations (Anderson, 2012). This will involve assessing the completeness of the transformation (checking against the objectives) and handing over any continuing implementation activities and the ongoing monitoring of benefits and risks. It will also include transferring knowledge to the relevant service and operational teams and finalizing any documentation and handing it over along with any collected data.

Identifying the value of the consultancy support

The aim of any consultancy is to deliver value through sustainable change. Consulting is about value realization, about proving that consultants can add value that will last. Consultants should be clear on the change they deliver, on what it is they are doing that is different and the value of that, and should have confidence that it is going to last. This means that throughout the consultancy cycle consultants must ensure that they manage how they are adding value. As outlined in Chapter 1 there are two aspects to value: value management and value differentiation (Nagle and Holden, 1995). By ensuring that the client understands the value that the consultant has provided there is a greater likelihood that there will be further opportunities for work for the consultant with the client. So during the transition phase the consultant must confirm how the outcomes from the change have tangibly delivered improvements and benefits. They must ensure that the added value they have provided is clearly understood by and communicated to the client as well as to other stakeholders.

Facilitating client learning

Consultants should aim to leave behind something of lasting value. This means not only enhancing clients' ability to deal with any immediate issues but also helping them to evaluate and learn from the transformation. According to Beer *et al* (1990) what is required is 'a learning organization capable of adapting to a changing competitive environment. The organization has to know how to monitor its behaviour – in effect, to learn how to learn.' The objective of sharing learning across the organization is to develop practices that support the desired transformation, to remove barriers to its success, and to implement regular evaluation and renewal that encourage appropriate and necessary alterations and avoid stagnation (Anderson, 2012). To achieve this the consultant should arrange a meeting with the client and other stakeholders to review the final outcomes and benefits of the change (Weiss, 2003), agree what went well and things that could be done differently, the strengths and weaknesses of their approach, lessons learned and how they can be applied to future change initiatives. The key learnings should also be shared with appropriate teams/individuals. Even if the change fails there are still key learnings, evaluations and transition activities to be conducted.

An approach that can be used for reviewing learning is *After Action Review*, which was developed by the US Army for extracting lessons from military exercises and applying them to others (Darling *et al*, 2005). This method can be used in a similar way for reviewing organizational transformations. It starts by reviewing the intent (stated at the start of a change) with what subsequently happened using the following questions: What was supposed to happen? What actually did happen? Why did it happen this way? What has been learned? What should be taken forward to use next time? Under each of these questions are sub-questions (outlined below) to help probe in more depth.

- What was supposed to happen?

  - What was the objective of the change?
  - How clear was the outcome?
  - How clear were the stakeholders about the impact of the change?
  - How were the measures and expected benefits communicated and understood?

- What actually did happen?

  - Where is the organization now?
  - How does this compare to where the organization wanted to be when the transformation began?
  - What was the actual outcome?
  - What does each person perceive to be the outcome and what are the perception gaps?
  - What explicit evidence is there?
  - What anecdotal or intangible evidence is there?

- Why did it happen this way?

  - What gaps were there between what was expected to happen and what actually happened?
  - How is the outcome rated against expectations?
  - What worked well, and why?

- – What did not work, and why?
- – What helped the success, and why?
- – What caused failure, and why?
- – What alternative courses of action might have been more effective?
- What has been learned?
  - – What are the key lessons learned?
- What should be taken forward to use for the next transformation?
  - – What lessons should be applied to i) consultancy assignments; ii) organizational change?

These questions provide a framework to share views about the content (what) and the process (how) of the transformation, which enables tangible learning to take place that can be transferred across the organization. This can also help the consultant to identify what they should build upon and what they should do differently in future engagements.

What is missing from this approach, however, is an explicit focus on evaluating the impact of change on people. Consultants therefore need to ensure that they include specific questions that elicit feedback about how the change affected individuals in terms of their attitudes, behaviours and feelings, such as, 'How do you feel about the change?' or 'How do you feel about changing your behaviour?' Such questions help to find out about the emotional elements of change.

Learning during transformation initiatives is a joint process. In every engagement, clients will learn what works well and what in their organization can be improved upon with transformational change, and consultants will learn how to be more effective in designing and conducting change interventions and building and maintaining relationships with clients. Taking time for reflection can help to create an awareness of what has been learned and can enable individuals to make sense of situations, identify cause and effect, develop corrective routines and challenge beliefs and assumptions (Hayes, 2014). So time needs to be built into the transition phase to reflect on learning from the whole consultancy cycle and to identify possibilities for improvement.

Letting go

Throughout the consultancy cycle the consultant will be building and maintaining their relationship with the client, but as this relationship grows so does dependency between both parties. Ultimately, however, the consultant needs to ensure that all unnecessary levels of dependence have gone from both sides of the relationship and that the client can fly solo because 'to have a situation where there is chronic dependence on consultants is an implicit admission of ineptitude' (O'Shea and Madigan, 1997). A dependent relationship may give short-term gain but will lead to longer-term problems, such as the client being unwilling to let go of the consultant's expertise and help, or the client being left without the confidence or ability to take the transformation forward themselves. As a result, the organization may revert back to the state that existed before the change. Withdrawal and disengagement can increase the risk of clients feeling vulnerable, particularly if they do not feel well prepared for their continuing role in implementing and sustaining change and perceive the consultant as integral to it, which can lead to the client re-engaging the consultant in order to continue working with them (Cope, 2010). Consultants may also find it hard to disengage and consequently make themselves too available and too compliant, and thus create client dependency.

To avoid dependency, the consultant's role and the client's expectations about the outcomes for the piece of work have to be agreed during contracting, so that the transition feels both appropriate and timely. Consultants will then be able to hand over ownership of the project in such a way that the client is able to continue to sustain the change.

Sustaining change

Building sustainability into implementation

The *sustainability* of organizational change is crucial to the development, growth, success and survival of any organization operating within an ever-changing environment (Farjoun, 2002). If this challenge is not addressed as part of the consultancy engagement then enormous resources will be wasted and the change initiative may fail. It is therefore vital to build into the implementation plan ways of sustaining the change, such as evaluation, realizing benefits, risk management, feedback and performance management. All of these are outlined briefly below.

Evaluation

There is often so much of a rush to claim victory by consultants and clients that they do not take the time to find out what is working and what is not working, nor to adjust what is happening accordingly. A survey by

PwC revealed that many organizations involved in transformation efforts fail to evaluate their progress (Aquirre *et al*, 2013). This is often due to the many challenges and barriers to conducting an effective and thorough evaluation for, as Burke and Noumair say, 'The evaluation process... can be compared to an annual physical examination – everyone agrees that it should be done, but no one, except a highly motivated researcher, wants to go to the trouble and expense of making it happen' (2015: 248).

Despite such difficulties, there are many good reasons for evaluation. It allows the consultant and client to return to the original objectives of the engagement, to be specific about what outcomes were expected and to find out if they have been achieved (Burke and Noumair, 2015). The results of an evaluation can facilitate planning for the next steps of the transformation, identify any barriers to implementing change that need to be addressed, help to understand aspects of the change that did or did not work as anticipated, and enable the consultant to learn from the experience and apply the lessons to future transformations. 'The creation of learning moments during and after the change process can offer the insight needed to boost the success of future change initiatives' (Koster *et al*, 1998: 10).

To illustrate the benefits of evaluation, Acquirre and Alpern (2014) in an article entitled '10 Principles of leading change management' provide the example of a global consumer products company that executed a change programme in order to reduce costs across the business. To ensure that people understood the ongoing nature of the change a series of pulse surveys were rolled out and focus groups convened to evaluate the progress. The first round of surveys found that only 60 per cent of respondents understood the rationale for change and the new behaviours expected from them. To address this the company asked leaders to play a bigger role in evangelizing for the initiative. They continued to run these surveys and focus groups to measure the results until a larger majority of the staff had shown they were prepared to be engaged and committed to making the change happen. Such an approach provided the company with the necessary information about how to support the process of change until it was effectively sustained.

The joint process of evaluation

Evaluation is a joint process between the consultant and the client that needs to be incorporated into the contract agreed during the contracting phase (see Chapter 3 for details on contracting) and runs throughout the consultancy cycle. It should cover task issues (what was done), process issues (how it was done) and people issues (what the impact on individuals was). The value of evaluating these three areas includes: identifying major areas of concern for remedial action; having a barometer of opinion at various times; being able to compare the situation in different departments, functions, locations and teams and so identify issues; getting people to think about the issues and to promote dialogue about the issues; and providing a benchmark against other organizations going through similar changes. The integration of evaluation into the consultancy for change cycle thus allows the impact of the change to be measured.

Evaluating the impact of change

Measuring the impact of change is a key aspect during the consultancy cycle for a number of reasons: it is a means of monitoring the progress of the change ('what gets measured gets managed'); what gets measured is likely to have a significant impact on how people behave; and it enables an assessment to be made of whether the selected interventions are having the desired impact and if they continue to be valid and beneficial.

Transition phase evaluation

During the transition phase a final review needs be conducted. This should reflect back over the consultancy cycle to see what has been learned that will contribute to future projects. The consultant can lead this review, or some clients may prefer to use an independent team to conduct the review in order to ensure objectivity.

Questions that need to be included as part of the agenda for the final review are:

1 In the client's view, was the issue addressed/problem solved?

2 Were the key objectives/success factors achieved? What helped/hindered?

3 What did not go well or caused problems for the change?

4 What was the final outcome – were the expected outcomes achieved?

If the answer is 'no' to questions 1 and 2 then the reasons for this should be identified, as well as what can be done to make sure the answer is 'yes' for future consultancy assignments. Equally, if the answer is 'yes' what was done well should be clarified so that it can be improved upon next time. The final review should also discuss the overall capabilities of the consultants, considering areas where the consultants performed well and areas where they could have done better. Finally, there should be a conclusion as to how successful the transformation has been and whether the client is satisfied with the work and would use the consultant again (Wickham and Wickham, 2008). This provides a final view as to how well the transformation was implemented and an acknowledgement as to whether or not the client is committed to working with the consultant again. In this way, the client will be formally aware that the contract with the consultant has come to an end and that the accountabilities and responsibilities for further reinforcement and fine-tuning of the transformation as well as ensuring that it is embedded in the business now rest with the client and the business.

Realizing benefits

Benefits realization is a core part of the consultancy cycle and depends on the process of organizing and managing the transformation so that potential benefits arising from investment in change are actually achieved (Ashurst and Hodges, 2010). Yet research indicates that less than a quarter (24 per cent) of the FTSE 250 multinational and public sector organizations measure the benefits of transformation projects properly – equating to some £850 million in potentially wasted investment in projects that do not have clear benefits or outcomes (Moorhouse Consulting, 2009). What is concerning about these findings is the risk of the lack of measurement on the impact of these projects that are perceived as critical to the success of the business and cost significant amounts of financial investment. It is unwise to embark on implementing change without first establishing that success can be probable and beneficial (Paton and McCalman, 2008). As part of the planning process for any change, the benefits to be achieved need to be identified so that the cost of the change is calculated, understood and monitored.

Benefits are broadly defined as the outcomes of change that are perceived as positive by a stakeholder (Bradley, 2010). Conversely, disbenefits are outcomes of change perceived as negative, while managing benefits is described as the process of organizing and managing, so that potential benefits arising from investment in change are actually achieved (Bradley, 2010).

The process of benefits realization management does, however, have limitations, which are highlighted by its critics. For example, Jenner (2009) refers to the phenomenon of 'optimism bias' whereby the benefits of potential projects are consciously or unconsciously inflated in order to secure their approval, and hence are neither robust nor realizable. In some cases this amounts to 'benefits fraud' where deception is involved, on the assumption that those responsible will never be held to account for knowingly inflating the benefits of their project. Despite such criticisms, taking time to identify, monitor and control benefits prevents getting to the end and discovering that the change has not achieved what was expected. Solutions for combating optimism bias include more independent scrutiny, greater use of evidence-based data and accountability mechanisms across the whole project life cycle (Jenner, 2009).

It is not about measurement for the sake of measuring, but about measuring the impact of the change so that adjustments can be made in order for change to be successfully implemented and sustained.

Risk management

A key factor in realizing benefits is the effective management of risks. A risk is the probability of an event or issue being realized that may lead to an undesirable effect on an intervention (Frame, 2003). The key elements of *risk management* are the planning, monitoring and controlling of actions that will address the threats and problems identified so as to improve the likelihood of the risks not occurring. Risks need to be identified and mitigated during the consultancy cycle.

Identifying risks in a way that will add value and help to manage the transformation better is not easy. Much of what will happen during a transformation is uncertain anyway, so when do uncertainties become risks? One way to address this question is to review each task that is part of the implementation schedule, looking for elements of uncertainty, such as the use of new technology or a lack of suitably experienced people. If any uncertainties do not have serious constraints then they do not need to be flagged as a risk; for instance, if an organization currently lacks employees with specific skills that are easy to recruit then this is not a risk.

Once the risks have been identified, an assessment has to be made of whether the probability of the risk occurring is high, medium or low (Hopkin, 2014) and the decision then needs to be made as to how to manage the risk and whether it should be avoided, transferred or mitigated. The most appropriate response will be dependent on the likelihood and probability of the risk occurring and its severity, as well as the cost of minimizing the impact of the risk should it occur and the availability of resources to avoid, transfer, mitigate or accept the risk. These actions have to be tracked through a risk register and the status of the risk and actions agreed and regularly updated, since events (internal or external) can occur that might reduce or increase the impact and probability of the risk. Proactive risk management will reduce not only the likelihood of an event occurring, but also the magnitude of its impact on the success of the change.

Feedback

Tailored feedback mechanisms facilitate the monitoring and control of change (Nadler, 1993) and can also help to sustain change. Feedback provides information not only on what people are thinking and therefore doing but also on why. Knowing the 'why' enables consultants and clients to engage with the issues of those involved in change and to identify which behaviours and actions need to be stopped or changed – either because the behaviours are representative of the past or because they are new but creating unhelpful interpretations of the change – and which behaviours and actions need to be encouraged because they are fostering positive interpretations of the change (Balogun, 2006).

Consultants can help to obtain this kind of feedback by designing feedback mechanisms, such as focus groups or surveys (see Chapter 4 for a discussion about methods for data gathering). Once the feedback has been gathered it needs to be analysed and then shared with participants and other stakeholders who should be encouraged to discuss the feedback in order to provide an opportunity for them to raise any issues, queries or ideas and to help them to agree on commitment to agreed actions (Appelbaum and Steed, 2005). In this way feedback can help to stimulate dialogue about what is working and what needs to be improved. It can also help to identify any required modifications to the change intervention or the way it is being implemented.

Performance management

Managing performance and rewarding individuals for their performance in change initiatives are important requirements for sustaining change. Performance management systems, which are aligned with change, help to reinforce the concept that individuals are responsible for implementing and embedding change (Sackman *et al*, 2009). When change initiatives become part of individuals' personal objectives, they remain the focus of their attention rather than getting lost in their daily operational tasks. Recognition of behaviour that is consistent with the desired change will reinforce the behaviour of individuals concerned and send signals to others about what is expected (Burke and Noumair, 2015). The appropriate use of performance objectives and a performance-based reward system can therefore be effective instruments for reviewing and evaluating the progress of the implementation and sustainability of change.

In conclusion, failure to measure and review the way a change is being implemented and managed can affect the achievement of the benefits.

It can also undermine staff commitment to the organization, cause reputational damage and tie up resources in managing unintended consequences. As a result it can ultimately adversely affect the impact and sustainability of organizational change.

In the following case study Dinah Bennett OBE, Founder and Director of International Consultants for Entrepreneurship and Enterprise (ICE) Ltd, shares her experience of how to implement and sustain change in order to ensure that it achieves a positive impact.

CASE STUDY

Creating a positive impact with organizational development and change consultancy

Introduction

A consultancy project in which I have been engaged with a large international financial services institution provides a useful basis for demonstrating how to create a positive impact with organizational development and change consultancy. The client institution had recognized the need to develop its ability to capitalize on an existing market sector (namely small and medium sized businesses), which presented significant growth potential. The institution could increase its market share, through increasing focus on the sector but, just as importantly, by seeking to broaden and intensify support offered to its existing customers in this sector; this in turn would improve customer satisfaction and retention, and also develop new customers for other parts of the institution.

Unearthing areas for development

On commencement of the project we had the option of focusing on customer service development – to respond to the obvious need that had been identified by the client. Adding new experience and knowledge into an organization to support the process of driving forward organizational development and change is an obvious benefit associated with commissioning consultancy services. However, as a practising consultant I have recognized that uncovering the ulterior, and sometimes unconscious, goals of the client is as important as reading those written in the brief.

To achieve the client's desired end-point, the consultant may need to play the role of: disrupter, to unhinge the status quo to allow for the desired change to take place; apolitical ambassador, to cut through prevailing intra-organizational contingents; and independent 'voice of reason' who has no direct stake in the organization. Discovering covert goals at the outset paves the way to a significantly improved result – for both parties – and ensures that the organizational methods to be deployed are designed accordingly.

Added to this, the symptom that the client has identified as the target for change is invariably derived from a combination of people, communication and process. In this case, the institution had not been sufficiently clear in communicating its goals and priorities, therefore the people were unable to respond. Furthermore, the processes and systems in place were working against the people achieving the required goal. These key findings were unearthed not by plunging into tackling the institution's perceived problem, but by reviewing the full picture from which the symptoms had emerged, so all aspects could be tackled in a holistic fashion.

A positive response from our client gave us permission to undertake a far-reaching, deep analysis in advance of the project development process, to ensure that whatever solutions were designed, they would genuinely achieve the outcome required. The objective of the analysis was to thoroughly understand the service being delivered to customers, but also to understand the institutional context in which the service was being delivered.

First a 'mystery shopping' approach was adopted. This was completed in advance of any intra-organizational meetings, to provide an objective, 'bird's eye' view of the customer experience, but also to ensure that consultants were not recognized. The observations from the mystery shopping exercise proved to be extremely valuable throughout the project, providing case study examples of both good and poor practice. However, importantly, individuals were not identified at any stage, as it was recognized that this could potentially disrupt the organizational development programme.

Discussions were then undertaken with staff and managers across all departments, including, amongst others, those working in the particular area of focus for the development project. This provided a clear view of the perception of the service by those in a delivery role, but importantly also provided a valuable insight into the institutional culture associated with both the niche customer sector and the service being delivered to it.

Finally, discussions with existing customers provided first-hand feedback, and as customers were selected by the consultancy team, this allowed for the emergence of multiple perspectives, avoiding an exclusive focus on those the institution considered to be its 'happy customers'.

Avoiding a 'whitewash'

Through evaluating the findings of the service review it became clear that, to support the institution to improve customer loyalty and profitability, a realignment of values, people and process would be required. The project reach would therefore be significantly wider and deeper than the institution had originally intended. This can present a significant challenge for any consultant – diverting the focus of the change project from the symptoms to the cause, and often, in practice, this means putting the spotlight on the institution's own leadership, communication and processes as the root cause of the manifestations that have led to the desire for change.

Being perceived to be 'biting the hand that feeds you' can obviously present a threat; however, I have found that it is an essential component of the consultancy process, in order to avoid ultimate service delivery becoming nothing more than a 'whitewash', and therefore ultimately pointless. Through building a robust, trust-based relationship between consultant and client from the outset, and being clear that any review process will be all-encompassing and may throw up surprises, some of which may be uncomfortable to the client or institution, the risks associated with being honest can be mitigated. In the case I have described, on presentation of the findings of our analysis the client fully embraced the need for change at all levels of the organization. The multifaceted evidence we provided to support our conclusions undoubtedly helped in this regard. Another point of learning was that the accurate presentation of facts assures objectivity.

Supporting the implementation process beyond the exit

Organizational development can only ever be acknowledged as having been effectively achieved when the desired change is wholly embedded and sustained long after the departure of the consultants. I have found that this can only be achieved through engaging people in delivering and owning the required development, and recognizing that the resistors to change within an organization are often even more critical to its ultimate attainment than the converts.

A key factor in embedding our example client case was to ensure that people were motivated to adopt new behaviours and attitudes because this would lead to fulfilment of their personal priorities, avoiding a linear focus on the higher organizational goals. Importantly, career advancement, job security and recognition and rewards had been recognized as critical, and were therefore clearly incorporated into the value and process elements of the change plan.

Another important element of successful implementation of the recommendations of our review involved enabling 'learning by doing' as a priority over classroom-based training. This extended the learning period and new knowledge and skills were embedded incrementally, leading to a significantly more robust development in the longer term.

The greatest risk identified by our client was the potential for progress to be undone following the conclusion of the 'formal' change programme at the departure of the consultancy panel. By introducing consultants the institution was indicating that they did not have the internal capacity and/or capability to drive the desired change, so it was clear that we needed to build both of these as a legacy of the change programme to avoid the long-term impact being lost. By ensuring new processes were embedded early in the change process: we were able to confirm that these effectively supported (and in some cases required) the desired change in practice; we identified and put in place internal change leaders to continue the momentum; and we documented all learning through the project to ensure that this would be embedded in all future induction and training to avoid dilution over time.

My experience has led me to understand that substantive change can rarely happen without a shift in culture – beliefs, attitudes and behaviours – and it has become clear through my work that culture change can only be possible when values, people and process are realigned. To achieve this through the act of delivering consultancy services, building trust and discovering the covert goals of the client early in the relationship is critical to achieving a successful outcome for both parties.

In summary, the points of learning that I would apply to assure organizational development and change consultancy have a sustainable positive impact are:

- Take responsibility for designing the approach, and base this on hard evidence.
- Build trust from the outset, to provide a foundation for open discussion.
- Be prepared to challenge the status quo associated with people, communication, process, values and leadership.
- Build the capacity for sustaining change throughout the project.

Discussion questions for the case

1 What were the key risks of the consultancy outlined in this case and how were they addressed? What might you do differently to avoid such risks?

2 How might you apply the lessons identified in this case to a consultancy you are working on?

What to do when change starts to fail

Change can be a success, a failure, or, in in many cases, a mix of both. For instance, the change initiative may have been delivered on time and within budget, but met only 60 per cent of the required benefits. Many changes will go well and have a positive outcome but some, inevitably, will be negative and fail because change can be complex and involve a 'rich tapestry of intellectual and human engagement' (Wickham and Wickham, 2008: 283). To avoid reaching the transition phase and finding that the change has been a total failure, there are a number of strategies that consultants can consider for turning the situation around as change starts to fail. These are outlined below.

- *Ensure that roles and responsibilities are clear.* Poorly defined roles mean that individuals will lack clarity about what they are responsible for, how their roles interlink with others, or about the authority they have to resolve problems and make decisions. This can lead to confusion and frustration and result in poor performance from key players. So the key roles and responsibilities of everyone involved in the change need to be clear.

- *Review the implementation plan.* The rules of effective project planning apply here. There may well be pressure to take swift action and cut corners to save time and resources, but careful planning and monitoring are essential. Milestones (ie key targets) need to be defined clearly and problems anticipated and acted upon swiftly (Boddy, 2002). For instance, if there is opposition to the change then the consultant will need the ongoing support of the client and other managers to secure engagement and commitment and, if necessary, additional resources to ensure the implementation progresses.

- *Focus on how people are engaging with the change.* Organizational change is an emotive event, as 'change is a process of unfolding and conflicting feelings – before, during and after the event' (Fineman, 2013: 121). Change can create a mix of emotions – simultaneously positive and negative. Part of consultancy for change is being able to acknowledge and understand emotions. In order to understand emotions during change, consultants need to recognize them as complex and evolving. Employees may experience several emotions throughout changes. The emotions that they have experienced during previous changes may impact on their appraisal process of subsequent changes. Consultants need to recognize that one change often follows after another change, or simultaneously, with multiple orchestrated changes occurring at the same time. So individuals are often experiencing sequential and simultaneous changes and the emotions that go with them. It is therefore important to appreciate employees' perspective in relation to change (Hodges, 2016).

- *Be honest with the client when things start to go wrong.* Consultants need to be honest even when the news is bad because it is better for the client to know how things are really going. Any bad news should be balanced, of course, with solutions: 'Here is the problem, and here is how we are going to fix it', otherwise there is a risk that the client will be left with the impression that failure is inevitable.

- *Identify and address the mistakes and avoid blaming others.* Although ultimate accountability for the change resides with the client, the responsibility for it is part of the consultant's role. It is too easy for the consultant to blame the client for the failure of a change, or vice versa. Consultants need to ensure that there is coordination of effort and that everyone shares successes and challenges.

- *Plan for all contingencies.* Possible contingencies have to be identified, should events not go as planned (Turner, 2016). This means planning for what the consequences of the change might be and identifying the likelihood of each consequence occurring (such as very likely, likely, possible, unlikely, or very unlikely). This approach can help to identify and manage the possible consequences of change interventions.

- *Recognize failure.* If change does start to fail and is irretrievable then it is important to take time to learn from the failure and apply the lessons learnt to future change (Cannon and Edmondson, 2005).

Making change sustainable

There is no one right way to sustain change because the success of any approach is to a great extent dependent on its context. What may work in one team or organization is likely to fail in another and vice versa. When change efforts fail or fade over time, employees tend to drift back to their old ways of working and behaving, resulting in a move backwards to 'initiative decay' or 'improvement evaporation' (Doyle *et al*, 2000). This relapse may occur for several reasons:

- The change is often more difficult than expected, requiring more conscious energy, emotion or attention, which can be difficult to maintain as individuals have to change their behaviours and habits and stick with those changes, which 'requires on-going focus, attention, and discipline on their part because of the challenge of maintaining new behaviours in the face of on-going work challenges' (Longenecker and Rieman, 2007: 7). Such challenges, as well as the psychological demands of maintaining conscious attention to the change, can result in the demands of personal, team and organizational change being too much to maintain (Hodges and Gill, 2015).

- Individuals might lack the skills and knowledge to adapt to the new way of working and require training and development, which may take weeks or months to acquire. As a result, 'without the patience to push through the natural and awkward phases of trial and error and the inevitable initial mistakes, many organizational members may claim that the change has failed and return to the old way' (Anderson, 2012: 311). So without the required capabilities to embed the change, individuals may resort to previous ways of working and behaving that they are more comfortable with using.

- The existing culture may be too entrenched to shift and consequently prevent employees from fully adopting the change (Bate, 2012). For instance, a manager who receives coaching to become more assertive in her style of management might be pushed back into old habits when she receives feedback about being too confrontational; or the escalation of complaints may force the customer services department to continue to produce customized reports that were supposed to be eliminated with the installation of a new CRM system. Cultural forces and established ways of working can therefore present intractable barriers to change.

To prevent the benefits of change from being lost and new practices and behaviours being abandoned, change must cease being something separate from normal business practices, and become 'baked in the organization' (Nadler, 1988). That is, it becomes an integral part of business as usual and is no longer labelled as change. Unless this happens, and the change seeps into the bloodstream of the life of the organization, then the change may prove to be just a passing fad that reaps no benefits. So attention needs to be given to sustaining change for as long as it is beneficial to do so; this caveat is important because there may be circumstances where it may not be beneficial to continue to maintain a change (Hodges and Gill, 2015). For example, sustaining change can be counterproductive when: changes in the external environment render recently implemented working practices obsolete; or maintaining recently implemented practices impedes further and more significant developments; or the change has produced unanticipated negative consequences (Buchanan *et al*, 2005).

Client and consultant influences on sustaining change

Sustaining change starts with the intentions and actions of individuals who can influence the sustainability of change through a number of activities that I have outlined in my book *Sustaining Change in Organizations* (Hodges and Gill, 2015) and revised for clients and consultants below.

Influences from clients

Clients can influence the sustainability of change by:

- recognizing the need for change, as well as the what, how and when of change;
- ensuring that the purpose and vision for change are clear for everyone;
- ensuring that there is a readiness for change;
- gaining engagement and commitment from people;
- maintaining commitment until the change becomes business as usual;
- not declaring victory too soon – give change time to become embedded;
- encouraging learning, reflection and development throughout the change;
- gaining the commitment of key internal and external stakeholders;
- engaging HR to ensure that people have the support to transition success-fully through the transformation;
- gaining input from stakeholders into decisions about change;
- appreciating the impact of decisions and the consequences of the actions of people involved in the change;
- being a champion who supports the transformation throughout its journey;
- maintaining the sponsorship and profile of the transformation;
- engaging in dialogue across the organization about the change and encouraging others to share creative ideas.

Influences from consultants

Consultants can play a key part in sustaining change by:

- fostering support, trust and participation among employees;
- encouraging dialogue across teams, groups and the organization;
- identifying whether or not there is readiness for change;
- involving employees in the diagnostic and intervention phases;
- managing the benefits and risks of the implementation;
- managing the timing, sequence and pace of change;
- working with HR to provide support to address the stress, anxiety and uncertainty that change may cause;
- being highly proactive and constantly reminding all involved about the aims of the change and what steps should be taken next to keep the change progressing;

- identifying training and development to build capability for change across the organization;

- raising any concerns and issues that may impact on the success of the change.

The most successful organizations will, according to Edward Lawler and Christopher Worley, learn not only how to master these practices but how to use them in shaping future transformations, which means 'creating an organization that encourages experimentation, learns about new practices and technologies, monitors the environment, assesses performance, and is committed to continuously improving performance' (2006: 21).

The key for consultants and clients is to maintain commitment and energy themselves and also from other key stakeholders. In the following case study Colin Campbell, Senior CRM Consultant at cDecisions, shares the importance of involving people in change and maintaining their engagement throughout the process.

CASE STUDY

Consultancy facilitated change in the private education sector

This case study describes a consultancy engagement with an organization seeking to drive significant change in how it manages its relationship with its customers. The consulting methodologies used are described and the case is evaluated with an appraisal of the key success factors, what did not work, and where the consultancy approach added value and contributed to the success of the change initiative.

The subject organization was a private higher education college in the UK education sector delivering a range of programmes to students, including formal degrees in affiliation with the University of London. The organization's business model was principally orientated around selling courses to students, with repeat sales for a minority of individuals who wished to go on to higher educational qualifications.

However, mandatory changes in reporting requirements to a specific governmental Higher Education Agency required a deeper understanding of student background and formal tracking of students through the course life cycle of enrolment through to graduation. This meant that the organization had to make significant changes in how it processed its student intake and how it maintained its student database as students progressed from enrolment through to graduation. As a consequence of this mandated change programme the organization was also presented with opportunities to deliver additional services, such as an enhanced alumni programme with services such as a job board to promote re-engagement with past students and the organization, with the prospect for additional revenue opportunities.

The organization's student management IT systems had no provision for managing these additional requirements. Salesforce, a cloud-based CRM system, was being used to manage sales of courses and subsequent enrolment of students and, once they were enrolled, a number of other disparate systems were used for managing day-to-day activities of the students, such as timetabling and course management.

As a result, the organization came to the conclusion that in order to facilitate the changes required they had to start by extending their CRM system to manage and track student progress from enrolment to graduation and beyond. The CRM consultancy company I worked for at the time, Xenogenix, was approached to propose a solution for delivering this change and, after an initial fact-finding meeting and the presentation from us of a brief proposal, we were awarded the consultancy assignment.

The consultancy engagement was structured into three phases: diagnosis; visioning; and implementation. The intention of each of these phases is to open up the conversation between client and consultant using suitable consulting tools, where the consultant can listen and learn about the client's business, and then narrow down the conversation to arrive at conclusions leading into the next step.

Diagnosis

The diagnosis phase in this engagement was principally structured around a business process mapping exercise using the software tool Tibco Nimbus to map the relevant areas of the organization in terms of the processes they currently performed and the business areas involved in each process. The diagnosis phase took place over four days and involved detailed discussion with representatives of all the business functions covering the student life cycle from sales and marketing of the courses, enrolment and course progression, to graduation and alumni. Client roles included the heads of sales, marketing, administration and finance to ensure that all relevant questions could be answered and a complete map of the organization developed.

Visioning

Following the diagnosis phase and the completion of a detailed process map, the visioning phase took place, which was the consultant's opportunity to present recommendations for addressing the issues uncovered and how the required goals could be achieved. This resulted in a detailed proposal that documented:

- a revised data model and system architecture to meet the new requirements of the business;
- recommended process changes and additional technical components for solving the issues uncovered in the diagnosis;
- timescales and costs;
- a detailed plan for implementation and delivery.

All of the above effectively form the ingredients for success and the role of the consultant at this stage was to demonstrate how these ingredients would solve the client's fundamental problems and provide a platform for enabling the successful change programme.

The areas of emphasis in this assignment were:

1 The proposed system built on the current use of the sales force CRM system with the necessary redesign to accommodate the new requirements. This was important because it meant that the client was minimizing risks involved. They were not expected to start afresh but instead build on what they currently had.

2 Based on the understanding of the current processes built up through the detailed enterprise map, areas were identified for significant performance improvement through the use of technology such as digital signing for student enrolment forms for faster processing and a reduction in the time by the enrolment team in chasing for the return of forms.

3 Presenting a delivery plan with a phased approach so that the client could see steady progress towards the objectives. In this case the plan detailed how changes would begin with the sales and enrolment department, followed by the new administration facilities in line with the start of the next academic year, and finally the complete Higher Education Agency reporting enhancements to meet their deadlines.

Implementation

Implementation of the solution followed the visioning process. The key element to highlight here is that this was based on an Agile process with repeated cycles of delivery in conjunction with customer feedback. Agile recognizes that traditional up-front planning methods through project management techniques such as Waterfall are problematic because ultimately people do not understand what they will get until they see it. The principles of Agile therefore encompass a series of planned deliverables with continual feedback from stakeholders and realignment of the implementation objectives based on this.

In this fashion the following components were delivered:

- a redesign and rebuild of the CRM system to deliver an enhanced sales system and process that allowed for creation of a lifetime student record and effective handover of the student relationship to administration upon enrolment;
- a system for managing student progressions from enrolment to graduation and beyond;
- training and handover to the sales team and administration;
- updated reporting capabilities to meet the Higher Education Agency requirements.

Through the Agile process continual reprioritization and review of timescales and budgets led to reducing scope in the planned support for alumni facilities and financial integration. Both these areas did not significantly impact the delivery of the core components to solve the immediate fundamental issues and facilitate a successful change initiative.

Conclusion

The above engagement process took place over a time period of four months. The phased approach taken allowed for an initial deliverable to the sales team for live use with the current student cohort intake as a test-bed for the changes undertaken. This was followed by additional work to introduce administration to the system and formally complete the new Higher Education Agency reporting requirements in line with their timescale deadlines.

In terms of the key objectives of enabling the organization to have a better understanding of its student customers and create a platform for delivering on the external reporting requirements, it was declared a success. In a follow-up customer survey from our consultancy the key client sponsor rated the consultant 10 out of 10 across the following categories:

- the consultant's skill set;
- initial project scoping for price and deliverables timelines;
- initial expectation setting for customer participation;
- communication between consultant and customer;
- adherence with project timeline;
- value of project delivery;
- the process for documentation, training and hand off.

In reviewing the project, the key factors that stand out as major contributors to the success of the change programme were:

- a sense of urgency imposed by the external Higher Education Agency deadline;
- bringing together the appropriate and relevant stakeholders across the business – sales, administration, finance and alumni;
- a clear vision on the objective – student management from intake to alumni and meeting the external commitments;
- An Agile approach that delivered short-term wins and refined the solution throughout the change process.

Something that became apparent during the project as not working so well was the overemphasis on some proposed technical components that were not fully necessary for delivery of the successful change programme. For example, the document digital signing technology was initially envisaged as being introduced across all student correspondence through the education programme. It was quickly realized that this was a difficult undertaking with limited value. When technology is concerned, it is easy to lose sight of the objectives.

A key learning point from my perspective was the reliance on the people aspects of the change programme. Despite being a technology-driven deliverable, the fundamental consulting processes of diagnosis was heavily reliant on the buy-in from the range of business functions involved, and the continual contribution from those individuals as the project progressed through the implementation phases. From my point of view, this was a learning point which led to making this a focal point on further engagements – the emphasis that ultimate success of a change programme is not a black box deliverable but requires significant people input

The ongoing consulting relationship

The maxim for any consulting work is that the consultant closes the engagement, but never closes the relationship, unless of course things go terribly wrong. The value of the consultant maintaining the relationship with the client can manifest in future projects, referrals to other clients, and an increase in credibility, reputation and consulting capability (Weiss, 2003).

Consultancy firms recognize that their most profitable business comes from their relationships with existing clients. This is because the cost of sales is lower for existing clients than for new clients, as less input is required to achieve a sale (Wickham and Wickham, 2008). This only works, however, when the client is satisfied with the work done by the consultant. This means asking for regular feedback from the client about what the consultant needs to stop, start and continue doing and then taking time to rectify any issues so that the client is more open to considering working with the consultant again.

Repeat business is not just something that external consultants should aspire to achieve but also something that internal consultants should aim for, as this can help to build their credibility and reputation across the organization. They need to have the courage to build on the engagement in order to continue to build a partnership with the client. So, rather than the transition phase being a time for the consultant to say 'goodbye', it is a chance for the consultant and client to reflect on their relationship and jointly decide if they want to move towards a longer-term partnership.

Visibility

Maintaining *visibility* is often undervalued or ignored by many consultants, especially internal ones, but unless visibility is attended to it is almost impossible for the consultant to begin to attract repeat business or the kind of work to which they aspire. If the client does not see the consultant other than solely through their perception of the consultant's current assignment then they are unlikely to risk offering an assignment of a different kind. For this reason consultants should make sure that the transition phase is complete and that the client is clear and able to articulate both task benefits (what got done) and process benefits (the way it was done). To help achieve this the consultant needs to capitalize on the benefits in various ways: such as raising awareness of them with relevant managers, peers and so on; encouraging the client to publicize them to his/her colleagues; using the company intranet site/newsletter to publicize them; and referring to them when talking to potential or actual clients about future assignments.

Maintaining visibility once the engagement is complete can be done in various ways such as:

- Arranging regular follow-up or audit meetings. Agreeing to meet with the client regularly to review progress provides an opportunity to keep in touch with how the change is being sustained and to discuss potential opportunities for other work.

- Sharing good practice. The transformation (if successful) could be written up as a case study, with, of course, the client's permission and even involvement, and shared across the organization. Taking into account confidentiality issues, the good practice from the change project could also be shared with other companies.

- Responding to the client's personal interests. To get to know clients better, consultants should find out what the client's interests are outside work, such as sport, culture or hobbies, and provide support and appropriate information that will be of interest to the client in these areas, such as inviting the client to local events.

- Sending the client business information that they will find of interest. To keep on the client's radar, send them research reports, articles, links to websites, blogs and so on. This can also provide an excuse to arrange to meet for at catch-up to exchange ideas.

- Inviting clients to participate in external committees or boards. Identifying a mutually beneficial external opportunity in which to involve the client, such as a committee or board, will help to continue the relationship and help the client in terms of their professional reputation and credibility.

Visibility is just as vital for internal as well as external consultants.

Summary

Transition from an engagement is as important as the initial contact with a client. The transition phase has to be carefully planned and considered rather than the engagement being just left to fade away. To help move towards effective transition, the progress of the change should be measured as it is happening, as this enables amendments to be made to help realize benefits and also provides feedback on how people feel about the change whilst it is still being implemented.

Monitoring the progress of change needs to be ongoing and frequent, because things rarely progress exactly as planned, and even when plans are implemented as intended there are often unanticipated consequences. Indeed, change is often more like a series of loops rather than a straight line (Burke, 2008). There is often a need to backtrack and fix things to keep the change on track. Asking for, and addressing, feedback is essential if consultants are to monitor whether or not the change is working. Yet consultants often fail to deliberately seek out feedback, and only realize that change is failing or producing unintended consequences when something unplanned happens to draw their attention to it. Too often, the discomfort of establishing a robust series of meaningful objectives and benefits is avoided and this can result in consultants having to deal with the agony of a stalled transformation initiative. So it is important to monitor and review change in order to identify areas that need to be adjusted and adapted to ensure that the change is effectively implemented and achieves the intended benefits. This is more likely to lead to repeat business from clients.

Transition also involves letting go of the current client–consultant engagement. This can be a challenge for both parties, as mutual dependency is usually built into the relationship. The mutuality can be powerful and become very seductive, which requires strong boundaries and ongoing self-awareness and reflection, especially on the part of the consultant. The challenge for consultants is to ensure that they have the capabilities for successfully achieving transition.

Implications for consultants

There are several practical implications for practising and aspiring consultants that arise from the issues discussed in this chapter.

- *Confirm that there is clarity about the aim and outcome of the change intervention.*
  To ensure that the intervention starts with a clear intention of what will be improved consider the following:
  - What links are there between the change and the organization's vision, purpose, values and strategic plan?
  - How clear are the strengths, weaknesses, opportunities and threats and how will the intervention influence them?
  - How will the outcomes and benefits be measured?
  - Which changes will have the greatest impact with the least risk?
  - How much change is too much?
  - How realistic are the timescales?

- *Hand over ownership.*
  The transition phase is a critical step in the consultancy cycle but one that is often neglected. Consultants need to ensure that they hand over ownership of the transformation to the client in a predefined way that

ensures that all unnecessary levels of dependency have gone from both sides of the client–consultant relationship. This involves ensuring that business benefits, KPIs and outstanding actions have clear owners and are integrated into performance objectives.

- *Identify change champions.*
  Consultants need to lay the groundwork for their disengagement well before the transition phase occurs. This can be done by preparing the client in advance, and stipulating expectations and transition timelines during the contracting phase. It can also be achieved by having a change champion, or group of champions, on site to monitor the change and who are enabled to take decisive action to make any adjustments, as necessary.

- *Evaluate, evaluate, evaluate.*
  Evaluation is not a one-time-only task, but rather an ongoing activity that should be conducted regularly through the consultancy for change cycle. Success in evaluation requires specific, measurable, achievable, realistic and time-bound (SMART) objectives that translate into benefits. It also requires time to reflect, for as the Buddhist teachings say: 'better [than] a hundred years lived in ignorance without contemplation is one single day of life lived in wisdom and deep contemplation' (Mascaro, 1973).

- *Learn from failure.*
  Not all transformations will be successful nor the consultancy experience positive. Consultants should accept the failures as part of the consultancy for change cycle and learn from them and apply the learning to future consultancy assignments.

- *Re-engage.*
  During the transition phase, look for opportunities to re-engage with the client and to identify opportunities for future work.

- *Ensure that the change is sustained.*
  Before exiting from the engagement, consultants need to ensure that the change is embedded into practice and put mechanisms in place to sustain it.

- *Celebrate.*
  Once the formal closure is complete and based on the assumption that the transformation is a success then it is time to celebrate.

References

Aguirre, D and Alpern, M (2014) 10 principles of leading change management, Strategy+Business. [Online] http://www.strategy-business.com/
article/00255?gko=9d35b

Aguirre, D, von Post, R and Alpern, M (2013) Culture's role in enabling organizational change, Strategy &. [Online] http://www.strategyand.pwc.com/reports/
cultures-role-organizational-change

Anderson, D (2012) *Organization Development: The process of leading organizational change*, 2nd edn, Sage, London

Appelbaum, SH and Steed, AJ (2005) The critical success factors in the client–
consulting relationship, *Journal of Management Development*, **24** (1), pp 68–93

Ashurst, C and Hodges, J (2010) Exploring business transformation: The challenges of developing a benefits realization capability, *Journal of Change
Management*, **10** (2), pp 217–37

Balogun, J (2006) Managing change: Steering a course between intended strategies
and unanticipated outcomes, *Long Range Planning*, **39** (1), pp 29–49

Bate, SPP (2012) *Strategies for cultural change*, Routledge, London

Beer, M, Eisenstat, RA and Spector, B (1990) *The Critical Path to Corporate
Renewal*, Harvard Business School Press, Cambridge, MA

Benson, JR (2010) Forgetting to put on new skin, in *Consultation for
Organizational Change*, ed AF Buono and D Jamieson, pp 269–92, Information
Age Publishing, Charlotte, NC

Boddy, D (2002) *Managing Projects: Building and leading the team*, FT/Prentice
Hall, London

Bradley G (2010) *Benefit Realisation Management*, 2nd edn, Gower, Farnham

Buchanan, D, Fitzgerald, L, Ketley, D, Gollop, R, Jones, J, Lamont, S, Neath, A and
Whitby, E (2005) No going back: A review of the literature on sustaining organizational change, *International Journal of Management Reviews*, **7** (3), pp 189–205

Burke, WW (2008) *Organization Change: Theory and practice*, 2nd edn, Sage
Publications, Thousand Oaks, CA

Burke, WW and Noumair, DA (2015) *Organization Development: A process of
learning and changing*, FT Press, London

Cannon, MD and Edmondson, AC (2005) Failing to learn and learning to fail
(intelligently): How great organizations put failure to work to innovate and
improve, *Long Range Planning*, **38** (3), pp 299–319

Cope, M (2010) *The Seven Cs of Consulting*, FT/Prentice Hall, London

Darling, M, Parry, C and Moore, J (2005) Learning in the thick of it, *Harvard
Business Review*, **83** (7), p 84

Doyle, M, Claydon, T and Buchanan, D (2000) Mixed results, lousy process:
The management experience of organizational change, *British Journal of
Management*, **11** (s1), pp S59–S80

Farjoun, M (2002) Towards an organic perspective on strategy, *Strategic Management Journal*, **23**, 561–94

Fineman, S (2013) *Emotions at Work*, Sage, London

Frame, JD (2003) *Managing Risk in Organizations: A guide for managers*, Wiley and Sons, London

Hayes, J (2014) *The Theory and Practice of Change Management*, 4th edn, Palgrave Macmillan, Basingstoke

Hodges, J (2016) *Managing and Leading People Through Change*, Kogan Page, London

Hodges, J and Gill, R (2015) *Sustaining Change in Organizations*, Sage, London

Hopkin, P (2014) *Fundamentals of Risk Management: Understanding, evaluating and implementing effective risk management*, Kogan Page, London

Jenner, S (2009) *Realising Benefits from Government ICT Investment: A fool's errand?* Academic Publishing, Reading

Koster, E, Bouman, W and Foods, FCD (1998) *The Balanced Change Card: A framework for designing and assessing organizational change processes*, Universiteit van Amsterdam, Department of Information Management

Lawler, EE and Worley, CG (2006) Designing organizations that are built to change, *MIT Sloan Management Review*, **48** (1), pp 19

Longenecker, CO and Rieman, ML (2007) Making organizational change stick: Leadership reality checks, *Development and Learning in Organizations: An international journal*, **21** (5), pp 7–10.

Mascaro, J (1973) *The Dhammapada*, Vol. 284, Penguin, London

Moorhouse Consulting (2009) *The Benefits of Organisational Change*, Moorhouse, London

Nadler, DA (1988) Concepts for the management of organisational change, in *Readings in the Management of Innovation*, 7th edn, ed ML Tushman and WL Moore, pp 718–32, Ballinger, New York

Nadler, DA (1993) *Feedback and Organizational Development: Using data based methods*, Addison-Wesley, Reading, MA

Nagle, TT and Holden, RK (1995) *The Strategy and Tactics of Pricing*, Prentice Hall, London

O'Shea, J and Madigan, C (1997) *Dangerous Company*, Nicholas Brealey, London

Paton, R and McCalman, J (2008) *Change Management: A guide to effective implementation*, 3rd edn, Sage, London

Rothwell, W and Sullivan, R (eds) (2005) *Practicing Organization Development: A guide for consultants*, Vol. 27, John Wiley and Sons, London

Sackmann, SA, Eggenhofer, P and Friesl, M (2009) Sustainable change: Long-term efforts toward developing a learning organization, *Journal of Applied Behavioral Science*, **45** (4), pp 521–49

Turner, R (2016) *Gower Handbook of Project Management*, Routledge, London

Van Eron, A and Burke, WW (1995) Separation, in *Practicing Organization Development: A guide for consultants*, W Rothwell, R Sullivan and G McLean, pp 395–418, Pfeiffer, San Diego

Weisbord, M (2012) 'The organization development contract', in *Handbook for Strategic HR: Best practices in organization development from the OD Network*, ed J Vogelsang, M Townsend, M Minahan, D Jamieson, J Vogel, A Viets, C Royal and L Valek, pp 53–60, AMACOM, New York

Weiss, A (2003) *Organizational Consulting: How to be an effective internal change agent*, Wiley and Sons, London

Wickham, P and Wickham, L (2008) *Management Consulting: Delivering an effective project*, 3rd edn, Prentice Hall, London

PART THREE
Consultancy capabilities

Building capabilities for consulting

07

KEY POINTS

- Capabilities comprise skills, knowledge, attitudes and experience, and provide consultants with the ability to engage more confidently with clients and to address the challenges and complexities of change.
- To effectively build capabilities means being able to identify the capability gaps, designing and delivering development interventions, and sustaining and monitoring how the learning is being applied.
- The most relevant capabilities required for consultancy for change are: building and maintaining relationships; managing emotions; being self-aware; gaining commitment and engagement; facilitating creative dialogue; being resilient; tolerance for ambiguity and uncertainty; being politically astute and managing power dynamics; and being an effective communicator.
- To build capabilities requires learning and development that provide consultants with the knowledge, ability and skills necessary to adapt to new and different ways of working and to reinforce the required behaviour in order to work more confidently with clients.

Introduction

To take an organization on a change journey is challenging, invigorating and deeply rewarding and will affect consultants in numerous ways. As Jennifer Todd says a consultant will 'experience the real pain of generations and cries for relief from thousands of people who have worked in difficult, even impossible, situations. [They] will also have the honor of seeing the heart and soul of [the] organization emerge as the true desires, creativity, power and passion of people gets unleashed' (quoted in Scherer *et al*, 2010: 69–70).

To cope with this and be able to implement and sustain change successfully requires consultants to possess what Nada Kakabadse and colleagues (2006) refer to as a sort of 'gift' specific to the consulting industry – a 'natural consulting skill'. It is like being a musician; most people can play badly but it is the people who are good who can become excellent. To become excellent requires not just skill but specific capabilities.

Capabilities comprise skills, knowledge, attitudes and experience (Hodges, 2016) and provide consultants with the ability to engage more confidently with clients and to address the challenges and complexities of change. In contrast, a lack of capabilities can impact negatively on organizational change. This is highlighted in a survey conducted by the Katzenbach Centre which suggests that the biggest obstacle to change was a lack of capabilities needed to make change last (Aguirre and Alpern, 2014). Similarly, the Barometer on Change survey carried out by Moorhouse Consulting (2014) shows that accessing the skills, experience and knowledge needed to deliver change is a growing concern amongst business leaders and that the percentage of organizations who are confident that they will be able to access these skills has dropped from almost half (47 per cent) to around a third (35 per cent). The need to have relevant capabilities for change is a significant enabler for ensuring the success of organizational change.

The aim of this chapter is to examine capabilities for consultancy for change. The chapter begins by providing insight into the capabilities that consultants need to be effective in organizational change, which include: building and maintaining relationships (including developing and sustaining trust); managing emotions; being self-aware; gaining commitment and engagement; facilitating creative conversations; being resilient; demonstrating a tolerance for ambiguity and uncertainty; political astuteness; managing the power dynamics; and being an effective communicator (listening, questioning and summarizing). Dr Katie Best outlines in her case study the key capabilities required to influence the client and build a partnership with them. This chapter goes on to look at how these capabilities can be built and the resulting ramifications for training and development.

Learning outcomes

By the end of this chapter you will be able to:

- appreciate the importance of the capabilities required for consultancy for change;
- identify relevant capabilities for effective consulting;
- build and maintain relationships with clients using appropriate skills;
- develop the appropriate capabilities required throughout the consultancy for change cycle.

Individual capabilities for consultancy

There have been many attempts to define the capabilities that a consultant needs in order to be considered fully competent. Some of these efforts have been conducted by individual researchers, some have been sponsored by professional associations, and others are part of executive education or university postgraduate programmes, such as an MBA. For example, the Institute of Management Consultancy highlights the key core capabilities that are essential for delivering management consultancy as: client focus; building and sustaining relationships; applying expertise and knowledge; and achieving sustainable results. The Institute of Business Consulting also has its own capability model that determines training and development requirements against a matrix covering three levels, which are termed: development; independence; and mastery. This matrix provides recognition of the skills required for moving up through the levels. Similarly, large consultancy practices often have their own capability requirements allied to career progression, which typically range across levels such as junior consultant, consultant, principal consultant up to partner level.

Research has also identified various consultancy capabilities. Roffey Park's Management Agenda survey (McCartney and Holbeche, 2004) highlights the core skills required by a consultant as: facilitating and understanding the nature of change; relationship building; and active listening skills. Other research has identified significant larger numbers of capabilities. Leon de Caluwé and Elsbeth Reitsma (2010) list ten capability categories, or domains as they refer to them, which are: enterprising, showing resilience, organizing, performing, analysing, considering, facilitating, influencing, managing, and inspiring confidence. Sullivan and Sullivan (1995) present no fewer than 187 essential capabilities. Donald Anderson (2012) also presents a daunting list, including the subsets of core and advance skills. It is, however, unlikely that any single consultant will be highly skilled in all of the areas outlined in such long lists.

Instead of breadth in a large number of competencies, some researchers suggest the need for deep expertise in a small number of areas (for example, McLean, 2006). Kenton and Moody (2003), for example, describe three areas where consultants need to be skilled: personal and interpersonal effectiveness; working as an agent of change; and consulting skills. In a survey of consultants Kakabadse and colleagues (2006) found that the following five skills were necessary to become an efficient consultant: experience; functional skills; ability to listen and question; objectivity; and self-awareness. In order to meet the challenge of consulting, Wickham and Wickham (2008) say that the consultant must develop a skill profile that allows them to call upon abilities in three key areas: an ability to manage the consulting exercise as a formal project; an ability to manage the analytical skills necessary to gain an understanding of the client business and the possibilities it faces; and an ability to communicate ideas and positively influence others. Such expertise in a small number of specific areas enables a consultant to build in-depth capabilities rather than be a 'jack of all trades'.

The majority of research tends to focus on specialized skills required for external consultants. The capabilities identified for internal consulting are often informed by a generic skills base, and adapted from existing management competency frameworks (Kenton and Moody, 2003). This leads to a reduced emphasis on operating as a consultant, with less value accorded to, and therefore time spent in, contracting activities at the beginning and throughout an intervention. This is evident in Alan Weiss's (2003) suggestion that the most important behaviours for internal consultants are: perseverance; high self-esteem; perspective about the work and its impact; willingness to take risks; and innovation. The risk of such lists is that they tend to be generic and ignore consultancy-specific skills.

As with consultancy capabilities, there are also numerous lists of desirable capabilities for change. For example, Ann Gilley and colleagues (2009) suggest that the following broad competencies are associated with the successful implementation of change: the ability to motivate employees; the ability to communicate effectively; and team building. Using a case study in a German tourism company undergoing a major transformation, Stefan Krummaker and Bernd Vogel (2013) investigated change-related capabilities and produced a model that reflects change capability based on readiness for change and ability to change. The former comprise: desire to challenge the status quo; disengagement from routines; change goal orientation; intention to act in change; purposefulness; and willingness to change. The latter comprise: assertiveness; political skill; and timing and shaping of change tasks.

In conclusion, there appear to be different sets of capabilities for consultancy and for change rather than a single approach for both. These different sets of capabilities differ in whether they describe interpersonal skills, behavioural skills or knowledge of content areas needed to be successful. Such lists are useful but some are very long and lack a focus specifically on consultancy for change and the context in which it is taking place.

Context for capabilities

To some extent, the capabilities required will be specific to the context in which the consultant is working and are therefore for them to determine. Context is the situation in which the consultant carries out interventions or in which the transformation takes place. Context has its roots in Lawrence and Lorsch's (1986) contingency thinking, the essence of which is that the best way to organize is specified by the situation. This means that the right way to change in organizations is derived from a cluster of variables that play a dominant role in the situation. De Caluwé and Reitsma (2010) say that the two main variables that play a significant role in establishing the context are: 1) the objectives of the change; and 2) the characteristics of the situation in which the change will take place. These variables create contextual factors, such as appropriateness of change and support for the change. So possessing the capabilities to consult for change within the given context is necessary.

Key capabilities for consulting for change

Trying to identify relevant capabilities for consultancy for change from the vast lists that prevail is a daunting prospect. In an attempt to address this Mark Wilcox and Mark Jenkins (2015) suggest grouping capabilities under the four headings of exploration, envisioning, engagement and execution.

- Exploration – carrying out deep environmental scanning; a diagnosis of the internal and external environment.
- Envisioning – creating a new, or modifying an existing, strategy in response to the opportunities and threats identified during the exploration phase.
- Engagement – engaging people and gaining their commitment to the change.
- Execution – delivering the change.

Such groupings are helpful in that they tend to mirror the key stages of most consultancy approaches. A similar method could be applied in this book, to identify the distinct skills, knowledge and experience required for each of the phases of the consultancy for change cycle. However, taking into account that consultancy for change is a cycle rather than a step-by-step approach then it seems more appropriate to consider the capabilities that run throughout the cycle as these will be required by all consultants, whether internal or external. An attempt has therefore been made to define the most critical capabilities for consultancy for change.

To identify the most relevant capabilities, I conducted a survey with over 1,000 consultants from 20 countries and 25 different organizations, along with over 500 client managers from 30 organizations to help identify the key capabilities. Internal consultants accounted for 45 per cent of respondents and external consultants 55 per cent. The managers were primarily from the private sector (70 per cent), while the majority of consultants responding were OD (40 per cent); HR (20 per cent); IT (15 per cent); operations (15 per cent); and finance (10 per cent). The findings indicated that the most relevant capabilities required for consultancy for change are: building and maintaining relationships; managing emotions; being self-aware; gaining commitment and engagement to change; facilitating creative dialogue; resilience; having a tolerance for ambiguity and uncertainty; political astuteness; managing power dynamics; and being an effective communicator. Each of these is described below.

Building and maintaining relationships

Consultancy is about people and therefore the consultant's role is to first establish a sound relationship with the client and attempt to make them feel 'comfortable with the consultant and the process' (Pellegrinelli, 2002: 353). Jamieson and Armstrong (2010) rightly point out that this foundation is critical to the openness, sharing and honesty that are necessary during organizational change.

The client–consultant relationship has to be built and maintained throughout the consultancy cycle. To understand the evolution of the relationship between consultants and clients, Stumpf and Longman (2000) say that there are different stages in the process of building the relationship. The first one is the development stage, where the aim is to create a 'ready-receiver' (client) who is willing to invest time in a conversation with the consultant about a specific issue that needs to be addressed. The second stage enlarges the scope of the relationship, and through conversations a common interest between the consultant and the client is developed. This common interest allows the consultant to gain the respect of the client and appear credible via a particularly good understanding of the client's industry or company. The third stage consists of identifying the real and relevant needs that will change the client's perception of the consultant. These stages show that it requires a great deal of patience and persistence to develop positive relations with a client.

The need to create a sound relationship is vital. A consultant interviewed by McLachlin said that 'climate is critically important... if you find that your thinking and the client's are not on the same wavelength, don't hang around' (1999: 399). In contrast, Werr and colleagues (1997) say that the consultant and client must be expected to have quite different views of the change process at the beginning of the project. This divergence of opinions forces consultants to learn to deal smoothly with delicate situations. According to Stumpf and Tymon it means that the consultant has to develop the skill of telling clients they are wrong in such a way that they thank the consultant for giving helpful advice, and this means learning 'how to disagree without being disagreeable' (2001: 49). Kubr supports this and says that the key to a successful relationship between consultants and clients depends on the proactive behaviour of the consultant which 'implies that the consultant thinks even of those needs and requirements of which a client has not been aware, and helps the clients to realize all their possibilities, and needs' (1996: 489). To achieve this requires a positive client–consultant relationship that is built on trust.

Developing and sustaining trust

Guanxi is a Chinese term used to describe relationships that may benefit both parties. To develop good guanxi, one must build trust. The relationship between the client and consultant needs to be based on trust. Erin Meyer (2015) describes the importance of developing trust in an example of an acquisitions expert from Nestlé, who found himself in a challenging situation when he was negotiating a joint venture in China. During the initial meetings with the Chinese executives the expert and his team had tried to be friendly and transparent and provide all of the details the Chinese wanted, but found them to be unwilling to negotiate on any of their demands. The expert and his colleagues met with a Chinese consultant to try to find out what they needed to do differently. The consultant told them that their approach was wrong, that they were going too quickly and that they were not going to get what they wanted from the Chinese executives until they developed guanxi with them. The expert took the consultant's advice and invited the Chinese executives out for dinner. During the dinner the two groups were able to socialize with each other and begin to build mutual trust. Consequently, during future business meetings the Chinese were much more willing to cooperate and the teams were able to move forward together as guanxi had started to be built. As seen in this example, the type of culture in which a company operates can impact on how trust needs to be built with them and also the type of trust needed for effective business relations.

Types of trust

There are two basic types of trust: cognitive trust and affective trust (Johnson and Grayson, 2005). *Cognitive trust* is trust from the head and based on the confidence an individual feels in another person's capabilities and credibility. *Affective trust*, on the other hand, comes from the heart and is based on how someone feels about another person. In cultures that are more task-based, such as the US, Denmark, Germany, Australia and the UK, business people are more likely to develop work bonds based largely on cognitive trust, whereas in countries such as China, Brazil, Saudi Arabia and Nigeria trust is relationship-based and is built through developing a personal bond (Meyer, 2015). For consultants from task-based cultures who are working with relationship-based clients the consultants need to put more time and effort into organizing social events, such as meals, with clients and to make time to talk about social rather than work issues, which will help to build personal connections. Consultants from relationship-based societies who are working with task-based clients should not discard socializing altogether but should focus primarily on the business engagement. So consultants need to be cognizant of how country cultures will affect the different types of trust that are important to clients. In the business world of those cultures, however, cognitive and affective trust may not always be so blatantly separate but may be more subtly woven together.

A client's willingness to share information will depend on how much they trust the consultant (Stumpf and Longman, 2000). Mike Cope (2010) has developed the mnemonic TRUST to reinforce this:

- Truthful. The consultant and the client must be truthful to one another. It is easy for the consultant to tell the client what they think the client wants to hear, whereas the truth may be painful. However, being truthful is a prerequisite for a sound business relationship.

- Responsive. The consultant needs to engage totally in the client's world – seeing life from their perspective – and being responsive to the client's needs.

- Uniform. A consultant must be consistent in their ideas and attitudes towards the engagement. If they continually change their mind, the client will become confused and begin to doubt the ability of the consultant to complete the task.

- Safe. Given some of the emotions a client may feel it is important that the client feels safe working with the consultant. This may be done formally through confidentiality agreements or informally through dialogue and reassurance.
- Trained. It may sound obvious, but it is important that the client believes the consultant is competent in the area of expertise that they are being consulted about, which will be based on their work experience and credibility, and if they are external consultants then also on the reputation of the consulting firm for which they work.

The ability of a consultant to build trust and gain the trust of the client is a key factor for building an effective client–consultant relationship.

Managing emotions

The relationship existing between consultants and clients is much more than professional, and involves a psychological dimension that must be taken into account when considering the capabilities required to effectively manage the relationship (Kakabadse *et al*, 2006). Stumpf and Tymon describe the relationship existing between the consultant and the client as an 'emotional duet' in which the consultant, if trying to be effective, has to learn to 'recognise, deal with and respond to the client's emotions' (2001: 49). Lundberg and Young (2001) go as far as to say that consultants who are called in to provide expertise and solutions on pragmatic problems such as change are in fact implicitly called in to provide emotional support. This view is shared by Stapley (1996), who says that organizational transformation is not only about dealing with the change but also about dealing with feelings and emotions of the different members involved in the process. Lundberg and Young take this a step further and say that 'turning emotional distress into positive organizational action, even excitement, after all is what consultants really are all about' (2001: 537). This is important to recognize because the consultant needs to avoid finding themselves in a situation where, although a good piece of consultancy was delivered, the client is disappointed because emotions were not managed carefully.

Emotions are involved in every phase of the consultancy cycle, hence consultants must be able to create a climate where clients feel that they can trust the consultant; however, in order to reach such a stage, the consultant must provide exclusive and sole attention to the client and their objectives and place the client's interest ahead of their own (Shenson, 1990). This involves consultants using emotional intelligence to manage and understand their own emotions and those of the client (Mayer and Salovey,1997). David Maister (2004) provides a list of the common emotions that clients feel when using consultants:

- Insecure. The employment of a consultant to address issues the organization is facing and which the client is unable to deal with may create insecurity for the client.
- Threatened. The client may feel threatened by a consultant who is carrying out a diagnosis into one of their business issues and feel concerned that it will highlight areas of weakness.
- Personal risk. The client may feel that they are losing control by giving a consultant responsibility for looking at their business.
- Impatient. A consultant is often called in as a last resort when there is an urgency for change, so the client may be impatient for something to be done quickly.
- Worried. The client might be worried about what the consultant will discover and whether it will be to the detriment of the client.
- Exposed. External consultants will be able to look at the confidential inner workings of the client organization and this may make the client feel exposed and open to criticism.
- Ignorant. The client may not fully understand what the consultant is proposing and find it hard to articulate this without appearing incompetent.
- Sceptical. Often when clients have had unsatisfactory outcomes with previous consultants, they are naturally wary of others.
- Concerned. Clients will worry that they will get a standard 'off-the-shelf' solution instead of a bespoke one for their business.
- Suspicious. Clients may feel worried that the consultant is selling them solutions that are of no value.

Such emotional responses show that what clients need is someone who understands their concerns, and will put their interests first. Ultimately, they want someone who will be able to develop an emotional depth to their relationship with them.

Collective emotions

There are often situations during organizational transformations when consultants have to deal not just with the emotions of their clients but also with the emotions of large groups and/or teams of people. For example, executives facing the news of an organizational restructure or frontline staff facing redundancy. This need to be cognizant of emotions is evident in the case of Nokia, described by Quy Huy (2015) in an article entitled 'Leaders who can read collective emotions are more effective'. Huy says that one of the reasons Nokia lost the iPhone battle was not only because of its lack of speed and inability to react to changing circumstances but also due to a collective fear among the company's middle managers of losing status and resources within the organization. The latter reason was, however, ignored by the company and as a result this oversight cost Nokia dearly – its precipitous decline in the iPhone business and a loss of about 90 per cent of its market value. As Huy rightly points out, the loss of market value and market share could have been avoided with a better understanding of the collective emotions within the organization.

Being able to understand and appreciate collective and individual emotions can help consultants respond effectively to how people respond to change. So consultants need to be aware of the impact of change on the emotions of individuals, as well as their own emotions, and this requires self-awareness.

Self-awareness

Carved into the stonework above the entrance to the principal examination centre of the University of Edinburgh in Scotland are the Greek words for 'know yourself'. An important capability for a consultant is to know themselves – to be self-aware. Self-awareness requires awareness of one's own strengths, limitations, interests, likes, dislikes, motivational drivers, values, beliefs and attitudes as well as an awareness of how these affect the ways in which an individual perceives and responds to other people. Kakabadse and colleagues (2006) believe that if consultants have not been through in-depth analysis of their own strengths and weaknesses then there is a risk that they will be influenced by the culture of the organization that they are working for and start working on change initiatives that they do not have the experience or skills for, rather than admitting that the client needs someone else's experience.

In order to understand client issues, the consultant must be aware of their own emotions and be able to assess their own strengths and weaknesses. Lundberg and Young say that 'successful consultants need to be in touch with and have ways of dealing with, their own anxiety, their own moods and affective reasons, so as to feel reasonably alert, secure, comfortable and centred to interact with their clients' (2001: 536). This involves self-reflection.

Self-reflection is an important skill for consultants. Being able to 'hold a mirror up' to themselves to reflect on their own emotions and practice – with the organization and the client – helps the consultant to gain balance and grounding in challenging situations (Keep and Ash, 2001). To aid reflection the following questions can be used (Weiss, 2003):

- What, if anything, should I have done differently to improve the final outcome?
- In what areas, if any, did I have to request help that should not have been necessary? (I should have been able to handle it myself.)
- What were my greatest learning points in each of these areas:
  - new skills or new application of existing skills;
  - new knowledge or new application of existing knowledge;
  - new experience;
  - new relationship?
- How specifically will I use the learning in future engagements?
- What weaknesses emerged, if any, that I must correct, and how will I correct them?
- How did I react emotionally and what was the impact on the client and consultancy assignment?
- What resources do I need to include, access or utilize better in the future in order to add to my value?
- How will I manifest these new talents and abilities to existing and potential clients?
- Using what I have learned, how can I more assertively market my talents and ability to help clients?

After reflecting on these questions consultants need to be able to integrate what they have learned into their behaviour. To do so, they must go through three steps from unconscious incompetence to unconscious competence. The first step is to move from unconscious incompetence to conscious incompetence. The second step is to move from conscious incompetence to conscious competence and requires a tremendous amount of attention, practice and persistence. The third step is being able to do something without thinking and hence move from conscious competence to unconscious competence.

So consultants need to be aware of their own abilities and emotions and their strengths and areas for development.

Gaining commitment and engagement

Getting *commitment* to a change is part of the process of engaging people in organizational transformations. John Kotter and Lorne Whitehead (2010) say that anyone who is trying to help an organization to go through a transformation needs to help people not only to understand it but also to engage and be committed to it. Consultants will often talk about this in terms of 'getting buy-in' for change. There is, however, a significant difference between buy-in and true engagement.

Engagement is the intellectual, emotional and spiritual commitment to what one is doing, shown by discretionary attention and effort devoted to it (Hodges and Gill, 2015). The UK's Chartered Institute of Personnel and Development defines employee engagement as 'a combination of commitment to the organisation and its values plus a willingness to help out colleagues (organisational citizenship)... [going] beyond job satisfaction and... not simply motivation' (CIPD, 2009). Clients who are engaged with an organizational change initiative devote discretionary effort to it willingly, even eagerly. If a client or other key stakeholders are not actively involved and ready to change, a consulting engagement is very unlikely to be successful (McLachlin, 1999). This argument is supported by Schein (1997), who says that it is the client who owns the problem and the solution and if during the transformation the client disengages and rejects their responsibilities, then according to Schein the war is over. Engagement and commitment with the change are, therefore, a determinant of successful, sustainable change.

Engagement and commitment need to come primarily from the client but also from stakeholders. For example, frontline employees are the ones responsible for behaving in ways conducive to proposed change and often have to learn new ways of doing things. Commitment to change is therefore an important enabler of change; if employees are not engaged then very little will change. One way to build commitment is for consultants and clients to create an environment in which the people most affected by change have a role in shaping it. Such involvement was carried out by the Indian manufacturer Larsen & Toubro, which managed to include 7,000 employees in defining the purpose for a company-wide organizational change (Meaney *et al*, 2010).

Employees need to understand what will happen and why they need to know what the rationale is for the change. They will then either engage with the change and see its implications for their future, or have a negative perception of it. Involving frontline staff in the diagnosis and joint problem-solving to identify solutions will help to gain commitment at an early stage as people are more likely to react positively if they have been involved in defining the solution rather than if it is imposed on them. Gaining commitment and engagement requires engaging in dialogue with individuals.

Facilitating creative dialogue

Dialogue is a key bolt of the consultancy for change cycle (see Chapter 1 for further discussion on this). Positive and creative conversations can help the client and other stakeholders to articulate what the real issues are and potential ideas/solutions for moving forward to gain commitment and engagement. To achieve this requires the ability, on the part of the consultant, to facilitate creative conversations.

The Mobius Model

An approach for encouraging creative conversations is the Mobius Model, which was developed by William Stockton and colleagues (Ryder-Smith, 1998). The model provides a guide to respond to different viewpoints by moving from a monologue that is based on the speaker's assumption that they know the whole truth and do not need to share it or listen to others, to a creative dialogue where all participants listen for understanding, seek common ground and build commitment for action (Demarest *et al*, 2004). For example, in a monologue a consultant may not fully share their opinion with the client, especially on the points that they think the client does not, or will not, understand or accept; whereas in a dialogue the consultant will be willing to listen, understand the client's perspective and seek mutual understanding. The model maps the six stages of effective dialogue, which are:

1 Mutual understanding. Each person feels understood and understands the other(s).
2 Possibility. This is the common ground that leads to everyone recognizing something new that is desirable and can realistically be created.
3 Commitment. This involves agreement about priorities, objectives and values.
4 Ability. This is a recognition of the shared skills, knowledge and resources to meet commitments.
5 Responsibility. An agreement around who will do what to meet agreed commitments.
6 Acknowledgement. Mutual awareness of what has been accomplished and what is still missing.

- These elements for effective dialogue need to be present for all stake-holders involved in the conversation and none of the elements can be skipped. To get real commitment each member needs to recognize that what they are being asked to commit to is possible, otherwise they may simply comply with what needs to be done without genuinely agreeing with the proposed actions.

Resilience

Resilience is a critical capability for consultants. *Resilience* requires developing an ability to think positively, maintaining perspective, developing a strong network of supportive relationships and taking care of one's mind and body (Wicks, 2015). In an article entitled 'Increase your resilience to change' Audra Proctor (2014), Director and Head of Learning at Changefirst Limited, identifies the characteristics of resilient people as optimistic, self-assured, focused, open to new ideas, willing to ask for support, structured and proactive. These components of resilience all play a vital role in enabling consultants to manage the stressors in a more proactive, adaptive and positive way. Resilient consultants are able to draw on these qualities at the right time and understand when, for example, being proactive is more important than seeking support. Developing resilience takes work and time, but there is evidence that it can boost confidence and ability. According to Judith Proudfoot and colleagues (2009), building resilience can improve sales and reduce turnover among financial advisers.

So, resilience can help to maintain higher performance levels, improve a consultant's sense of well-being and help them cope with fluctuating emotions. It also helps them to deal with different types of clients and organizational transformations within different contexts without being overwhelmed.

Tolerance for ambiguity and uncertainty

Consultants must be able to cope with ambiguity and uncertainty. Ambiguous situations can be defined as completely new situations with no familiar cues or precedents, or apparently insoluble situations that cannot be solved in the usual way. Such ambiguity creates uncertainty and is uncomfortable, and can lead to individuals wanting to quickly resolve issues (Inglis, 2000). The desire to achieve quick solutions may be compounded by a client who questions the capability of the consultant when the consultant responds to the client's 'what's next' questions with 'I don't know' or 'I am not sure where this is going at present' (Ainsworth, 2010). Rather than agreeing to a quick fix, tolerating ambiguity means being able to delve into the root causes of an issue. In such situations and in order to probe deeper and explore potential problems, a tool such as the 5 Whys can be used.

5 Whys technique

The 5 Whys is a technique for uncovering the root cause of a problem. The process starts with identifying a problem and asking 'why' it is occurring. Answers should be grounded in fact and focus on what actually happened and not on what might have happened. The question 'why?' should be repeated (use five as a rule of thumb) until the root cause of a problem is reached and a countermeasure that prevents it recurring has been identified. For example, to find out why patients are always late in arriving at the operating theatre the 5 whys can be used as follows:

Why? There was a long wait for a trolley.

Why? A replacement trolley had to be found.

Why? The original trolley's safety rail was worn and had eventually broken.

Why? It had not been regularly checked for wear.

Why? There is no schedule for repairing trolleys. So the root cause is that there is no equipment maintenance schedule.

The 5 Whys tool can be used on its own or as a part of the Fishbone analysis (see Chapter 4 for a description of the Fishbone tool) which can help to explore all potential or real causes of an issue. Once all inputs are established on the Fishbone, the 5 Whys technique can be used to drill down to the root causes.

Political astuteness

Just providing the right solution is not enough; consultants have to be able to deal with the politics within the client organization. Organizational politics are often described as a turf game involving a competition of ideas (Buchanan and Badham, 2009) which consultants may be forced to play. Kumar and Thibodeaux (1990) acknowledge, and indeed advocate, the use of *political strategies* when planning change. In support of their argument they identify three levels of change: first-level change, which involves improving team or departmental effectiveness; second-level change, which involves introducing new perspectives to organizational subsystems; and third-level change, which concerns organization-wide shifts in values and ways of working. While first-level and second-level changes require political awareness and political facilitation respectively, third-level change entails political intervention. In other words, the more widespread the implications of organizational change, the greater the political involvement required by consultants. This highlights the need for consultants to intervene in the political system of the organization in order to legitimize the rationale for change, particularly when they are faced with opposition to it. Keep and Ash (2001) use a theatrical metaphor to describe the political intervention of consultants who need to decide if they are a 'front-stage' worker or a 'back-stage' worker or whether they feel comfortable working in both worlds. Each area requires different political astuteness; for example, some organizational transformations require a lot of back-stage preparation prior to front-stage activity, while others may require only back-stage working.

Politics are a naturally occurring phenomenon in organizations and are resistant to attempts to stifle or eradicate them. Rather than attempting to do so, the more effective response is for consultants to recognize and address them, when appropriate. Accordingly, there is a need to learn how to read the political context of a change initiative (Lewis and Seibold, 1998), its political manoeuvring and informal social network, in order to bring about the desired outcomes (Salancik and Pfeffer, 1978).

Managing the power dynamics

Power is the energy needed to initiate and sustain action or, to put it another way, the capacity to translate intention into reality (Bennis and Nanus, 1985). The prominent role that power plays in organizational change is evident in Kanter's comment that no new change will occur 'without someone with power pushing it' (1983: 296). Consultants need to know where the power lies when dealing with organizational transformations, which means not only 'positional' (appointed) power but also 'relational' (people) power, since without this knowledge the progress of change can be severely impeded. Consequently it is important to know who has power, how to recognize other people's exercise of power and what power tactics to use.

Power tactics

Consultants can apply *power tactics* to influence others. Robbins and colleagues (2010) have identified nine distinct tactics from the research, which are:

1 Legitimacy. Relying on one's position of authority and stressing that a change is in accordance with organizational policies and rules.

2 Rational persuasion. Presenting logical arguments and factual evidence to demonstrate that a change is reasonable.

3 Inspirational appeals. Developing emotional commitment by appealing to an individual's values, needs, hopes and aspirations.

4 Consultation. Increasing an individual's motivation and support by involving them in deciding how the change will be achieved.

5 Exchange. Rewarding an individual with benefits or favours in exchange for supporting a change.

6 Personal appeal. Asking for compliance based on friendship or loyalty.

7 Ingratiation. Using flattery, praise or friendly behaviour prior to making a change.

8 Pressure. Using warnings, repeated demands and threats.

9 Coalitions. Enlisting the aid of people to persuade an individual or assuring the support of others as a reason for an individual to agree to a change.

Some tactics are more effective than others. Specifically, rational persuasion, inspirational appeals and consultation tend to be most effective, while pressure tends to backfire and is the least effective tactic (Yukl, 2006).

Power tactics should be used to: ensure the support of key power groups (stakeholders); generate energy and enthusiasm in support of the change; use symbols and language to create energy and commitment for change; and build stability to ensure some things remain the same, such as location and hours of work. Such sources of stability are anchors for people to hold onto during change, and this is important since people need to know what will remain stable and what is likely to change. Consultants need, therefore, to actively use tactics to effectively manage the power dynamics in a client organization.

Powerlessness

If consultants lack power they may find it challenging to get their ideas accepted and implemented. Kotter (1985) traces this problem to what he describes as the 'power gap'. This is a discrepancy between the resources and authority attached to formal positions and the power needed to obtain cooperation and support from the different groups on which a successful change depends. Such a gap can lead to consultants feeling frustrated because they are in a position of powerlessness in which the performance expectations placed on them exceed their resources and capabilities. The successful implementation of change means consultants overcoming not only powerful vested interests but also the powerlessness that can impede any initiatives, since the power to influence the actions and reactions of others is critical for achieving change.

A lack of power can lead to ineffective interventions due to a lack of commitment from stakeholders who view the consultant as powerless. Internal consultants, in particular, do not always have positional power, particularly if their primary role is not that of internal consultant and they are performing this role as an additional function. For instance, the trainer or other 'expert' who moves into the role of the internal consultant must learn to deal with the ambiguity and frustration that will inevitably come from a lack of positional power (Kenton and Moody, 2003). Gaining power comes, however, with a word of caution. Stanford GSB Professor Brian Lowery suggests that in order to avoid the misuse of power as an individual's power grows, they should ask others to help them check their behaviour, because if they just rely on themselves to do this they may end up missing something important (quoted in Lynch, 2016). So consultants need to identify their own personal power for each engagement, as well as that of their clients and other stakeholders, as they must feel confident in the power vested in them and be able to demonstrate it in a positive way.

Communication skills

The ability to communicate with people is a core element of consultancy for change. Quality dialogue between consultants and clients can be achieved through effective listening, questioning and summarizing.

Listening

Tuning in and listening actively will connect a consultant more to their client. Listening is, however, the most used but the least understood communication skill. Hearing is automatic, but listening is something that people choose to do. Crucini and Kipping (2001) stress the importance of consultants being careful not to scare clients with an uninterrupted flow of words and ideas but rather taking time to listen. Listening is a complex activity that involves interpreting and understanding verbal messages, clarifying ambiguous information and encouraging meaningful communication.

There are different modes of listening – 'listening about' and 'listening for' (Brownell, 2015). 'Listening about' is often value laden and may lead to questions such as, 'Do I like what this person is saying?', 'Do I believe it?', 'Do I have evidence to refute it?' 'Listening for', on the other hand, is often about hearing possibility and opportunity: 'What are they saying?', 'Do I understand it from their perspective?', 'How does that relate to what

I know?' 'Listening for' is listening actively without judgement. Active listening involves paying attention to the client without interrupting, but instead making sounds occasionally to indicate understanding or encouragement, maintaining eye contact, looking interested, being interested and being at ease. It means that the person talking feels that the listener is fully present and not being distracted, such as by checking social media, e-mail or phone calls. Listening also means being aware of the non-verbal behaviour of the speaker, noticing their emotional cues such as facial expressions, which can provide information about how the speaker is making sense of the discussion and allow the consultant to tailor their responses and questions. Consultants should also listen for 'pings' or 'hooks' to enable them to identify what to hang their next question on, such as the person saying 'I have always had concerns in that area'. Active listening is closely tied up with questioning.

Questioning

Effective questioning involves asking open questions (such as when, where, what, how) to obtain more information and using reflecting and closed questions (for example, is that right?) to obtain confirmation. There are three levels of questioning that can be used during the consultancy cycle to gain mutual understanding: data, meaning and importance.

- *Level one: data.* Questions at this level are simple data-gathering questions, relatively easy to answer, and which do not require a high level of trust to be answered. For example, 'How are you today?' or 'How many people are in your team?'

- *Level two: meaning.* This level involves questions that probe the meaning or consequence associated with the facts, such as 'What do you feel about x?' 'What does that mean to you?' 'What interests you about x?' 'How do you know that is the problem?' Such questions need more thought and require a higher level of trust as they are starting to ask about what someone feels as well as thinks.

- *Level three: importance.* Questions at this level move to the other person's perspective and involve wanting to know the value or importance associated with the meaning or consequences of something, such as 'Why is that important to you?', 'Why do you feel that?', 'Why does that concern you?' These questions need the highest level of trust and often require a considerable degree of thought in order to gain an understanding of why individuals value the things they do.

If a client does not answer a question immediately (especially an open-ended one), consultants should not rush in and fill the space – there is power in silence, especially with level three questions when the client is likely to need time to think about their answer.

Listening can be actively done in response to each of the three levels of questioning as follows:

- Level one – In response to data questions, listen for facts, figures, information and content.

- Level two – In response to meaning questions, listen for feelings, preferences, views and opinions about the facts.

- Level three – For importance questions, listen for attitudes, beliefs and what is important and valued.

Along with listening and questioning, consultants need to *summarize* or paraphrase what has just been said and also recognize feelings, for instance 'You seem very angry about...' or 'So, let me reflect back to you what you have just said to check that I understand correctly...'. Summarizing is also a good technique for moving a conversation forward.

Listening, questioning and summarizing may appear to be basic skills but they are very powerful if used effectively and actively – which can be hard to do and require practice and patience.

In the following case study Dr Katie Best, Consultant and Researcher, describes how during her time as MBA Director at BPP she was asked to design a bespoke MBA for a top city law firm. Katie outlines the key capabilities required to influence the client and build a partnership with them.

CASE STUDY

Designing a bespoke MBA for the legal sector

The law firm we were asked to design an MBA programme for had conducted research in house and concluded that i) trainees felt inadequately prepared for life as a lawyer following their legal training and ii) partners wished that trainees were more able to engage with clients. We were a new business school and ready for our first corporate clients. But what was unclear was how we might design and deliver what they wanted.

We had a small team, and less than six months to go from no programme, to a validated, written and staffed MBA welcoming 20–30 incredibly bright students to the course. We needed an approach that would provide a simple way for a few staff and a lot of freelancers to think about this niche degree: MBA (Legal Services). The challenge – and the main advice that we needed to provide to the client – was to use the client's requirements but also work within the constraints that apply in the UK if you are going to run a degree programme or an MBA programme that you might like accredited at some point. In between these many regulations and requirements, we wanted to try to make something that everyone would be delighted with – the client, the students and BPP. There were a lot of stakeholders, in that all London-based partners were welcome to have a say. We spent a lot of time talking to the client but not to our future trainees who had, by this time, finished their legal training and were backpacking around South America for the most part.

'What do you want them to be able to do?' we asked the client.

'Be clued up on business,' the client said.

'What does that mean?'

'Know the figures, the facts, not be scared off by them.'

We started trying to design an MBA that did this, and it would have been fine, but it did not feel very different to what anyone else was doing. Something was missing. But a door-handle comment from one partner, over his shoulder as he left a meeting, made something click: 'You know, last week, a trainee went mute in front of a client. The rest of the legal team was stuck on a train and it was just him. I want this MBA to prepare our trainees to be able to cope if they're the first one to the clients, or stuck at a dinner alone because everyone else is on a broken-down train.' And in my memory (although it probably did not happen like this at all) we all looked at each other as though we had struck gold: this was the leitmotif we needed to design an innovative MBA that was just right for the market. Our mission was 'to make sure the trainees can talk the talk if they are locked in a room with a CEO for two hours'. It meant that the students needed modules that taught them how to read the *Financial Times*, how to present a good understanding of marketing, accountancy and innovation, and anything else the board of directors might care about, without necessarily being able to do it, and how to talk knowledgably about each of the core sectors that the legal firm specialized in.

But it was not as simple as that. We needed to design an MBA that could be validated, that students would want to study, and that might – if we were lucky – end up with accreditation from the major MBA bodies. Our design process was iterative, cycling between what the client wanted, what the accrediting bodies and the Quality Assurance Agency for Higher Education demanded, and what BPP's policies were about classroom time, lecture format and so forth. We would get everything right in one way only to realize that it let us down in another way. But once we had weaved our way amongst the obstacles, we ended up with an MBA with teaching days that looked quite school-like. We recognized that the best way to get the students engaging with the material and thinking on their feet was to get them in class almost every morning and have highly interactive lectures and workshops that required their constant engagement. In the afternoons, and occasionally for week-long blocks, we wanted them to prepare for a range of business-appropriate assessments and activities such as researching presentations on the core sectors, analysing accounts, running marketing simulations or reading the financial press.

There were other important aspects that emerged from conversations. These were not driven by the client but came out of our early conversations with them: 'We have to show this in the partner meeting before we can get it signed off.' Or, from the more cynical, 'Why do trainees need an MBA? The chances of them staying with us and becoming partners are miniscule.'

The legal sector, being a professional services sector, has an operating structure and set of issues which are all its own. As well as teaching the students about business as a whole, would it not be great to make them reflexive practitioners in their own field? We added two modules at the end of the course – one behavioural, and the other more strategic, looking at the opportunities, challenges, research and theories that were about the sector. So often, these theories never reach the people they are about, and we wanted the students to be able to understand the world that they were entering in a way that most of their colleagues would not. The partners took some convincing: 'We want them to learn about everyone else, not us.'

'They will. They'll be able to compare and contrast your industry with the others. You learn what a zebra is by seeing that it's a horse with stripes.'

Throughout, I sat in an odd place – internal to the project and having part-ownership of the final MBA programme that we would create, and yet external to the client. It meant I had a degree of pushback if I needed it – I could use the regulations and the validation process to argue for or against particular features and approaches. But because we had to design something that would work and could be validated, the client sometimes had to be persuaded. In particular, we had to do some work to show the client that the degree they wanted was not just a law degree with different content. It was about a mindset change. And this was hard. But opportunities arose during our regular engagement with them. For example, one day a partner phoned me up, upset that the slides had spelling mistakes.

'A student is very unhappy and says he can't study accounting any more.'
'Why not?'
'There are errors on the lecturer's slides.'
'I'm sorry about that. What kind of errors?'
'Spelling mistakes. He's struggling to concentrate.'

(And here was a choice. And because of the way it turned out, I'll paint myself as a hero, but it could have ended very badly.)

Deep breath. 'Well, there are spelling mistakes in the real world. I think the best thing this student could do for his education is to try to get used to them.'

A business lesson in a mistyping of the word *balance*.

We were atheoretical in our approach. By necessity (short timescales and busy people), everything was done through brief, informal conversations, mainly over coffee in our offices or theirs. This added to the sense that what we were designing was highly iterative – there was never really a sense that it was done but rather that everything was all right until the next conversation. I now wonder whether that might have been a mistake. Some of the partners were slightly intimidated by the idea that their trainees might be more clued up than they were on some aspects of business. Perhaps if we had all taken the time to spend days together, working things through, some of these barriers could have been dismantled. We had asked some of the partners to come in to watch student presentations and they had mostly said, publicly or not so publicly, that they had learned an awful lot.

Possibly a model or a way of seeing things to share the vision, other than just diagrams and validation documents, could have helped us to share our ideas with them and brought them on board in a less threatening way.

I learned to stand up to clients in a way that I may not have learned to do if I was working for myself, desperate for my first piece of consultancy business. Rather than feeling that I had to agree with them because otherwise they might have walked away with my consultancy fee, I could be contrarian in the knowledge that what I was doing was helping them to do the right thing. It meant that I saw the power of a decent partnership between client and consultant, and the value that it can have. It has meant that, in the work that I have done since, I've been brave enough to tell a client if they're off the mark, knowing that I'm ultimately going to be delivering value to them. I want to be paid to tell them the truth rather than what they are hoping to hear. Idealistic, perhaps, but I am fortunate that I am not only a consultant but also a lecturer and academic researcher so I don't have to rely solely on consultancy work to pay my mortgage.

Experience

Capabilities comprise experience as well as skills and knowledge. Having experience and expertise in a particular field is vital for the reputation and credibility of consultants, since they must demonstrate their expertise to enhance their professional standing and in order to make a valuable contribution to an organization. In a survey of consultants Nada Kakabadse and colleagues found that experience combined with a solid knowledge of a particular industry is what gives consultants credibility in the eyes of their clients. This was highlighted by one respondent in the study who said that 'it is not so much technical knowledge, it is much more about business knowledge and actually being there and [having] done it... you have to have a sound business grounding or technical grounding in your field of expertise otherwise people say, why shall I believe you' (2006: 72).

Expertise gives credibility to internal just as much as it does to external consultants. If an internal consultant is viewed by their colleagues as having limited or outmoded expertise or is unable to demonstrate ongoing value and the capacity to apply their work to other parts of the organization, then their credibility and effectiveness will suffer (Sturdy and Wiley, 2011). Clients are more likely to see a consultant as credible when their opinion is based on experience.

Overcoming barriers to developing capabilities

Most individuals will face a number of obstacles to developing their capabilities, such as lack of time, energy and focus. To overcome such barriers Jean-Francois Manzoni (2014), INSEAD Professor of Management Practice, says that individuals need to have focus, mindfulness and persistence.

- *Focus.* Instead of spreading time and energy across several capabilities, consultants should select one skill that is of significant importance and where improvement will deliver a high return on investment. Development objectives should be agreed that are positive (as in 'I will start to...') instead of negative (as in 'I will stop...'), and broken down into small, manageable targets.

- *Mindfulness.* Consultants can spend a great deal of time on automatic pilot – on anticipating the future by trying to predict what will or might happen and on thinking back to the past. As a result they are rarely completely in the here-and-now – what is happening at this moment, in this place, and with these people. To be present here-and-now requires consultants to be mindful, and there is a growing amount of evidence showing the benefits of mindfulness and how to develop it (Keep and Ash, 2001). The growing scientific consensus for mindfulness was discussed at the 2014 World Economic Forum and was summarized in a *Time Magazine* cover story entitled 'The mindful revolution' (Pickert, 2014). Developing the ability to be mindful is an essential enabler for the implementation of new knowledge and the development of new skills.

- *Persistence.* Even when a consultant's resolve is strong and their efforts well focused, implementing new knowledge and developing a new skill are not an easy, linear process. It is more likely to be frustrating at times, and there is no doubt that there will be some setbacks along the way. Consultants need to try to understand what the setback is teaching them about themselves, about others and/or about the situation.

So consultants need to be focused, mindful and persistent in developing their capabilities throughout the consulting cycle as they work with the client.

Summary

There is a variety of capabilities that must be grasped in order to become an efficient consultant. In addition, the level of expertise and the mastery of certain skills will fluctuate in relation to the level at which consultants operate. In this chapter we have highlighted the importance of capabilities required by consultants throughout the consultancy for change cycle, which are: building and maintaining relationships; managing emotions; being self-aware; gaining commitment and engagement; facilitating creative dialogue; resilience; having a tolerance for ambiguity and uncertainty; political astuteness; managing power dynamics; and being an effective communicator. The relative emphasis on each capability will depend upon the situation, but all are vital in consultancy for change.

To build capabilities requires learning and development, which provide consultants with the knowledge, abilities and skills necessary to adapt to new and different ways of working and reinforce the required behaviour to work more confidently with clients. As Warren Bennis says, capabilities can be learned: 'we are all educable, at least if the basic desire to learn is there and we do not suffer from serious learning disorders. Furthermore, whatever natural endowments we bring to [our role], they can be enhanced' (cited by Manzoni, 2014).

Developing capabilities has benefits for both the client and the consultant. It enables consultants to maximize their contribution to sustainable organizational change for the benefit of the organization and their clients (Kerber and Buono, 2010). At the same time, the benefits specifically for the consultant include: an increase in competitive advantage; an improvement in the ability to execute a greater number of changes more effectively; and an increase in repeat business. In order to achieve such benefits, consultants must continue to develop and enhance their capabilities.

Implications for consultants

There are several practical implications for practising and aspiring consultants that arise from the issues discussed in this chapter.

- *Build and maintain trust.*
  The foundation of the client–consultant relationship has to be based on trust and to build such trust consultants must demonstrate that they are capable of helping the client and that they will act with integrity, honesty and fairness. Every month ask for an opportunity to meet with the client informally – over lunch, for coffee or in a similar setting – not primarily to talk about the assignment but to get to know them better. This will also give the client an opportunity to raise any issues they may have in an 'off the record' setting, which is how you may get the first early warning of any problems or opportunities.

- *Connect with peers for feedback.*
  Arrange regular sounding board meetings with fellow consultants (ideally people not working on the same assignment) at which you describe progress and prospects on the assignment and ask them to critique both the task (content) and process (relationship) aspects.

- *Maintain visibility.*
  Maintaining their visibility can be done by consultants in different ways, such as: meeting with clients to catch up over a coffee or lunch; inviting them to relevant in-house or external events; connecting with them through appropriate social media forms, such as LinkedIn, and e-mailing them information that may be of interest, such as articles and research reports.

- *Focus on different development opportunities.*
  Apart from formal development events, another way for consultants to develop capabilities is to get involved in associations and/or online communities where different types of consultants meet up in order to compare viewpoints and share experiences. Being involved with such specialized associations and communities not only enables consultants to share their views and to benefit from the experiences of other consultants who might have been through similar situations, it also broadens their knowledge and allows them to share experiences with their peers.

- *Consider learning and development as a lifelong activity.*
  To ensure that individual learning and development are ongoing, consultants need to take time to reflect on their learning, as they can learn a lot

from reflecting back on past situations and interactions so as to try to identify what they did well and did less well, as well as why they reacted in the way they did.

References

Aguirre, D and Alpern, M (2014) 10 principles of leading change management. [Online] http://www.strategy-business.com/article/00255?gko=9d35b

Ainsworth, D (2010) Into the rabbit hole: Variations on traditional approaches to diagnosis and discovery, in *Consultation for Organizational Change*, ed AF Buono and D Jamieson, pp 247–68, Information Age Publishing, Charlotte, NC

Anderson, D (2012) *Organization Development: The process of leading organizational change*, 2nd edn, Sage, London

Bennis, W and Nanus, B (1985) *Leaders: The strategy for taking charge*, Harper Row, London

Brownell, J (2015) *Listening: Attitudes, principles, and skills*, Routledge, London

Buchanan, DA and Badham, RJ (2009) *Power, Politics and Organizational Change*, 2nd edn, Sage, London

CIPD (2009) Employee engagement, Factsheet, Chartered Institute of Personnel and Development, London

Cope, M (2010) *The Seven Cs of Consulting*, FT/Prentice Hall, London

Crucini, C and Kipping, M (2001) Management consultancies as global change agents? Evidence from Italy, *Journal of Organizational Change Management*, **14** (6), pp 570–89

De Caluwé, L and Reitsma, E (2010) Competencies of management consultants: A research study of senior management consultants, in *Consultation for Organizational Change*, ed AF Buono and D Jamieson, pp 15–40, Information Age Publishing, Charlotte, NC

Demarest, L, Herdes, M, Stockton, J and Stockton, W (2004) *The Mobius Model™: A guide for developing effective relationships in groups, teams, and organizations*, Farrar & Associates, Minneapolis, MN

Gilley, A, McMillan, HS and Gilley, JW (2009) Organizational change and characteristics of leadership effectiveness, *Journal of Leadership & Organizational Studies*, **16** (1), 38–47

Hodges, J (2016) *Managing and Leading People Through Change*, Kogan Page, London

Hodges, J and Gill, R (2015) *Sustaining Change in Organizations*, Sage, London

Huy, Q (2015) Leaders who can read collective emotions are more effective, Knowledge@Insead. [Online] http://knowledge.insead.edu/strategy/leaders-who-can-read-collective-emotions-are-more-effective-4002#EH8GKwIHxfRtvkTb.99

Inglis, IR (2000) The central role of uncertainty reduction in determining behaviour. *Behaviour*, **137** (12), 1567–99

Jamieson, D and Armstrong, T (2010) Consulting for change, in *Consultation for Organizational Change*, ed AF Buono and D Jamieson, pp 3–13, Information Age Publishing, Charlotte, NC

Johnson, D and Grayson, K (2005) Cognitive and affective trust in service relationships, *Journal of Business Research*, **58** (4), pp 500–07

Kakabadse, N, Kakabadse, A and Louchart, E (2006) Consultant's role: A qualitative inquiry from the consultant's perspective, *Journal of Management Development*, **25** (5), pp 416–500

Kanter, RM (1983) *The Change Masters*, Simon and Schuster, New York

Keep, J and Ash, K (2001) Change agency practice: The future, in *Organizational Change and Development: A reflective guide for managers, trainers and developers*, ed R Hamlin, J Keep and K Ash, pp 297–303, FT/Prentice Hall, London

Kenton, B and Moody, D (2003) *The Role of the Internal Consultant*, Roffey Park Institute, London

Kerber, K and Buono, A (2010) Intervention and organizational change: Building organizational capacity, in *Consultation for Organizational Change*, ed AF Buono and D Jamieson, pp 79–112, Information Age Publishing, Charlotte, NC

Kotter, JP (1985) *Power and Influence*, Free Press, New York

Kotter, JP and Whitehead, L (2010) *Buy-In: Saving your good idea from getting shot down*, Harvard Business School Press, Boston, MA

Krummaker, S and Vogel, B (2013) An in-depth view of the facets, antecedents, and effects of leaders' change competency: Lessons from a case study, *The Journal of Applied Behavioral Science*, **49** (3), pp 279–307

Kubr, M (1996) *Management Consulting: A guide to the profession*, International Labour Office, Geneva

Kumar, K and Thibodeaux, MS (1990) Organizational politics and planned organization change: A pragmatic approach, *Group and Organization Management*, **15** (4), pp 357–65

Lawrence, PR and Lorsch, JW (1986) *Organisation and Environment: Managing differentiation and integration*, Harvard Business Press, Boston, MA

Lewis, LK and Seibold, DR (1998) Reconceptualizing organizational change implementation as a communication problem: A review of literature and research agenda, in *Communication Yearbook 21*, ed ME Roloff, pp 93–152, Sage, Thousand Oaks, CA

Lundberg, CC and Young, CA (2001) A note on emotions and consultancy, *Journal of Organizational Change Management*, **14** (6), pp 530–38

Lynch, S (2016) The dangers of power, Insights by Stanford Business School. [Online] http://www.gsb.stanford.edu/insights/dangers-power

Maister, D (2004) The consultant's role, in *The Advice Business: Essential tools and models for management consulting*, ed CJ Fombrun and MD Nevins, Pearson Prentice Hall, Upper Saddle, NJ

Manzoni, J (2014) Breaking the bad habits of leadership. Knowledge @Insead. [Online] http://knowledge.insead.edu/leadership-organisations/breaking-bad-leadership-habits-3173

Mayer, JD and Salovey, P (1997) What is emotional intelligence? In *Emotional Development and Emotional Intelligence: Educational implications*, ed P Salovey and D Sluyter, pp 3–31, Basic Books, New York

McCartney, C and Holbeche, L (2004) *The Roffey Park Management Agenda 2004*, Roffey Park Institute, London

McLachlin, RD (1999) Factors for consulting engagement success, *Management Decision*, **37** (5), pp 394–402

McLean, GN (2006) *Organization Development: Principles, processes, performance*, Berrett-Koehler, San Francisco

Meaney, MC, Pung, C and Wilson, S (2010) *Voices on Transformation*, McKinsey, New York

Meyer, E (2015) Building trust across cultures, Knowledge @Insead. [Online] http://knowledge.insead.edu/blog/insead-blog/building-trust-across-cultures-3844

Moorhouse Consulting (2014) *Barometer on Change 2014*, Moorhouse, London. [Online] http://www.moorhouseconsulting.com/news-and-views/publications-and-articles/barometer-on-change

Pellegrinelli, S (2002) Managing the interplay and tensions of consulting interventions: The consultant–client relationship as mediation and reconciliation, *Journal of Management Development*, **21** (5), pp 343–65

Pickert, K (2014) The mindful revolution, *Time Magazine*. [Online] http://content.time.com/time/subscriber/article/0,33009,2163560,00.html

Proctor, A (2014) Increase your resilience to change. [Online] https://www.linkedin.com/pulse/20141209100529-8521084-increase-your-resilience-to-change

Proudfoot, JG, Corr, PJ, Guest, DE and Dunn, G (2009) Cognitive-behavioural training to change attributional style improves employee well-being, job satisfaction, productivity, and turnover, *Personality and Individual Differences*, **46** (2), pp 147–53

Robbins, SP, Judge, TA and Campbell, TT (2010) *Organizational Behaviour*, FT/Prentice Hall, London

Ryder-Smith, J (1998) The secret of good conversation-investing in success, *Health Manpower Management*, **24** (1), pp 38–39

Salancik, GR and Pfeffer, J (1978) Who gets power – and how they hold on to it: A strategic-contingency model of power, *Organizational Dynamics*, **5** (3), pp 3–21

Schein, EH (1997) The concept of 'client' from a process consultation perspective: A guide for change agents, *Journal of Organizational Change Management*, **10** (3), pp 202–16

Scherer, J, Lavery, G, Sullivan, R, Whitson, G and Vales, E (2010) Whole system transformation: The consultant's role in creating sustainable results, in *Consultation for Organizational Change*, ed AF Buono and D Jamieson, pp 57–77, Information Age Publishing, Charlotte, NC

Shenson, HL (1990) *How to Select and Manage Consultants: A guide to getting what you pay for*, Lexington Books, New York

Stapley, LF (1996) *The Personality of the Organisation: Psychodynamic explanation of culture and change*, Free Association Books, London/New York

Stumpf, SA and Longman, R.A (2000) The ultimate consultant: Building long-term, exceptional value client relationships, *Career Development International*, 5 (3), pp 124–34

Stumpf, SA and Tymon Jr, WG (2001) Consultant or entrepreneur? Demystifying the 'war for talent', *Career Development International*, 6 (1), pp 48–55

Sturdy, A and Wiley, N (2011) *Internal Consultants as Agents of Change*, Economic and Social Research Council, RES-000-22-1980/A

Sullivan, R and Sullivan, K (1995) Essential competencies for internal and external OD consultants, in *Practicing Organization Development: A guide for consultants*, ed W Rothwell, R Sullivan and G McLean, pp 535–49, Pfeiffer, San Diego

Weiss, A (2003) *Organizational Consulting: How to be an effective internal change agent*, Wiley & Sons, London

Werr, A, Stjernberg, T and Docherty, P (1997) The functions of methods of change in management consulting, *Journal of Organizational Change Management*, 10, (4), pp 288–307

Wickham, P and Wickham, L (2008) *Management Consulting: Delivering an effective project*, 3rd edn, Prentice Hall, London

Wicks, R (2015) Personal and professional development, in *The Effective Change Manager's Handbook*, ed R Smith, D King, R Sindhu and D Skelsey, pp 492–534, Kogan Page, London

Wilcox, M and Jenkins, M (2015) *Engaging Change: A people-centred approach to business transformation*, Kogan Page, London

Yukl, G (2006) *Leadership in Organizations*, Simon and Schuster Trade, London

The ethical side of consultancy 08

KEY POINTS

- Ethics are highly individual beliefs which distinguish between what is right or wrong, good or bad. These beliefs provide a basis for judging the appropriateness and the consequences of behaviour, and guide consultants in their dealings with other individuals, teams and organizations.
- Consultancy for change needs to be underpinned by a set of ethical values that influence the behaviours and actions of consultants and the outcomes and consequences of change initiatives.
- It is not just the consultant that needs to take responsibility for ethical behaviour, but also consultancy firms and client organizations, which have a responsibility to develop and enforce commonly understood, and adhered to, ethical guidelines.
- The consequences of ethical malpractice have the potential to lead to the darkening of the credibility of consultancy for change.

Introduction

Consulting ethically, responsibly and effectively through change so that it is sustainable is not an altruistic 'nice to have', but a business imperative. Consultants have a responsibility to engage in behaviour that is not only efficient and effective but also ethical. Consultancy for change needs to be underpinned by a set of ethical values that influence the behaviours and actions of consultants and the outcomes and consequences of change initiatives. The impact of unethical practice can translate into irretrievable damage, as was evident with Arthur Andersen, the accounting firm that once counted itself as one of the world's big five professional firms, until its criminal handling of the energy company Enron led to its downfall. Ethics are therefore a vital part of consultancy, and as such consultants need to recognize this and act in an ethical way.

In order to explore the importance of ethics and consultancy for change this chapter considers what constitutes unethical as well as ethical behaviour. The chapter begins by defining what is meant by ethics and why they are critical to consultancy for change. A critical perspective is then taken on the individualization of ethics with the examination of the implications of the shift of responsibility for ethical practice from the organization onto the individual. The assumption behind this individualization is that if consultants themselves are ethically responsible, then consulting practice will be ethical. In his case study Peter Gerlach describes how he was faced with unethical practices that left him as the 'scapegoat' when working for a consultancy firm.

The second part of the chapter discusses the importance of the ethical dimension of consultancy as a means of ensuring that consultants act in the interests of the people within the organization. The key ethical issues in carrying out change, especially culture change, are explored, along with a review of the types of unethical behaviour that can occur during the consultancy cycle. In a personal reflection Dr Olga Matthias explores the ethical aspects of consultancy. The chapter concludes with the implications for consultants, and organizations, in pursuing an ethical approach to change.

Learning outcomes

By the end of this chapter you will be able to:

- appreciate the importance of the ethical aspects of consultancy for change;
- identify the ethical issues that can arise during the consultancy cycle and how to handle them successfully;
- apply an ethical approach to consultancy for change.

Business ethics

The importance of ethics

Organizational leaders are still allowed to put their own self-interests before those of others (and even rewarded for it), often with disastrous results and consequences (Hodges, 2011), as was evident in the 2008 global financial crisis. Consequently, there are increasing calls for organizations to act in a more ethical fashion. Prominent in this respect is the promotion of corporate social responsibility linked to employee social responsibility. However, this has not necessarily led to a diminution of unethical behaviour. Consider the issue of Apple's tax avoidance. For more than 20 years, Apple's business in Ireland was the beneficiary of an extraordinary deal that enabled it to avoid paying any tax on almost all profits in Europe and other global markets (Beesley and Barker, 2016). As Joseph Stiglitz (2010), the Nobel Prize-winning economist, says, unethical behaviour appears to have escalated out of control in many organizations as society seems to have encouraged the individualistic motto of 'Every man for himself' in place of 'One for all and all for one'.

The long-term, sustainable interests of the many are often sacrificed to the short-term greed and arrogance of the few, which is evident in employees having to compromise ethical standards in favour of business objectives. In an article in *The Times* newspaper entitled 'Ethics versus profits: the fight goes on', Carly Chynoweth (2015) writes that employees feel that they sometimes have to choose between doing the right thing and doing the right thing by their boss. This dilemma is further highlighted by nearly a third of the 1,600 workers and managers in the UK who participated in the Management Agenda survey feeling under pressure to compromise their individual ethical standards to meet business objectives (Lucy *et al*, 2015). This was found to be especially true in the public sector, where it was felt by 40 per cent of respondents, against 27 per cent in the commercial world and 31 per cent in the not-for-profit sector. It appears, therefore, to be a matter of whether an individual is willing to behave in an ethical manner and whether an organization is willing to ensure that ethical standards are adhered to.

In an attempt to ensure that ethics are entwined in the culture of companies the Ethisphere Institute, a US-based independent research centre, promotes best practices in corporate ethics and governance and conducts research into the state of ethics in business. The Institute assesses the world's most ethical company based on five key categories: ethics and compliance programme (35 per cent), corporate citizenship and responsibility (20 per cent), culture of ethics (20 per cent), governance (15 per cent) and leadership, innovation and reputation (10 per cent). Among the 132 ethical companies identified in 2015 were four consultancy firms: Accenture and Capgemini, the management and IT consultancies; CBRE, the real estate advisor; and Wipro, the Indian IT consultancy (Consultancy.uk, 2015). This is a positive step forward. However, to avoid repeating the errors of past decades and the considerable damage that has been done to organizations and especially to the people within them due to unethical behaviour, there is a need to focus on what is ethical and unethical consulting for all consultants, not just the few who work for global companies.

Defining the ethics of consultancy

Most people would agree that child labour is clearly unethical, but would they recognize which consultancy for change practices are unethical? To be aware of the ethical dimensions of consultancy, consultants and clients must have measures for judging what it is potentially ethical or not. A starting point for this is to understand what is meant by 'ethics'.

Ethics can be described as the science of morals, concerned with the distinction between right and wrong, good and bad (Hamlin *et al*, 2001). As such, ethics are moral values or beliefs about what is right versus what is wrong and what is good versus what is bad. These beliefs provide a basis for judging the appropriateness of motivation and the consequences of behaviour and they guide people in their dealings with other individuals, groups and organizations and help to distinguish between ethical and unethical behaviour (Singer, 1994).

Unethical behaviour is often labelled as coercing employees into certain actions. Coercion occurs when an individual forces another individual to behave or refrain from behaving under threat of severe deprivation, such as the loss of their job or a negative impact on their well-being (Warwick and Kelman, 1973). This means that a consultant can be said to be acting in an unethical way if they coerce others into certain behaviour; or use manipulative tactics that involve deceit, threats, fear, secrecy and dishonesty to gain the commitment of individuals to organizational change.

Many of the same issues that are associated with coercion can also be raised with respect to manipulation. Manipulation generally implies a type of interpersonal influence in which the manipulator intentionally deceives the target. Seabright and Moberg say that 'manipulation operates by robbing the victim of autonomy either in choice (situational manipulation) or in self-definition (psychological manipulation) for the sole purpose of advancing the perpetrator's objective' (1998: 167). The results are actions that are not freely undertaken. In the context of organizational change, 'manipulation and coercion can occur when the organizational development effort requires organizational members to abridge their personal values or needs against their will' (White and Wooten, 1983: 691). For instance, consultants may manipulate clients into implementing a specific change intervention by the use of flattery or lies and play on the emotions of the client to get their own way. Coercion and manipulative tactics that involve deception, threats, fear, secrecy and dishonesty can therefore be considered unethical.

Ethics for consultants are not, however, set in stone – there is no rule-book for them. Consistent, responsible and ethical decisions are, however, vital for ensuring sustainable change (Stokes and Harris, 2012). Although consulting companies and client organizations often have their own code of ethics or code of conduct, responsibility for behaving ethically still tends to lie with the individual consultant.

Individual or institutional responsibility

The individualization of ethics

Despite the burgeoning interest in ethical codes and ethical practices in consulting it is, in the eyes of some critics, not getting any better (O'Mahoney, 2011; Power, 2004). The reason for this is that ethics are increasingly being made the responsibility of the individual consultant rather than that of the institutions and structures that envelop consulting practice.

The assumption behind this *individualization* is that if consultants them-selves are ethically responsible, then consulting practice will be ethical. This means that ethics as a concern is 'removed from institutional or systemic operation and is, instead, imposed upon individuals or groups that can be held responsible when things go wrong' (O'Mahoney and Markham, 2010: 322). The benefit of this for not only the consultancy firm but also the client organization is significant as it means that where unethical practice does take place responsibility is firmly placed on the individual consultant and they can be held up as the scapegoat. The identification and responsibility for ethical behaviour at an individual rather than organizational level have the potential to lead to individual dissent, such as in the case of Eric Ben-Artzi, who blew the whistle on false accounting at Deutsche Bank in 2016 (Skapinker, 2016).

Such individual dissent is often viewed as a nuisance by management, whereas so-called 'whistleblowers' say that they do it because they care about ethical conduct. This is evident in a study conduct by Croucher and colleagues (2016) of 889 employees in companies in the US, UK and Australia. Findings from the study show that employees are one of the key elements not only in fostering an ethical corporate reputation but also in preventing the loss of it. When things go wrong in organizations, there are almost always people inside who could see it coming and may decide to expose the ethical malpractice. The risks of doing so are that it may cause tremendous damage to the reputation of the company and to the individual who reveals the information. The individualization of ethics thus places individual consultants in a difficult position, as is evident in the following case study by Peter Gerlach, the Managing Director of Peter Gerlach International.

CASE STUDY

The consultant as a scapegoat

This case is based on one of my clients in the banking and financial services sector that operates worldwide. The company provides its clients with retail, commercial financing, investment banking, asset management and private banking services. The company's goal was to reduce its processes and to provide a leaner, less bureaucratic and more customer-focused service to its clients Europe-wide. To help to implement this vision, which was decided by senior management, 100 employees from various divisions volunteered to be involved at various levels of commitment.

The company subsidiaries that agreed to lead the change and to be the first to take part in the implementation were those based in Germany and the UK. To make the change stick, it was decided to get an experienced external consultancy firm involved to help with the change implementation.

My role was to support the change as a 'senior expert' and I was hired by the consultancy firm to support their client with the coaching, facilitation and delivery of 'coach the coach' and 'train the trainer' workshops.

Given the very short timescale in which to prepare, I immediately began gathering data about the issues the business was facing and the goals they wanted to achieve. In order to dig deeper into the key issues, I interviewed and spoke with as many internal and external stakeholders as possible over the telephone, asking questions such as 'What does ideal look like?' and 'How do you envisage the transformation?' Based on the work my client – the consultancy firm – had already done in their initial data-gathering exercise, there appeared to be a good level of energy from the individuals I interviewed, which removed the need to ask any deeper emotional questions such as 'How do you feel about the transformation?' and 'How will the change affect you and your work personally?'

My next task was to deliver a keynote presentation and a workshop to employees from the German and UK subsidiaries. The aim of the 90-minute workshop was for participants to get to know each other, to find commonalities and to strengthen engagement with the proposed change. The 30-minute keynote presentation consisted of 13 PowerPoint slides with very basic material, such as the change curve (originally created by Elisabeth Kubler-Ross in 1969), a sales pitch on the added value the consultancy firm would bring during the change process and an overall message to all delegates and leaders to stick to the change process and to be patient, as the change would take time.

The consultancy that had hired me, and the bank, had prepared the content and material for me to deliver at both events. Based on the information I had gathered from the interviews, I decided to slightly adjust and tailor my delivery.

Unfortunately, neither the workshop nor the keynote presentation were a success. The material did not fully fit the needs of the audience, especially as some of the participants were apprehensive about how the change would personally affect them. I felt very uncomfortable delivering the content as I sensed that the material that was given to me did not fit the purpose. In fact, it was too basic and the content was not what I would have produced. At the same time, I felt I had to do a good job for both my client and the bank.

During the workshop, the level of engagement, commitment and ability of participants varied massively. A high percentage of the Germans were in limbo and demanded a lot more structure and information about the change, in terms of why, how and when – more than there was time to address. In my view, this should have all been clarified at the start of the project by the senior management and the CEO. They should have checked the levels of understanding and emotional buy-in when they announced the change to all employees. A few of the participants also raised their concerns during the breaks in the workshop. They whispered amongst themselves that they would rely on their 'work council' (which in Germany represents and acts in the interest of the employer and employees, negotiating working conditions, wages and labour agreements) to protect them against any redundancies due to the changes. Such concerns indicated to me that there was a certain level of fear and anxiety about the proposed transformation, which was also evident in the way people communicated and behaved during the workshop. For instance, some of the participants' communication styles were aggressive and defensive, while others asked very specific, deep and detailed questions on issues that might happen. The level of openness and excitement, which should have been high, was very low.

Participants from the UK subsidiary had a very different outlook as they seemed already to be miles ahead. First, their work culture had always been service orientated, which enabled them to adapt a lot faster to the change. Second, since the UK does not have work councils for bankers, each employee had to take personal responsibility for their own situation and for driving added value for their clients.

After I had delivered the workshop and the keynote presentation, I was heavily criticized by the banking client for not delivering exactly what they had asked for. The client felt that the delegates were more confused than they were in the beginning. The consultancy firm did not back me up either. The fact that prior to the workshop most people were very apprehensive, intrinsically afraid and too set in their current ways of working was not taken into account. I was the scapegoat and the delegates were happy that they could go back to what they had always done and what they were familiar with – the status quo. This meant that the employees were able to do the job in the way they had always done it, and where they felt safe and secure.

It was a quantum leap for me in terms of learning experience from this consultancy assignment. My main learning points are:

- I will only get involved in a change event if all stakeholders are on board with it – physically and, most importantly, emotionally – and I will personally ensure that this is the case. Without emotional commitment, nothing works, and exercising the leadership's positional powers by prescribing what ought to be done is simply doomed to fail.

- I will engage with as many stakeholders as possible but in person rather than just by phone. It is so much better to see people's reactions face-to-face.

- Delivering a highly scripted keynote presentation from the client at a workshop that has also been prepared by a client simply does not work.

- It would have made sense for the German team to have worked together, prior to the workshop, with the help of some facilitation perhaps from the UK team, since the latter were miles ahead in their attitude to change. This would have improved team working and helped both teams to share best practices. It would have also created some success stories that could have been shared, showing everyone that it was possible to step up to the challenge and see success at the end, and not just another 'great' idea that senior management came up with.

While I take responsibility for some of the issues that arose, a major difficulty was with the consulting firm who took the work on and who wanted to change the culture with their own knowledge of processes, structures, technology and banking policies, instead of focusing on the interests of the stakeholders' personal feelings, emotions and fears, which are highly critical in the success of any change project.

My client – the consulting firm – did not take responsibility for the job and at the end did not even back me up, and in fact they turned against me. They were not able to build a sincere relationship with the client or the stakeholders involved and instead focused on processes, technology and banking policies.

What really works is to engage with consultants, facilitators and/or change agents who live and breathe what they do. Someone who does not just pay 'lip service' but has practical and multi-sector as well as cultural experience, who challenges the status quo and is dedicated to giving added value to their clients. Such consultants know and appreciate that every case is different and adapt their approach to the needs of the client.

Discussion questions for the case

- What were the main unethical behaviours in the case?
- What can a consultant do to avoid becoming a scapegoat?

Ethical codes of practice and professionalism

In consultancy the individualization of ethics is evident in the development of ethical codes of practice and the rise of professionalism (O'Mahoney and Markham, 2010).

Ethical codes of practice

Organizational *ethical codes* of practice or conduct are formalized rules and standards that describe what the company expects of its employees. Such codes encourage ethical behaviour by aiming to eliminate opportunities for unethical behaviour, and consequently the company's employees know both what is expected of them and what the punishment is for violating the rules.

Ethical codes are increasingly commonplace in consultancies and their professional associations such as the International Council of Management Consultancy Institutes. Members of the UK's Management Consultancies Association, for instance, must comply with a code of practice which states that each member will always:

- put their client's interests first;
- focus on delivering sustainable value to the client;
- employ people with the right skills and experience to help their client and continually develop their expertise;
- be clear and transparent with the client;
- be trustworthy, independent and objective;
- be financially strong enough to deliver on their commitments.

Similarly, the American Association of Management Consultancy Firms has a code of ethics that member companies and their employees are expected to conform to, which prescribes how members will behave with regard to clients, engagements and fees (see www.amcf.org for details of the code). This type of code is mirrored, in different ways, by professional consultancy firms. For example, Accenture has a code of ethics with an ethical fitness decision-making model, while Deloitte has a code of ethics entitled 'Personal accountability: Recognizing the power of one'. The basis of such codes is that if, individually, consultants are ethical, then the company becomes ethical, which removes the responsibility for ethics from the boardroom to the individual consultant.

Criticisms of ethical codes of practice

There are serious flaws in ethical codes of conduct and little evidence that they are effective (Schwartz, 2004). The codes are often vague, leaving plenty of room for interpretation and subjectivity (Kaptein and Schwartz, 2008). Adhering to these codes is also primarily a voluntary activity and not imposed by relevant legal sanctions, so ignoring or breaking these practices is not illegal unless it contravenes other legal restrictions. The enforcement of the ethical practices relies on members reporting violations of the code (Shawver and Clements, 2008). However, research suggests that less than half of the individuals who witness code violations actually report them (Nitsch *et al*, 2005). In a survey of the ethics of consultancy, Kamath (2007) found a disparity between different professional associations regarding the way in which they handled the enforcement of ethical standards. Out of the 26 professional associations surveyed, only nine did anything about ensuring that ethical standards were adhered to, which is a concerning result especially since one would expect self-regulation to be enforced by professional associations that oversee the work of consultants.

Critics point out that codes of ethical practice are central to perpetuating the individualization of ethics because they make the individual responsible for ensuring an ethical approach to the consultancy (Beck and Beck-Gernsheim, 2002). For example, Enron had a 65-page code of ethics, but when things went wrong it was Jeff Skiling and Ken Lay who were held up as responsible and imprisoned (Beck and Beck-Gernsheim, 2002).

So ethical codes may be open to criticism because such codes are often ignored and when things go wrong the organization can use them as a stick to beat the individual rather than admitting corporate responsibility.

The Issue of professionalization

Professions, by developing industry norms and institutionalized practices, are frequently cited as providing the individual with support and guidance for ethical practice (Brien, 1998). Yet, in consultancy *professionalization* is open to criticism for several reasons, which are outlined by O'Mahoney (2011). The first is that few consultants are members of a professional association; according to the Institute of Business Consulting, only 2 per cent of consultants in the UK belong to a professional association. The second reason is that, unlike the accounting, medical or legal professions, membership of the consulting profession is voluntary, and the institute has no regulatory powers to monitor, intervene or punish firms that transgress the ethical norms, or codes, of the profession. Third, professional associations such as the Institute of Business Consulting have belatedly begun to license individual consultants rather than their member firms. This focus makes the individual consultant rather than their firm the focus of ethical regulation. Finally, some researchers (such as Greenwood and Empson, 2003) have suggested that it is the professional partnership (the organization rather than the profession) that forms the basis of professional ethics for the consultant. This suggests that there is still plenty of scope for improving the professionalization of consultancy practice.

The responsibility for ethics in the consulting industry is highly, though not entirely, individualized, through ethical codes and a lack, as yet, of professionalization. This benefits the organization by devolving responsibility for ethical decision-making. The consequence is that the institutional relationships and conflicts of interest that can encourage unethical behaviour are often neglected, leading potentially to the 'dark side' of consultancy.

The 'dark side' of consultancy

The issue of ethics is integral to the theory and practice of consultancy since the consequences of ethical malpractice have the potential to lead to the darkening of the credibility of consultancy for change. This so-called 'dark side' of consultancy seems to have gained currency in academic circles, especially amongst those who adopt a stance of decrying consultants and what they do (Clark and Salaman, 1998; Czerniawska, 1999; Kihn, 2005). The consulting industry has also come under attack from politicians and the press for a number of alleged offences due partly to its growing importance and influence and, partly, to the visibility of high-profile failures and scandals. These include wasting public money in government contracts, selling fads that do not work, selling unnecessary interventions to managers, and encouraging conflicts of interest with clients. Critics have also argued that consultants often use templates (boilerplates) that they have developed for other clients and maintain that this 'one size fits all' approach to change is one of the reasons, along with a hedonistic self-interest, why so many consultancy interventions fail (Craig and Brooks, 2006). Criticisms have also been made of breaches of client confidentiality, misrepresentation of results, deceptive practices, alleged misconduct and non-delivery, and this has led to close scrutiny and suspicion of consultants and the profession in general.

The charge that consultancy, and by association consultants, are occasionally unethical is a serious one that cannot be ignored. To address this charge there is a need to look closely at ethical approaches to change.

Ethical approaches to change

The very nature of change can impinge on the work as well as on the emotions of individuals, groups and teams within an organization (Hodges, 2016), and this raises a number of ethical questions to consider including:

- Is the change legal?
- Is it right?
- Who will be affected?
- Does it fit with the organization's values?
- How would it look in the newspaper or on social media?
- Will it reflect poorly on the company?

To address such questions consultancy for change needs to be underpinned by a clear and transparent system of ethics. That is to say, consultants must be instilled with a moral compass that fits the client organization. This means that consultants must make decisions in the interest of the many rather than the few and refrain from abusing the faith that is placed in them and the unique positions they often enjoy in organizations. Therefore, a key question – and one of considerable importance – is: how can consultants lead and manage change ethically?

To do this, consultants need to be clear about the ethical implications of the particular change interventions that they develop and promote. Currently there is often a damaging lack of clarity regarding the ethical values underpinning approaches to change and its management (By and

Burnes, 2013). Kamath (2007) identifies seven core values as being important for consultants:

1 *Confidentiality.* All the information that a consultant receives from a client remains confidential and cannot be used without authorization.

2 *Transparency.* Where a consultant has relationships with a third party that may result in a conflict of interest, the consultancy should declare such relationships.

3 *Integrity.* The consultant should work loyally for their client.

4 *Reliability.* The client trusts the consultant to comply with stated agreements and to keep to contracts.

5 *Objectivity and independence.* A consultant must act as an impartial third party.

6 *Expertise and competence.* Consultants should have the knowledge, expertise, skills and capacity for the assignment.

7 *Professionalism.* All requirements of the client should be met and the client should act in a professional manner in dealing with all aspects of the engagement.

Such values can be applied to consultancy for change and adapted for different organizational situations.

The ethics of culture change

It is especially important to be cognizant of ethical values when attempting to change the culture of an organization. Any attempt to change the cultural aspects of an organization assumes that people are malleable and open to change. This raises ethical issues relating to attempting to change individuals' attitudes, values and beliefs. Such issues, Jean Woodall says, 'do not just concern the inherent worth of the exercise or its benefit to the organization. They also include the impact on individual motivation to comply and above all the infringement of individual autonomy, privacy, self-esteem and equitable treatment' (1996: 35).

The ethical feasibility of doing this is open to criticism. As Gareth Morgan (2006) says, although the evolution of culture can be influenced it should not be controlled since individuals are not passive recipients of cultural interventions. This view is supported by Tony Watson, who asks, 'What right do managers have to engage with the deeper beliefs and conceptions of right and wrong held by organizational employees?' (2002: 267).

Such criticisms of culture change draw attention to the ethics of getting inside employees' heads, without requesting the explicit consent of individuals. For by attempting to change culture, consultants may be encouraging individuals to suppress or suspend independent thought and action. This raises ethical questions about the consequences of deliberately setting out to change the values, attitudes and beliefs of individuals, as well as the meanings and identities that they associate with the organization. Critics say that this risks treating individuals as objects to be manipulated (Watson, 2002). Any attempt at culture change needs to take into account individuals' own values and has to be participative and collaborative. This means that when attempting to change a culture, or parts of it, or even just considering such an intervention, consultants must ensure that they act in an ethical way, especially when considering how the change will affect employees in the organization.

Ethics in the consulting cycle

Ethics needs to be positioned at the heart of the consulting cycle. So how can consultants ensure that they are acting in a way that is ethical? We will attempt to address this question by considering when a consultant's actions and behaviour might be considered unethical during the consultancy cycle. This is challenging, since ethics is a highly subjective matter, and consequently opinions on what constitutes unethical behaviour will vary from consultant to consultant. To provide some guidance on this, White and Wooten (1983) define unethical behaviour for OD consultants as comprising anything that involves misrepresentation, collusion, value and goal conflict, and technical ineptness. During the consultancy for change cycle there are ample opportunities for such unethical behaviour to take place.

Unethical behaviour during initial contact and contracting

During the initial contact meeting with the client there are a number of opportunities for unethical behaviour on the part of the consultant. For instance, in order to be given the work the consultant may misrepresent their capabilities by telling the client that they have experience with similar problems, organizations or industries; or the consultant might misrepresent the potential for change to be a success by over-promising results that they know they cannot achieve.

In order to create an initial good impression and to start to build a relationship with the client, consultants may be tempted to collude with the client by quickly adopting the client's perspective on all issues and not voicing any concerns they may have in the initial stages of the consultancy. This can occur, for example, when a consultant implicitly or explicitly agrees to accept the client's framing of the issue without proposing the need for diagnosis in order to identify the root cause of the issue. Instead they agree to a short-term change that may have long-term negative consequences, or agree to focus on a limited aspect of change that will benefit only a particular group rather than the whole organization. Similarly, the consultant may agree to implement an intervention merely because the client wants it. Technical ineptness can occur during the initial phase, for example when consultants do not articulate their needs and expectations, or when they agree, without any formal contracting, to take on engagements that they know they will not succeed in, in order to maintain good relations with the client.

When the purpose of the change effort is not clear, or when the client and the consultant disagree over how to achieve the goals (again due to a lack of formal contracting), this can lead to value and goal conflict. This type of conflict can also occur when the objective for the consulting engagement violates one or more value principles of consulting, such as when the client wants to use the consultant as a 'spy' or observer, or when the client wants to hide the purpose of the consultancy engagement from other key stakeholders in the organization. Value conflict can also arise when consultants, who work for several clients, fail to be explicit about any potential conflicts of interest that may result from serving multiple clients.

A violation of ethics can, therefore, happen during the initial phases of the consultancy cycle when contracting is skipped or minimized (Anderson, 2012) and misrepresentation, collusion, value and goal conflict, and technical ineptness are enacted. Such behaviour, which results from not paying enough attention to the contracting discussions, is not only evidence of a poor consultancy process but is also unethical.

Ethics and diagnosis

The diagnosis and analysis phase of the consultancy cycle provides the potential for a number of unethical malpractices. Data gathering is itself a response to ethical concerns as its purpose is to avoid colluding with the client's initial views of the issue to be addressed. By gathering data the consultant is able to expand on the client's view in order to ensure that the right problem is solved for the long-term benefit of the organization. Due to technical ineptness the consultant may fail to conduct enough diagnosis to identify the root causes of the issue and as a result a change intervention may be identified and implemented that only addresses the surface issues of the problem.

Data gathering is also open to misrepresentation particularly when a consultant decides to disclose the data in a way that violates the anonymity of the participants (Anderson, 2012). For example, the consultant might choose to disclose to the client the name of the individual who made a particular comment during an interview or focus group session, after pledging to the participant/s that contributions would remain anonymous. Consultants might also leak inappropriate information or, under the guise of obtaining further information, gather data about whether a particular manager is good or bad and share it with others. Misrepresentation can also occur during the analysis of the data when a consultant decides to highlight, omit or distort particular findings for their own self-interest, or chooses to push their own point of view well beyond what the evidence of the diagnosis reveals because they want the client to do what they advise.

Ethics and evaluation

Misrepresentation of data can also occur during the evaluation phase. For instance, the consultant might choose to gather or report on evaluation data that only shows the positive impact of the change intervention, and to ignore the data that shows negative results; thus the data is misinterpreted for the benefit of the consultant. This can be especially true for internal consultants who have a personal stake in what data the client sees and chooses to address (White and Wooten, 1983). Alternatively the consultant may collude with the client by avoiding or minimizing data that the client does not want exposed. This misuse and withholding of data by consultants is unethical and tends to occur when consultants have not agreed during the contracting phase about how the data collected will be used. The client has the right to all the information that the consultant has collected (Block, 2011); therefore misinterpreting and withholding information from the client is unethical.

Ethics and interventions/implementation

The intervention phase of the consultancy cycle provides the greatest opportunity for unethical behaviour. As White and Wooten (1983) say, during this stage collusion of parties, technical ineptness and value and goal conflict can create dilemmas resulting in inappropriate choices of interventions due to a lack of skill, objectivity or differing needs and orientations. This can have a significant impact on the change, as critical to the success of any intervention is the selection of an appropriate intervention, which depends, in turn, on careful diagnosis of the issue to be addressed. Selecting an intervention is closely related to the consultant's own values, skills and abilities. Consultants will often emphasize their own favourite intervention or technique and let their own values and beliefs dictate the change intervention rather than what is best for the organization. Value and goal conflict can occur when the client and the consultant disagree over the most appropriate intervention, and in response the consultant may act unethically by withholding services unilaterally from a client who does not agree with the intervention the consultant has proposed.

In contrast, during the intervention phase the consultant can act unethically by colluding with the client by agreeing to a specific intervention despite having data that verifies it is not the right one to implement. Consultants can also act unethically by misrepresenting the time, cost or difficulty of an intervention in order to please the client, over-promising that a certain intervention will achieve specific outcomes and benefits, or by agreeing to carry out an intervention that they do not have the skills to design and implement effectively, just so that they can continue to work with the client. Such unethical behaviour will, however, ultimately impact on the realization of benefits and their sustainability.

Ethics and transition

During the transition phase the consultant can act in an unethical way if they delay the transition or make it happen too quickly (White and Wooten, 1983). If a consultant extends a consultancy engagement for too long this can be ethically questionable as it can increase dependency on the consultant by the client and lead to the consultant (especially if external) continuing to accept payment when the contracted services have been completed or when the client is no longer benefiting from the help of the consultant. Alternatively, consultants who feel that the client is not making enough progress or that the relationship is poor may look for reasons and ways to exit when things get difficult. A premature exit can also happen when the consultant believes wrongly that the client is ready to take over complete ownership of the transformation (Anderson, 2012). Transitioning out of an engagement too early can leave the client in a position of managing a transformation that they are not yet capable of doing; similarly, if the consultant extends the engagement for their own self-interest this is open to ethical malpractice. Instead, an honest assessment of the motivation of the consultant and the client to end the engagement is required in order to ensure that it ends ethically.

To decide whether or not something is ethical during the consultancy cycle, consultants should consider these questions: Does it feel right? Would you be embarrassed if others knew you had taken this action? How would it look in the newspapers? And could you sleep at night if you did it?

Question for discussion

- Identify the ethical considerations that need to be taken into account for change in the organization in which you work, or one you are familiar with.
- How can an ethical approach to consultancy be applied in your organization, or one you are familiar with?

Reflections on the ethical side of consultancy

In the following case study Dr Olga Matthias, Head of Operations and Information Management Department, University of Bradford, provides a personal reflection, gained from 25 years in several large consulting firms, of the ethical aspects of consultancy. As an illustration of the complexities encountered by consultants, Olga provides two examples of large projects that had different approaches and outcomes. In discussing these challenges, Olga raises awareness of the hidden difficulties that have serious and sometimes far-reaching consequences for both clients and consultants.

CASE STUDY

Shadows and reflections on the dark side of consulting

Whilst all consultancy firms genuinely have their clients' interest at heart, this can be manifested in different ways, and the client may not always be in tandem with this. In order to grow, firms require consultants to sell. This is done through extending work with existing clients and finding new opportunities elsewhere in that organization. It may not necessarily be in the client's best interest to have consultants there on multiple assignments, be they concurrent or consecutive.

Individual consultants succeed by pleasing the client. This pleasure is fed back to the consultancy firm and in due course comes promotion, greater responsibility and financial reward. So far, so simple. But what if putting the client first actually means not selling something else? In the world of meeting utilization and sales targets, not selling is not a welcome outcome for the consultancy firm. It might be for the client, though, who sees that consultant as genuinely aware of their needs. But how many of us would really compromise our own careers in the shorter term in order to please a client? Obviously, some of us do, but not all of us, and hence widely held negative views, mentioned earlier. That is a real ethical dilemma.

What if putting the client first means telling them what they really need, even though this is not what they asked for? Do you risk losing the existing contract whilst having no clue if you can persuade them of their real need? If you don't, you may well risk creating the oft-expressed criticism that consultants 'take your watch and tell you the time', especially if it later emerges that you could have advised a different path. Hindsight may well be a marvellous thing, but it is not often used to forgive a direction that subsequently turns out to have not been the best. Such operational tension can cause many sleepless nights and much anxiety.

This brings us to the question of how our work is measured. Progress, value-add and success are notoriously difficult to gauge in credence work such as consulting. There are contractual measures, but it is perception that carries greater weight and spreads more readily in the networked world of client and consultant. Clients may like what you are doing and how you are doing it, but their goalposts can move and your work can inadvertently become devalued because of those changing priorities. Also, there are many ways of measuring a consultant's work, some of which only become evident long after we are gone. Yet we all like to be proud of our work, so we tend to do our best. Commercial pressure tends to make consultants feel they always need to prove their value. This can lead to hiding issues, exaggerating progress or even inflating work to increase or legitimize costs.

Here are two examples of how behaviour affects process and outcome, and which highlight the shadows of consulting. The two case studies, ethically, are polar opposites and I leave it to you to decide which one actually put the client first. In the first project I led the process side of what was essentially the 'recovery'. In the second project I led the cultural and organizational change work-stream.

Case 1: Merging multiple call centres

This project was a major undertaking merging ten call centres into one centralized centre at head office. The project was long, and the work detailed, spanning everything from staff skills and numbers to the location, design and size of the office. The objectives were multiple, but could be summarized into economies of scale and simultaneously creating a centre of excellence for service and customer-centric knowledge.

Reality did not align with aspiration. Millions had been spent on systems, infrastructure and consultants. Client and consultant teams working on this project were both big, demonstrating the importance senior management ascribed to it. Call times increased by an order of magnitude, as did customer complaints. Dropped calls increased, the number of calls answered within target decreased. Staff morale plummeted, after already suffering from the relocation and job redesign hits. Six months passed, and still there was no sign of performance settling to requisite levels. So what happened?

Neither client nor consultant wanted to be seen as having not delivered. The relationship was strong, and between them they put a case to the board that phase 1, being the merging, had succeeded, as far as it went, and that phase 2 was required to realize further performance improvements that a unified, single office was now offering. Essentially, they were each legitimizing the previous work, using the new business case as an endorsement of the previous, unsuccessful project. Phase 2 was commissioned, the process work 'phase 1' had failed to do was redone, and was hailed as a great success.

How did this pass all the checks and controls embedded in any large organization? How was no one called to task over the fact that one piece of work had to be done twice to get the desired result? Simple. Careers lay on the line for this project. Those in charge, on both sides, had a vested interest in being associated with success. It was to the advantage of all to create another opportunity for 'success', and create the intended outcome. So that is what they did. Their second chance worked and all the senior people got promotions as a result.

Case 2: Transforming customer-contact systems

The objective of this project was to implement a new suite of systems within a vertical supply chain comprising five suppliers and nine companies, including the regulator, with the main organization being a new joint venture company (JV). After a lengthy procurement process, JV appointed a consulting firm as its 'transformation partner' for what was to be a 12-month project. All appeared to be going well. As the deadline for implementation approached, many of the systems people began to work even longer hours than usual. Glitches had started to appear, problems that required ever more time to resolve. The client could see consultants becoming visibly tired and felt the atmosphere change in the office. Yet the weekly and monthly governance meetings indicated no problems.

The consultants had decided to 'ride out' the problems, and put as many people onto the work as needed so as to deliver 'on time and to budget', one of the company's main claims to success. However, the client, sensing something was awry, and not wishing to incur any penalties from the regulator, decided to bring in another firm to carry out a quality audit of this critical project. The problems the main consulting firm were dealing with, unsurprisingly, came to light. The actions taken to mitigate the problems were also noted. The client's reaction was to hire the consulting firm that had carried out the quality audit to act as project manager and run the project office. This removed responsibility from the original firm and rendered them simply as an extra resource – the firm had not lost the work but had lost their position of providing expertise and merely fulfilled the role of extension.

When the project concluded on time and ostensibly on budget, because although extra resources had been injected they had not charged the client, and furthermore the client had charged the firm for the new consultants, thus wiping out any margin, the implementation had been the most successful one ever in that industry. It won several awards at international events based on the systems integration and implementation and on the way the JV had smoothly adopted all the new working practices and provided successful staff training.

To conclude, I found case 1 darker than case 2, because in case 2 the client was genuinely put first. Ironically, the relationship suffered because the consulting firm was not open about the problems and how they were being dealt with, and tried to hide them. Perhaps more than anything, the two examples highlight the fact that the nature and strength of the client–consultant relationship are a big influencer on shaping belief, and the importance of the impact of ethical behaviour on this relationship.

Ethical practices for consulting for change

Ethical consultancy is of crucial importance for organizational change. It means that consultants display a desire to benefit others in the organization and that their behaviour reflects empathy, care, concern and respect for others. Ethical consultants model pro-social and altruistic behaviour; they behave like good parents (Popper and Mayseless, 2003). It is, however, about more than just being authentic, it is also about being proactive in applying ethical practices.

To avoid ethical malpractice, consultants need to be cognizant of ethical standards. The minimum ethical standards required by OD consultants are highlighted by French and Bell (1999) as:

- Interventions must be selected that have a high probability of being helpful in the particular situation.
- The consultant should not use interventions that exceed their expertise.

- The client system should be as informed as is practical about the nature of the process.
- The consultant must not be working any personal hidden agendas that obtrude into high-quality service for the client.
- Commitments to confidentiality must be kept.
- Individuals must not be coerced into divulging information about themselves or others.
- The client must not be promised unrealistic outcomes.

Such lists are only useful if they are adapted and applied in practice. To do this Woodall (1996) says that at the very least there is a need to identify the process of reasoning by which decisions and acts are justified. This is supported by Ovretveit (1996), who suggests that an ethical approach means deciding which principle is the most important in the situation, and that the steps for such an analysis include looking at each of the choices or alternatives of behaviour and actions and considering the ethics of them, as well as thinking about the consequences of them and considering self-interest bias. Establishing ethical guidelines can help provide a framework for applying ethical standards of behaviour in practice.

Establishing organizational ethical guidelines

Ethical behaviour should not be left solely to the responsibility of the individual consultant. For instance, Citigroup has an entire committee focused on ethics and culture, and has implemented a series of web-based videos detailing real workplace ethical dilemmas. Bank of America is focusing its corporate culture transformation on encouraging employees to report and escalate issues or concerns, as well as incorporating a risk 'boot camp' into their current training. Organizations need to embed mechanisms that can guide ethical behaviour. Such mechanisms include appropriately communicated and implemented ethical guidelines, visible senior management commitment to, and role modelling of, ethical behaviour, and appropriate performance management, as well as repercussions for non-compliance with ethical standards.

During the consultancy cycle the client organization and the consultancy firm both have responsibilities to ensure that ethical guidelines are adhered to. For example, the ethical elements of the contractual negotiations are formalized, and all ethically related considerations in the relationship are discussed and defined during the contracting process, thereby ensuring an ethically sustainable and mutually beneficial client–consultant relationship.

Although the client organization and consultancy firm need to take responsibility for driving ethical behaviour, within the client–consultant relationship there are also obvious benefits of ethical parameters being developed at a profession level. For example, professional consultancy associations can play a role in helping to develop ethical behaviour, through mechanisms such as providing training in ethical standards to consultants, promoting membership and acting as a body that not only consultants but also clients can take ethical issues to for resolution. Implementation of these mechanisms will help to develop ethical practice and avoid the darkening of the credibility of the consulting profession.

Training and education in ethics

Training and education in ethics are of value for consultants since an effective ethics education programme will not only reinforce ethical standards and guidelines but will also show consultants how to engage ethically at multiple levels in an organization both internally and externally. An evolving and interactive ethics education programme can help to uphold the principles and standards of ethics (Ellis, 2013). Such programmes have been implemented across a number of companies in different sectors. For example, Carillion – a construction services company – retrained its 30,000 employees to make sure that they understood the company's policy on ethics. Osama Al Jayousi, the compliance manager at the company, advocates the benefits of such training and says, 'We needed to make sure [people] were aware of our policies, where to go if there are issues, where to go to raise concerns, and also to know they won't be victimized if they raise genuine concerns' (cited in Chynoweth, 2015).

Training is imperative for developing and sustaining the ethical behaviour required of consultants. Both consultancy firms and professional associations can play a major role in providing appropriate training, while companies should include, at the very least, ethical training in their induction programmes. Academic institutions can also play a significant role in developing the knowledge of ethical behaviour through promoting awareness of the need for, and implementation of, ethical parameters within consultancy. Education and training in ethics are undoubtedly a worthwhile investment to help ensure an ethical approach to consultancy for change, as well as creating a healthy organization.

Creating a healthy organization

As mentioned earlier in this chapter, ethics has to be the responsibility of not just individuals but also of the organization. Honest and ethical companies, according to Croucher and colleagues (2016), are healthy companies that see their reputations as central to their future, and promote people who feel the same – those who worry about the company's good name populate every level of the organization. However, as Michael Skapinker writes in an article in the *Financial Times* (2016), organizations that foster honesty are those that are honest in the first place. The challenge is to create an honest organization that is not just about setting up an ethics hotline but that has a culture which puts a stop to unethical behaviour before it gets out of hand. Fostering that sort of ethos, according to Skapinker, takes years, and while all ranks of the organization have to be infused with it, it will never take root unless those at the top believe in it too.

Addressing ethical issues

Consultants not only have to act ethically, but will also have to deal with ethical issues that arise during organizational change. To deal effectively with the ethical issues of change, Martin Bower (1997), who was a Director and Partner at McKinsey, outlines in his book entitled *Will to Lead* the following five responsibilities of a consultant:

1 The client's interests must be put ahead of the firm's interests.

2 The highest standards of truthfulness, integrity and trustworthiness must be adhered to.

3 The client's private and proprietary information must be kept secret.

4 A consultant must maintain an independent position and tell the client the truth.

5 A consultant must provide only services that have real value.

There are numerous other steps similar to those suggested by Bower that can help consultants manage the ethical dimensions of change. The following are suggested:

- *Identify that there is an issue.* This involves acknowledging that there is a problem that needs to be addressed, which means separating ethical issues from unethical issues. For example, if an individual does not attend a kick-off meeting to discuss changes to financial processes this may be considered bad manners and violate peer and team expectations; however, it is not an ethical problem involving right or wrong. Whereas deciding whether to make someone's job redundant during a restructuring exercise because of his or her gender is an ethical issue.

- *Determine who is responsible.* Once an unethical issue has been highlighted that needs to be addressed, the persons responsible need to be identified, as well as who is responsible for addressing the problem. For example, if a consultant is concerned that one of their client's suppliers is exploiting cheap labour they will need to inform them about it and agree with the client who should be responsible for dealing with it.

- *Gather the relevant facts.* Adequate, accurate and current information is important for making effective decisions of all kinds, including ethical ones. For instance, in deciding whether or not it is fair to suspend a colleague for being rude and aggressive about a proposed new HR system, a consultant will need to discuss the issue with the client and the individual concerned to determine the seriousness of the offence and the reason why the individual is criticizing the system, before making a decision.

- *Review right-versus-wrong issues.* To decide whether an issue or course of action is ethical or unethical consultants need to consider if it is right or wrong; gives them a negative reaction; would make them uncomfortable if it appeared on a social media site; or violates the ethical practices and standards of the organization.

- *Apply the ethical standards and perspectives.* If the organization has an ethical code of conduct, standards and/or perspectives then the consultant needs to decide which are the most relevant and useful to apply to the specific issue.

- *Make the decision.* At some point consultants need to make a decision that requires 'moral courage' (Kidder, 1995), which is an attribute essential to consultancy.

- *Revisit and reflect on the decision.* Finally, the learning from the decision taken needs to be reflected upon, including the lessons learned that can be applied to similar situations in the future.

Activity

How would you address the following ethical issues?

1 The client already knows the answer they want to their business problem.

2 The client wants you to omit information from your report about the findings from the diagnosis of the problem to be addressed.

3 The client wants proprietary information that you learned while working with another business/part of the organization.

4 You discover that your client is involved in fraudulent activity.

Summary

Ethical consultancy is of crucial importance for organizational change and consultants need to take responsibility for ensuring that they behave and act ethically. Ethical consultants display a desire to benefit others in the organization rather than their own self-interest. Their behaviour reflects the values of empathy, care, concern and respect for others and they understand how to avoid ethical malpractice. Ethical consultants are clear on what precisely constitutes unethical behaviours during change and are able to move beyond general statements of ethics, such as those found in corporate social responsibility statements and policies. They are able to evaluate their own ethical behaviours and their actions, and determine whether they are compatible with those of the client organization and its stakeholders. This means that consultants must consider the ethical consequences of their actions and behaviour in order to prevent misinterpretation, collusion, value and goal conflict and technical ineptness, all of which requires an understanding of the ethics of change.

It is not, however, just the consultant that needs to take responsibility for ensuring ethical consultancy, but also the consultancy firm and the client organization, both of which have a responsibility to develop and enforce commonly understood, and adhered to, ethical guidelines and standards. If ignored then the consequences of ethical malpractice have the potential to lead to the darkening of the credibility and reputation of consultancy for change.

Implications for consultants

There are a number of practical implications for practising and aspiring consultants and organizations based on the issues discussed in this chapter.

- *Ensure ethical standards and guidelines of behaviour are understood and applied.*
  It is critical that organizations and consultants take responsibility for establishing ethical standards and guidelines for values and behaviours.

Those standards and guidelines are the moral compass in the midst of the confusion and complexity that are typical at various times in organizational change.

- *Address unethical behaviours.*
  Client and consultancy organizations with a corporate policy on ethics need to reiterate it clearly to consultants, so that consultants are able to avoid any inappropriate behaviour that is not in line with corporate policy. If ethical malpractice occurs then it needs to be addressed by client and consultancy organizations.

- *Balance organizational and individual responsibility for ethical behaviour.*
  Ethical individualization needs to be balanced with organizational ethical practice. Consultancy firms and client organizations need to take responsibility for developing and enforcing commonly understood, and adhered to, ethical standards.

References

Anderson, D (2012) *Organization Development: The process of leading organizational change*, 2nd edn, Sage, London

Beck, U and Beck-Gernsheim, E (2002) *Individualisation*, Sage, London

Beesley, A and Barker, A (2016) Apple tax deal: How it worked and what the EU ruling means, *Financial Times*, 30 August. [Online] http://www.ft.com/cms/s/0/cc58c190-6ec3-11e6-a0c9-1365ce54b926.html#axzz4KLTjQJHy

Block, P (2011) *Flawless Consulting*, 3nd edn, Jossey Bass/Pfeiffer, San Francisco

Bower, M (1997) *Will to Lead: Running a business with a network of leaders*, Harvard Business Review Press, Cambridge, MA

Brien, A (1998) Professional ethics and the culture of trust, *Journal of Business Ethics*, **17** (4), pp 391–409

By, RT and Burnes, B (eds) (2013) *Organizational Change, Leadership and Ethics*, Routledge, London

Chynoweth, C (2015) Ethics versus profits: the fight goes on, *The Sunday Times*, 25 January.

Clark, T and Salaman, G (1998) Creating the 'right' impression: Towards a dramaturgy of management consultancy, *The Service Industries Journal*, **18** (1), pp 18–38

Consultancy.uk (2015) 4 consultancies named World's Most Ethical Company. [Online] http://www.consultancy.uk/news/1672/four-consultancies-named-most-ethical-company

Craig, D and Brooks, R (2006) *Plundering the Public Sector*, Constable, London

Croucher, SM, Zeng, C and Kassing, J (2016) Learning to contradict and standing up for the company: An exploration of the relationship between organizational dissent, organizational assimilation, and organizational reputation, *International Journal of Business Communication*. [Online] http://journals.sagepub.com/doi/pdf/10.1177/2329488416633852

Czerniawska, F (1999) *Management Consultancy in the 21st Century*, Macmillan Business, Basingstoke

Ellis, P (2013) Corporate ethics education yields rewards, *National Defense Magazine*, 8 August

French, WL and Bell, CH (1999) *Organization Development: Behaviour science interventions for organization improvement*, 6th edn, Prentice Hall, Upper Saddle, NJ

Giddens, A (1991) *Modernity and Self-Identity: Self and society in the late modern age*, Stanford University Press, Stanford

Greenwood, R and Empson, L (2003) The professional partnership: relic or exemplary form of governance?, *Organization Studies*, **24** (6), pp 909–33

Hamlin, R, Keep, J and Ash, K (2001) *Organizational Change and Development: A reflective guide for managers, trainers and developers*, FT Prentice Hall, Harlow

Hodges, J (2011) The role of the CEO and leadership branding: Credibility not celebrity, in *Corporate Reputation*, ed R Burke, G Martin and C Cooper, pp 181–98, Gower, London

Hodges, J (2016) *Managing and Leading People Through Change: The theory and practice of sustaining change through people*, Kogan Page, London

Kamath, G (2007) *The State of Ethics: Comparing and benchmarking codes of conduct*. Report prepared on behalf of The Ethics Committee of The International Council of Management Consulting Institutes, ICMCI

Kaptein, M and Schwartz, MS (2008) The effectiveness of business codes: A critical examination of existing studies and the development of an integrated research model, *Journal of Business Ethics*, **77** (2), pp 111–27

Kidder, RM (1995) *How Good People Make Tough Choices*, Morrow, New York

Kihn, M (2005) *House of Lies*, Warner Business Books, New York

Lucy, D, Poorkavoos, M and Wellbelove, J (2015) *The Management Agenda*, Roffey Park, London

Morgan, G (2006) *Images of Organization*, Sage, London

Nitsch, D, Baetz, M and Hughes, JC (2005) Why code of conduct violations go unreported: A conceptual framework to guide intervention and future research, *Journal of Business Ethics*, **57** (4), pp 327–41

O'Mahoney, J (2011) Advisory anxieties: Ethical Individualisation in the UK consulting industry, *Journal of Business Ethics*, **104** (1), pp 101–13

O'Mahoney, J and Markham, C (2013) *Management Consultancy*, Oxford University Press, Oxford

Ovretveit, J (1996) Ethics: Counsel or perfection, *The IHSM Network*, **3** (13)

Popper, M and Mayseless, O (2003) Back to basics: Applying a parenting perspective to transformational leadership, *The Leadership Quarterly*, **14**, pp 41–65

Power, M (2004) *The Risk Management of Everything: Rethinking the politics of uncertainty*, Demos, London

Schwartz, MS (2004) Effective corporate codes of ethics: Perceptions of code users, *Journal of Business Ethics*, **55** (4), pp 321–41

Seabright, MA and Moberg, DJ (1998) Interpersonal manipulation: Its nature and moral limits, *Managerial Ethics: Morally managing people and processes*, Lawrence Erlbaum Associates, NJ

Shawver, T and Clements, LH (2008) Whistleblowing: Factors that contribute to management accountants reporting questionable dilemmas, *Management Accounting Quarterly*, **9**(2)

Singer, P (ed) (1994) *Ethics*, Oxford University Press, Oxford

Skapinker, M (2016) Lessons from the Deutsche Bank whistleblower Eric Ben-Artzi, *Financial Times*, 24 August

Smith, A, Van Vuuren, LJ and Visser, D (2003) Client–consultant ethical relationship considerations within management consulting, *Journal of Industrial Psychology*, **29** (1), pp 83–92

Stiglitz, J.E (2010) *Freefall: Free market and the sinking of the global economy*, Allen Lane, London

Stokes, P and Harris, P (2012) Micro-moments, choice and responsibility in sustainable organizational change and transformation, *Journal of Organizational Change Management*, **25** (4), pp 595–611

Warwick, D and Kelman, H (1973) Ethics in social intervention, in *Processes and Phenomenon of Social Change*, ed G Zaltman, pp 377–449, Wiley, New York

Watson, T (2002) *Organising and Managing Work*, FT/Prentice Hall, Harlow

White, LP and Wooten, KC (1983) Ethical dilemmas in various stages of organizational development, *Academy of Management Review*, **8** (4), pp 690–97

Woodall, J (1996) Managing culture change: Can it ever be ethical?, *Personnel Review*, **25** (6), pp 26-40

Conclusions and reflections

In this final chapter a synthesis is provided of the main points made in the book.

Consultancy is based on the interactions between people and involves consultants guiding and influencing clients' decisions; assisting them with diagnosing and identifying the most appropriate intervention to address a specific issue; transferring knowledge and expertise; and helping clients to learn and build capability. This definition of consultancy derives primarily from an OD orientation, where there is traditionally a focus on the client–consultant relationship, which distinguishes consultancy from other forms of helping. This is especially relevant for consultancy for change, since working with and through people, by forming relationships, is an important aspect of sustaining change in organizations.

To provide value to clients, consultancy for change requires a mix of consulting roles (particularly expert and facilitative), but just as important is an emphasis on building and maintaining relationships; continuous learning; involvement and participation; and collaboration which can be provided by internal or external consultants. Although there are advantages and disadvantages to both types of consultants, there is not necessarily one that is better than the other. Instead there is a need to consider the best resource for achieving value, which is determined by the client. It is important for consultants to understand what the client perceives as value, since value must be identified and measured according to what the client expects in terms of benefits to be realized.

To mitigate the impact of disruptive change, consultants need to see their roles not simply as pushing out content that they have developed and sharing their expert knowledge, but also as facilitating the effort to help clients to address the issues they are facing. The goal of consultants is not merely to craft a change intervention but to curate the experience so that learning is achieved from it. This requires a shift in focus, especially from internal consultants.

Internal consultancy has begun to move away from 'a service-provider' mentality to becoming valued talent and involved in organizational change. Many internal consultancies are now deeply embedded in business through senior business-partner leadership roles, such as in HR. In this model internal consultants must be more change-orientated specialists possessing skills in design thinking and digital platforms and application, as companies begin to operate in different ways. Companies such as Philips and Nestlé are changing their learning and development environments to focus instead on learning experience design. Similarly, the Commonwealth Bank of Australia is focusing on user-centric design and design thinking to build new apps and new experiences for employees (Greenberg, 2015). This shift encompasses consultants not just delivering change interventions but also creating innovative new learning environments. Consultants must build a compelling and dynamic experience for clients and guide clients in how to learn from organizational transformations. Consultants must, therefore, help clients to learn from failure as well as success.

In order to help consultants support organizations with transformations and the resulting lessons, the consultancy cycle for change provides an iterative approach. The cycle comprises different phases: initial contact and contracting; diagnosis and analysis; intervention; implementation; evaluation; and transition. Each of the phases informs the orientation of previous and subsequent phases, and each varies in length and complexity depending on the nature of the change and the client's expectations. Each phase of the cycle is bolted together with *dialogue, feedback,* the *client–consultant relationship* and *stakeholder management.* Overall, the iterative cycle provides a route map to be used by a consultant during a transformation. However, like all conceptual frameworks, it does need to be adapted to the specific context in which it is being applied.

Some of the phases, such as contracting, are ongoing activities throughout the consultancy for change cycle. Consultants may need to return to contracting discussions each time they meet with a client in order to validate progress, correct any misunderstandings and agree on what to do next. Contracting is a critical skill for a consultant to learn, especially for internal consultants who may overlook the need for it and instead make assumptions about what the client expects and how those expectations will be met. The consultant, whether internal or external, therefore, needs to be familiar enough with the cycle to be able to use it flexibly and to revisit the different phases within it, when necessary.

The consultancy for change cycle is also a collaborative approach involving both client and consultant. For instance, diagnosis is a joint process that aims to understand the client's issue and its root causes so that appropriate change intervention/s can be identified to address them. However, this is the phase that clients and consultants may be tempted to skip on the assumption that they already have sufficient information about an issue and its causality. This is a misguided assumption that can lead to change interventions being implemented that address the symptoms and not the underlying causes of the problem. So diagnosis needs to be done collaboratively to provide evidence-based data to help identify potential solutions. The selection and design of appropriate interventions should also be done collaboratively and derive from careful diagnosis.

Since interventions may function differently in different organizations, so flexibility in the application of any intervention is necessary. The purpose of interventions is to improve the effectiveness of the organization, team/s and/or individuals and so care must be taken in selecting the most appropriate intervention since failed interventions cause significant costs in terms of time, money and motivation of organizational members. There is, therefore, a need for interventions to be practical and business-focused, while also being underpinned by a strong evidence-based foundation and rigorous learning methodology.

The ownership of the intervention has to be clarified so that the client and consultant both understand clearly how the consultant will help the client achieve the objectives of the intervention. The consultant should, whenever appropriate, be involved during the implementation of the intervention. However, they will eventually need to disengage because the responsibility for sustaining the change needs to be transferred to the client. Transition of ownership of the intervention to the client is, therefore, vital to ensure the ongoing sustainability of the change.

Being clear about the boundaries of the consultancy work, and knowing the correct time to withdraw, is essential. Disengaging becomes much easier and clearer when the contracting process has been done effectively. If the consultant's role and the client's expectations about the outcomes for the consultancy engagement have been clarified, the transition will be both appropriate and timely and the engagement not just left to fade away. To help move towards effective transition, the progress of the change should be monitored and measured as it is happening since this enables adjustments to be made to help realize benefits, and also provides feedback on how people feel about the change whilst it is still being implemented.

Knowing what influences and determines the sustainability of change is a key part of the consultancy for change cycle. Determining whether or not change has been sustained will involve measurement of the benefits achieved, as well as management of the risks associated with the change. Attempting to lead a transformation without metrics or a risk assessment is like trying to fly a plane without instruments. On a short flight on a clear day consultants might be able to reach the destination safely, but once they hit clouds they will find themselves in serious trouble. So it is important to monitor and review a transformation in order to identify areas that need to be adjusted and adapted to ensure that the change is effectively implemented and the intended benefits achieved.

There is a variety of capabilities that must be developed by consultants in order to effectively implement the consultancy cycle for change and ensure benefits are realized and these are: building and maintaining relationships; managing emotions; being self-aware; gaining commitment and engagement; facilitating creative dialogue; being resilient; having a tolerance for ambiguity and uncertainty; being politically astute; managing power dynamics; and being an effective communicator. The relative emphasis on each capability will depend upon the situation; moreover the level of expertise and the mastery of certain skills will fluctuate in relation to the level at which consultants operate. All the capabilities are, however, vital to the consultant's repertoire.

To build and enhance the capabilities require learning and development in order to provide consultants with the knowledge, abilities and skills necessary to adapt to new and different ways of working and also reinforce the required behaviour to work more confidently with clients. Developing the required capabilities has benefits for both the client and the consultant; however, it is not simply a matter of just having the right knowledge. The best swimmers do not win a medal in the Olympics by simply reading books or watching other swimmers: they practise and consequently they get better at the sport. The same is true for great artists, musicians and writers. Similarly, not only do consultants need to be taught about consultancy and change concepts, but they also need time to apply their knowledge and practise their skills. Furthermore, it is particularly important that they do this in an ethical way.

Consultancy for change needs to be underpinned by a set of ethical values that influence the behaviours and actions of consultants, as well as the outcomes and consequences of change initiatives. Consultants and clients, as well as the organizations they work for, need to take responsibility for ensuring that consultants behave and act ethically because otherwise, if ignored, the consequences of ethical malpractice have the potential to lead to the darkening of the credibility and reputation of consultancy for change.

The consultancy for change cycle moves the consultant's focus beyond traditional linear change approaches in favour of working in partnership with clients and other stakeholders to design a productive and meaningful intervention focused on an employee experience that is simple, compelling and sustainable. In a *Harvard Business Review* article Jon Kolko (2015) points out that people need their interactions with changes in technologies and other complex systems to be simple, intuitive and pleasurable, because it implicitly drives a more thoughtful, human approach to business. Many companies are relying on this approach. GE, for example, has made simplification a core new business strategy and, as a result, is introducing a simplified model for performance management, new mobile apps for goal management and collaboration, and a new set of principles for work. The company now uses agile methodologies throughout product development and is teaching managers how to help teams 'do less' and 'focus more' (Krishnamoorthy, 2015). A consultancy for change approach supports this by focusing on the people and not just on the process.

At its core, the consultancy for change cycle involves an OD approach through dialogue in order to understand people and the issues they face in organizations, and in order to implement interventions to develop and engage people. Applying the consultancy for change cycle compels consultants to ask 'What does a great change intervention that will engage individuals look like from end to end? How can we facilitate collaboration and learning in everything we do?' Successful consultancy for change integrates an understanding of how to engage people in change, it identifies what motivates people and it examines how they react to change. Through this approach, consultants and clients can gain important insights into key pain points, needs, and challenges.

Consultants need, therefore, to shift from a linear based approach to a people-centred focus using the consultancy for change cycle. Using the latter approach, interventions can be designed that improve productivity, boost engagement and increase employee satisfaction while also providing sustainable change. To help manage complexity and change, consultants must adopt a consultancy for change approach that puts the engagement and commitment of people at its heart.

References

Greenberg, A (2015) How 4 top employees use candidate experience for competitive advantage. [Online] recruitingdivision.com/4-top-employers-use-candidate-experience-competitive-advantage/

Kolko, J (2015) Design thinking comes of age, *Harvard Business Review*, **93** (9), pp 66–71

Krishnamoorthy, R (2015) GE's culture challenge after Welch and Immelt, *Harvard Business Review*. [Online] https://hbr.org/2015/01/ges-culture-challenge-after-welch-and-immelt

INDEX